HEART

BREATH

MIND

HEART
BREATH
MIND

WITHDRAWN

Train Your Heart to Conquer

Stress and Achieve Success

LEAH LAGOS, Psy.D.

Houghton Mifflin Harcourt

Boston   New York   2020

If you have a known heart condition, high blood pressure, diabetes, asthma, or another chronic health condition, speak to your health care provider before embarking on this program. *Heart Breath Mind* is not meant to be a substitute for treatment.

Names and identifying details of some individuals have been changed to protect confidentiality.

Library of Congress Cataloging-in-Publication Data
Names: Lagos, Leah, author.
Title: Heart breath mind : train your heart to conquer stress and achieve success / Leah Lagos.
Description: Boston : Houghton Mifflin Harcourt, [2020] |
Includes bibliographical references and index.
Identifiers: LCCN 2019057828 (print) | LCCN 2019057829 (ebook) |
ISBN 9781328604408 (hardcover) | ISBN 9781328603524 (ebook)
Subjects: LCSH: Stress (Psychology) | Stress (Physiology) | Stress management. |
Mind and body.
Classification: LCC RC455.4.S87 L34 2020 (print) | LCC RC455.4.S87 (ebook) |
DDC 155.9/042—dc23
LC record available at https://lccn.loc.gov/2019057828
LC ebook record available at https://lccn.loc.gov/2019057829

Book design by Greta D. Sibley
Illustrations by Mapping Specialists, Ltd.

Printed in the United States of America
DOC 10 9 8 7 6 5 4 3 2 1

To my daughters,
Madeline and Felicity:
may you always thrive by
embracing your resonance
and cultivating a life
based on your inner light.

CONTENTS

Preface   1

PART I
LAYING THE GROUNDWORK

1. The Importance of Training Your Heart   13

2. Building a Life of Resonance   23

3. How to Use This Book   32

PART II
REWIRING THE STRESS RESPONSE

4. Week 1: Finding Your Resonance Frequency   49

5. Week 2: Using Your Breath to Increase Energy   65

6. Week 3: Letting Go of Your Stress and
   Expanding Your Emotional Range   84

7. Week 4: Healing the Broken Parts   103

8. Week 5: Preparing for Challenge   120

9. Week 6: Mastering the Emotional Pivot   132

10. Week 7: Cultivating Resonance Under Fire   145

11. Week 8: Imprinting the Physiology of Success   162

12. Week 9: Using Your Heart Rhythms to
    Strengthen Your Relationships   175

13. Week 10: Anchoring Yourself in Resonance   192

PART III
BEYOND 10 WEEKS

14. Maintaining and Fueling Your Resonance   207

Your Week-by-Week Snapshot   219

Your HRV and Homework Tracking Notes   223

Acknowledgments   243

Notes   246

Index   262

PREFACE

We spend years of our lives training to perform, whether it's on the field, on a stage, or in a boardroom. No matter how well prepared we may be, the pressure of performance often sabotages us when it matters most. When a challenge presents itself, will you rise to the occasion and perform at your best? Or will you become overwhelmed, paralyzed, or derailed?

To a great extent, the answer depends on your physiological stress response. When facing a moment of intense pressure, whether you're an NBA player at the three-point line, a parent managing multiple children, or an executive preparing to give a presentation before a large audience, your body responds: your heart rate increases, you breathe at a faster rate, your blood vessels constrict, and you feel a burst of energy from the release of stress hormones.

All these things happen automatically because your body is biologically programmed to respond to stress as if you're in physical danger. The autonomic nervous system (ANS) — the master controller of those bodily functions that occur without thought, such as breathing, heart rate, and digestion — begins preparing you to either fight or flee. This is called the fight-or-flight response.

Here's the problem, though — none of the stressful situations I mentioned above actually require fighting or fleeing. And the fight-or-flight response leaves you in a physiological state that is hardly conducive to peak performance. It's nearly impossible to think clearly, make wise decisions, and perform confidently when your heart is racing, your breathing is ragged, and your hands are shaking. Surely, you've experienced this firsthand.

Thanks to the burgeoning field of sports science, we already have plenty of stress-reduction techniques to boost performance. A quick search reveals a multitude of books filled with well-researched cognitive and behavioral approaches to battling stress. Most of these focus on techniques to control your thoughts and modify your behaviors.

The problem with these methods is that our physical response to stress is not only in our head. It's not just our thoughts that are causing stress hormones to flood our system or creating an erratic heart rate and breathing pattern. We can't access a state for peak performance through mind-set alone. That's because your stress lives *in your body*.

There is, however, a scientifically proven, safe, natural way to rewire your body's baseline stress response and optimize your health and performance. The breathing exercises and peak performance strategies described in *Heart Breath Mind* will take you on a journey from merely surviving stress to thriving despite it. A critical part of our work together will be developing your somatic awareness — a heightened consciousness of how your body is feeling — so that you will recognize when you are stressed and can take action to shift yourself out of a state of stress and into what is called parasympathetic dominance. You will learn how to rewire and optimize your body's natural, immediate, and automatic response to stress. You will learn how to replace negative emotions such as anger, guilt, and anxiety with healthier responses such as compassion, forgiveness, and gratitude, changing your heart rhythms in the process.

You will become adept at accessing flow, or what I call resonance, during critical moments so that you can more consistently perform at your prime across all of life's arenas. We'll start by using technology to help you find your ideal breathing rate, but with dedicated practice, you'll be able to breathe without the technology, accessing your best self on demand and linking together your heart, breath, and mind in the way nature intended.

And it all begins in your body's most superb instrument: your heart.

THE NEW SECRET TO PEAK PERFORMANCE

Most people are under the impression that their heart beats with the monotony and repetitiveness of a metronome. On the contrary, when you inhale, your heart rate (the number of times your heart beats per minute) naturally rises; when you exhale, it slows down again. This is true for everyone.

But the exact amount the heart rate accelerates on inhalation and how quickly it decelerates on exhalation vary quite a bit from person to person. This range from your maximum heart rate to your minimum heart rate is your heart rate variability (HRV).

In an ideal world, if electrodes were connected to your chest, your heart rate would show up on-screen as big, beautiful oscillations that rise and fall like rolling ocean waves. The greater the difference between the peaks and the valleys, the higher your heart rate variability. High heart rate variability is what you need to thrive under pressure; it signifies the body's ability to quickly ramp up and feel a full range of emotions and energy — including stress, when needed — and then swiftly and efficiently let go, or recover. This dynamic allows you to effectively prepare for performance situations, navigate any challenges that arise, and then swiftly recover in between peak moments. Individuals with high heart rate variability have greater control over how their heart reacts under pressure and how quickly it recovers. If you've ever found yourself feeling in the zone, like you're sinking every shot you make (be it at work or on the court), then you know what this feels like. It's a state of flow when your mind clears, muscle tension dissipates, and you feel confident, making great performance easy.

But prolonged stress decreases heart rate variability, diminishing the amplitude, or height, of your heart rate oscillations. If I hooked you up to electrodes and studied your heart rate on a screen on a day when you had lost money in the stock market, had a clash with your spouse, or arrived 30 minutes late for an important meeting, those beautiful oscillations would decrease in size, and your heart rhythms might appear more erratic, signaling a system on high alert. With less variability in your heart rhythms and autonomic nervous system, you are unable to pivot efficiently between different emotional states or to adapt flexibly to the stressors in your specific situation, including work, competition, and relationships.

Low heart rate variability is, quite simply, the opposite of what you need for peak performance. Less variability between heartbeats indicates that the body is under stress, and can increase susceptibility to health conditions such as depression, diabetes, heart disease, and more. On the other hand, high heart rate variability is associated with psychological and physiological flexibility, cardiac resilience, and overall heart health. It is also known to enhance performance in a multitude of sports — golf, basketball, dance, baseball, gymnastics, and so on.

At the core of *Heart Breath Mind* is a scientific process to systematically gain control over your heart, rewiring your stress response and unlocking your highest potential for performance and positive health.

GET OUT OF YOUR HEAD AND INTO YOUR HEART

You see, the heart is a muscle with far more responsibility than just pumping blood. It is an essential part of your autonomic nervous system, featuring an acceleration system and a deceleration system that, together, function as your body's internal braking system. Heart rate variability is an indication of the balance within the two main branches of your autonomic nervous system: the sympathetic nervous system and the parasympathetic nervous system. The sympathetic nervous system controls the fight-or-flight response, enabling your body to ramp up quickly to meet the demands of a stressful moment or prepare for elite performance. This is the branch that activates, or increases, the heart's action. The parasympathetic branch slows the action of the heart, allowing your body and brain to rest, recover, and relax. The parasympathetic nervous system also handles your day-to-day vitals, like breathing, heart rate, digestion, and sexual arousal; it's sometimes called the rest-and-digest system. You can think of them as the gas pedal and brake of a car; the sympathetic nervous system is the gas, revving up when it detects stress or danger, and the parasympathetic nervous system is the braking system to slow things down.

In order to be able to accelerate and decelerate quickly, like a high-performance racecar, you need balanced and finely tuned sympathetic and parasympathetic nervous systems. Yet most adults have a dominant sympathetic nervous system and an underactive parasympathetic nervous system. They have no problem feeling stress and physiologically preparing to fight or flee, even if the "danger" at hand is not a nearby hungry predator but a looming deadline at work, a speech before a large crowd, or an upsetting conversation with a loved one.

This isn't surprising, given the world in which we live. In 2018, the most Googled medical symptom in the United States was stress, topping the list in one out of every five states. (Morning sickness was the front-runner in Utah, and Maine seems to have an issue with night sweats.) The American Institute of Stress lists the future of our nation, money, work, political climate, and crime and violence as the top five stressors for Americans. We are a nation besieged by stress, whether it's related to career, family, finances, romance, current events, or health problems.

Once you're ramped up, though, it's overly difficult for your physiology to recover. You're driving a car that has no trouble reaching a high speed but is incapable of slowing down. This is true for most of us. Think about it: When you narrowly avoid an accident on the way to work or school or get into a heated confrontation with a family member, do you feel your heart rate speed up in the moment, then swiftly return to normal as you proceed with your day? Or does it take you a while to stop ruminating or replaying the incident and release that stress? For most people, the latter scenario is more common and is indicative of sympathetic dominance — an overactive sympathetic nervous system that keeps you stuck in a state of fight-or-flight longer than necessary. Your physiology — your heart — is what's immobilizing you. And because your psychological well-being is governed by your physiology, you must address your heart's response before you can control your emotions or thoughts.

When faced with a challenge, will you become overwhelmed, paralyzed, or derailed? Or will you rise to the occasion and perform at your best level?

It's time to improve the way your mind *and* body react to stress.

THE MEETING THAT CHANGED EVERYTHING

Fifteen years ago, I was working as a sports therapist at a collegiate counseling center treating student-athletes. I was frustrated by the fact that many psychological approaches weren't time-oriented enough for my clients. They wanted a process that was scientific, short-term, and effective to gain control over their emotions and consistently be able to perform at their peak. Psychology was only getting them so far; all the positive self-talk in the world couldn't help a competitive golfer decelerate his heart and regain his fine motor skills when he was stressed before a putt on the eighteenth hole. When they were unable to self-regulate, their stress responses created poor performance that would undo countless hours, weeks, or even years of training.

In 2004, I attended a presentation by Paul Lehrer, PhD, a Harvard-trained behavioral psychologist and a recognized authority in the field of heart rate variability. After Dr. Lehrer finished his talk about HRV's link to health, resilience, and stress recovery, I introduced myself and asked him if HRV might hold promise for my athletes. Little did I know that question would alter the trajectory of my practice and career.

Dr. Lehrer introduced me to Russian physiologist Evgeny Vaschillo, PhD, and his wife, Bronya Vaschillo, MD, both faculty members at Rutgers University and pioneers in the field of HRV. Evgeny Vaschillo had spent years working with the Russian space program developing stress-alleviating breathing techniques for cosmonauts. Drs. Lehrer, Vaschillo, and Vaschillo had combined the principles of heart rate variability with a mind-body technique called biofeedback, in which one uses monitoring equipment to learn how to modify one's physiology with the intent of altering or enhancing some physical or psychological outcome. Classic biofeedback applications include learning how to lower blood pressure, control blood flow to the extremities, and reduce muscle tension. In doing so, the Vaschillos and Lehrer discovered a way to breathe at a specific frequency to increase heart rate variability at baseline and thereby regulate anxiety and enhance performance.

I went through their training myself and was blown away by the effects. My mind became clearer. I found myself letting go of stress more easily than ever before. It became easier to access positive emotions on demand. I knew I had found the missing link.

But I didn't want to leave my clinical research and practice behind as I embarked on this new physiological approach. For my clients to master the cognitive changes stemming from our psychological work, I believed, they first needed to learn to control what their hearts were saying to their bodies and brains.

I started to wonder if I could combine the two not only to train my clients' hearts to respond more optimally during moments of stress but also to expedite any mindfulness training or other psychological techniques my clients may be using. My goal was to develop an optimization program featuring a two-tiered training process for maximizing performance and health, starting in the heart and leading to the brain.

HRV: Your Path to Your Most Optimal Self

In *Heart Breath Mind* you have access to a scientifically proven, safe, natural way to increase your HRV and rewire your body's baseline stress response to perform at your peak level of ability despite pressure or distraction. This is a revolutionary approach to stress management that aims not just to tame your stress but to master it. Through 10 weeks of systematically training your heart, you can train your body to engage in a reflex that helps you tighten and rebalance the way your autonomic nervous system responds during moments of challenge and stress. You will not only perform better, but you will also be healthier.

Our objective is to increase your heart's ability to effectively and efficiently let go of stress. A key component of this involves relearning how to breathe the way nature intended — from your belly, not your chest. Learning to let go also requires an exploration of the negative thoughts and past upsets that have contributed to keeping you physiologically stuck in a state of fight-or-flight, whether you realize it or not.

The second objective is for you to learn specific heart protocols for anticipating stress, managing stress in the moment, and recovering quickly from stress to prepare for your next event, performance, or task. Using these heart protocols, you will learn to systematically create a heart state on demand, which gives you the ability to access any desired emotional state you need, in real time, to manage challenges. Together, these skills will provide you with system-wide control over your heart and mind to manage and release stress.

As a clinical health and performance psychologist with an expertise in psychophysiology — the relationship between the mind (psyche) and the body (physiology) — I'm endlessly fascinated by the body's ability to shape and influence our cognitive well-being. This protocol has proven so effective that my client base has expanded from collegiate athletes to include elite performers of all kinds — entrepreneurs, investment professionals, award-winning actors, best-selling authors, business executives, Olympic athletes, professional basketball players, and more.

My clients report that our work together helps them find their power and respond more flexibly to stressful situations; teaches them to let go of negative thoughts and emotions; and prepares them to be focused, confident, and in an enhanced state to compete and perform. The athletes I treat can get back to baseline more quickly after an unexpected challenge; financial executives can quickly recover between stressful meetings and can continue making levelheaded decisions; spouses and romantic partners can become more empathic listeners and feel more united as a team. By learning to control their heart, they can more tightly regulate their emotions, turn off their busy brain, and live in the present.

This process is transformative, and while I can see only so many clients in my private practice, I'm delighted to share this groundbreaking training program with a much wider audience than I could ever possibly treat individually. I'm so honored to guide my remarkable clients — and now readers — through this process, but the truth is that the solution lies within each of us. We all have the power to control how our heart responds to stress and the ways in which we connect, compete, and lead during challenge as well as everyday life.

PART I

▼

LAYING THE GROUNDWORK

1

▼

The Importance of Training Your Heart

Like all muscles, the heart has a memory. If you were a tennis player preparing for the US Open, you would practice hundreds of serves a day to teach the shoulder and arm muscles exactly how to respond on the day of the match. If you were a pianist whose professional success hinged on your concert performance skills, you would rehearse for days on end, searing the notes, rhythm, and dynamics into your mind. In *Heart Breath Mind* you will learn how to do the exact same thing with your heart — to train it with specific muscle patterns so that your most important muscle operates flexibly when you're under stress.

For example, if you've ever felt locked up by nerves, you may relate to one of my clients, an entrepreneur, who was preparing to pitch her company to investors. Halfway through her 10-week protocol, I taught her a technique called Heart Shifting, which involves shifting between a heart sensation she associated with being nervous and the way she wished to feel during her important presentation — confident, calm, and focused.

She practiced this regularly, including the night before and morning of her presentation, to teach her heart how to respond during her performance moment. After engaging in this training, she was able to let go of her hypervigilance and tap into a relaxed, open sensation in her heart when delivering her pitch.

THE HEART-BRAIN BOND

Up until the 1960s and 1970s, the prevailing belief was that communication between the heart and brain was one-sided, with the heart responding to the brain's commands and not the other way around. But thanks to groundbreaking work by pioneers like psychophysiologists (and husband-and-wife team) John and Beatrice Lacey; Harvard Medical School's Herbert Benson, MD; Doc Childre and Rollin McCraty, PhD, of the HeartMath Institute; the aforementioned Lehrer and Vaschillos, both at Rutgers University; Julian Thayer, PhD; and many others, we now know that the heart and brain are engaged in a nonstop, bidirectional dialogue, each organ influencing the other's behavior.

For example, McCraty's research tells us that when our heart rhythm pattern is erratic and disordered, the corresponding pattern of neural signals traveling from the heart to the brain inhibits higher cognitive function. The prefrontal cortex—the part of the brain that controls complex cognitive behaviors such as planning and decision making—goes "offline" when you are in a state of fight-or-flight. Evolutionarily speaking, this makes sense; your body prioritizes your survival by making sure you don't end up in a state of "paralysis by overanalysis" when your life is in danger. Unfortunately, this also impedes your ability to think clearly, remember, learn, reason, and make intelligent decisions.

In contrast, a body in rest-and-digest mode, with high heart rate variability, produces a more ordered and stable heart pattern, sending input to the brain that facilitates cognitive functioning and reinforces positive feelings as well as emotional regulation. High heart rate variability is associated with smooth, efficient prefrontal cortex activity and executive-function tasks including working memory and inhibitory control. This means that by increasing your heart rate variability, you improve your prefrontal lobe activity and with it your ability to self-regulate, inhibit negative thoughts, make objective decisions, and remember what you learn.

At its most basic level, heart rate variability (which I'll refer to as HRV from now on) is a measure of the beat-to-beat changes in the heart. In general, high HRV represents a flexible autonomic nervous system that is responsive to internal and external stimuli and is associated with fast reactions and adaptability. Diminished HRV, on the other hand, represents a less flexible autonomic nervous system that struggles to recover from stress and is associated with poor health and performance.

As we've discussed, variation in heart rate can be caused by several factors, including emotion, stress, and various physical and behavioral changes. But the same malleability that renders HRV susceptible to the stressors of everyday life also allows it to be impacted by breathing and visualization. By improving HRV, we can train our bodies to flexibly shift into positive states on demand. Instead of leaving a frustrating business meeting feeling anxious or resentful for the rest of the day, your heart kicks into parasympathetic dominance, allowing you to let go and reset for your next performance.

YOUR NEW PROGRAM FOR OPTIMAL PERFORMANCE

A typical initial HRV biofeedback session in my office would look like this: Your heart rate, respiration, and HRV are all displayed on a large monitor. Once we identify your baseline HRV, our first step is to follow the Lehrer and Vaschillo protocol for identifying your resonance frequency breathing rate (more on that to come in just a moment.) Then, we can begin to alter how your body manages stress through a series of novel strategies to clear your brain and identify the positive states you wish your heart could connect with in times of stress. Through this process, you learn how to break free from chronic cycles of anxiety and shift into an optimal performance state of calmness and confidence.

The fact that a trainable reflex can increase HRV so that your braking system works more efficiently is extremely exciting to me. Thanks to advances in neurocardiology, we know that strengthening the parasympathetic system (brake pedal) is just as crucial as dampening the sympathetic response (gas pedal). Slow and deep breathing does suppress sympathetic activity, but unless you do it systematically, it won't strengthen the parasympathetic branch at your baseline state. That's where the braking action happens, thanks to something called the baroreflex.

The baroreflex is one of the body's mechanisms for maintaining blood pressure. Receptors located in the walls of arteries trigger this reflex. Every time you inhale, your heart rate increases, followed by a rise in blood pressure approximately 4 or 5 seconds later. When you exhale, your heart rate slows, this time followed by a drop in blood pressure approximately 4 or 5 seconds later. This cycle is mediated by specialized receptors in the walls of your aorta and carotid arteries called baroreceptors.

The baroreflex is fixed and almost entirely mediated by unconscious mechanisms, but we *do* have control over our breathing rate. Most of us breathe at a faster frequency than our baroreflex, but when we purposefully slow our breathing to match the frequency of our baroreflex, we strengthen our control over it.

It turns out there is a particular rate of breathing, called resonance frequency, that maximizes the amplitudes of heart rate oscillations. For some people, it's 6 breaths a minute; for others it might be 5 or 7. Regardless of the specific number, when you breathe at this rate, something amazing happens: it strengthens the baroreflex, creating even greater overall increases in HRV.

When you are stressed, your heart rate and breathing rate fall out of alignment, propelling you into a state of dissonance. But when you breathe at your resonance frequency, your heart rate oscillations become perfectly in phase with your breath. You enter a state called resonance, or flow.

As you train your heart by breathing at your personal resonance frequency, you are exercising your baroreflex, making it stronger and more

High HRV demonstrated by parallel oscillations between heart and breath. *(This also illustrates the max to min HRV measurement).*

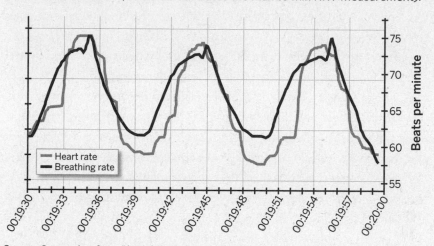

Source: Screenshot from Physiology Suite Software by Thought Technology, ProComp Infiniti Software, with permission

efficient so that your HRV remains high even when you resume normal breathing. Breathing at resonance frequency improves your baseline stress response and trains your body to reflexively kick into a state of resonance, even during moments of stress.

By strengthening your baroreflex, you can train your heart muscle so that the heart rhythms that you experience during relaxation and moments of gratitude appear, even when you are stressed. You develop an innate reflex.

The ability to physiologically let go of a difficult phone call or a missed putt and prepare for the next one in a matter of seconds is a hallmark of peak performance. My clients need to be able to quickly ramp up, act assertively, and get excited before a meeting or presentation, then quickly recover afterward. Our work increases their ability to deeply engage (turn on) as well as their ability to quickly let go (turn off). The more completely they can let go, the higher the peak of their performance grows. This ability to let go is a precursor to being able to perform at the very apex of your skill.

The effects of strengthening the baroreflex are far-reaching. I've watched in awe as clients battling several clinical conditions associated

with autonomic nervous system dysfunctions, including headaches, insomnia, and even depression, have curbed or eliminated their symptoms.
It also helps the CEOs and athletes I train gain tremendous amounts of
stamina and resilience.

When I worked with a university golf team, I measured their heart
rhythms before and after our training. Before experiencing HRV-biofeed-
back (BFB) training, their heart rates went up before they took a shot,
then remained elevated after the shot as they prepared for the next one.
After the 10 weeks of training, their heart rates increased less before each
shot and more quickly returned to baseline afterward. In other words,
they were less reactive prior to their performance and recovered faster
between shots. For many, this led to greater stamina and better overall
golf performance.

**Heart rate patterns averaged across 18 shots
for the virtual golf session.**

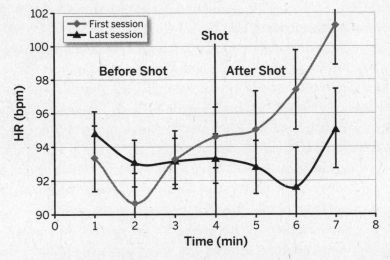

Source: Author, Biofeedback Magazine.

Some people start noting a difference in their stress response starting
around week 3 or 4, when the baroreflex begins exhibiting quantifiable
gains in strength. By week 6 or 7, the cognitive benefits, such as improved

focus, organization of thought, and executive functioning, will begin to kick in.

THE NERVE THAT UNLOCKS YOUR MAXIMUM POTENTIAL

But how do the baroreceptors in the heart communicate with the brain in the first place? Isn't the brain the organ in charge, sending messages and directives along neural pathways to the rest of the body?

As it turns out, communication between the brain and body is bi-directional, with countless signals being sent in both directions — from the brain to the body *and* from the body to the brain. These messages travel along the vagus nerve, a large nerve that connects the brain stem with nearly every one of our organs, including the heart. (*Vagus* is the Latin word for wandering; it shares its language roots with *vagabond* and *vague*.) The vagus nerve bears responsibility for the regulation of an impressive host of functions, from heart rate, respiration, and digestion to reflexive actions like coughing, swallowing, and sneezing. But the reality is that the vast majority — between 80 and 90 percent — of vagal nerve fibers spend their time sending messages "up" from the body to the brain. The phrases "listen to your heart" and "listen to your gut" aren't just clichés; they're accurate descriptions of real physiological processes.

The strength of your vagus nerve activity is referred to as vagal tone. People with good vagal tone have high HRV and vice versa. The stronger your vagal tone and the tighter the balance between the sympathetic and parasympathetic branches of the nervous system, the better your body is at distinguishing between real and perceived threats. With increased vagal tone, impulses from the baroreceptors travel more quickly to the brain so that you can hit the gas when you need to rev up or hit the brake when you need to recover. Those with poor vagal tone are often hyper-vigilant, erroneously interpreting sensory input as a threat to their safety and becoming stuck in a chronic state of fight-or-flight.

THE DIFFERENCE THAT HRV TRAINING MAKES

Let's say you frequently clashed with a parent who didn't allow you to set your own rules and schedules as a teenager. You might have been infuriated by the lack of control and the feelings of inferiority. You might not connect that experience with the anxiety and panic you now feel when another person — a colleague, romantic partner, or friend, for instance — tries to take control of a situation you are perfectly capable of handling. But the link is there, lingering in your heart and sending messages of stress up toward your brain via the vagus nerve. Or maybe you were fortunate not to experience any major battles with your parents but had a traumatic illness or invasive surgery when you were young and now demonstrate fleeting feelings of panic in situations where you feel out of control of your safety or health, like when flying in an airplane. These are examples of how painful experiences become stuck in our physiology.

In order to address our pain, which is an essential step toward mastering stress, we need to be able to identify and release the painful or unpleasant sensations that often get stuck within our physiology. *That* is how you address autonomic imbalance in the body.

This can be a tricky mental hurdle for people to conquer. Many of us are used to traditional cognitive approaches such as talk therapy, visualization, and goal setting, which call for us to tune into our minds; but the notion of clicking into our heart and asking it how it feels can seem foreign. We are afraid of facing our deeper pain because we have not learned a specific method for letting go of the physiological experiences. It is not so much the people who hurt us or the cognitive memories of the experience, but our own bodily sensations that have become our adversary. Anxiety about being hijacked by uncomfortable feelings keeps us paralyzed, and our minds transpose those past sensations onto new situations to seek release.

If you need evidence of how this dynamic plays out in real life, look no further than the last time you reached out to a friend or family member to vent about an upsetting experience. It's a common human instinct to reach out to trusted loved ones when we're feeling distraught. Our support network is there to catch us when we fall; these people know us intimately, and it can feel cathartic to unload, to rehash, even to cry with someone who cares for us.

But I'll bet that if you earnestly reflect on these moments, you'll realize that even though sharing your pain with a loved one seems like a calming, soothing experience, doing so often *rekindles* your adverse emotions. Whether you're recounting an argument with a friend, lamenting a harsh review from your boss, describing a fear, or just unloading after a really annoying day, you're revisiting a painful memory. My guess is that while you're talking, you don't remain totally calm and estranged from your emotions. Your heart rate escalates. You might raise your voice or weep. You might feel like you're right back in the unpleasant scenario even though you're in a totally neutral space like a friend's kitchen, a colleague's office, or a neighborhood café.

Many of my techniques require you to let go of the mind's processes, resist the urge to get into your head, and just trust in the somatic work. This is critical because the cognitive approach will block you from generating a physiological state that can be encoded into your body. Talk therapy, visualization, goal setting, and other cognitive techniques are certainly important, but to truly optimize the way your body interprets and manages stress, you need to gain control over your physiology as well. The skills in *Heart Breath Mind* merge the science of HRV biofeedback with novel psychological strategies designed to optimize the way you respond to stressful situations. One technique, for example, asks you to practice connecting to a daily stress as you inhale, then breathe it away on the exhale for a powerful result called a Heart Clearing. With the Bubble technique, you envision surrounding yourself with a protective forcefield that shields you from a specific stress — a couple arguing on the subway; a micromanagerial boss barking orders; an impossible relative at Thanksgiving dinner.

The 10-week *Heart Breath Mind* protocol is not only a process of sharpening your reflexes and adapting more flexibly to pressure, it's a healing process that lets you release the sensations associated with aversive experiences, all without becoming overwhelmed and retraumatized. You're about to train your most important muscle to maintain balance, enter stressful conditions from a stronger position, and perform at your peak when under stress and in daily life.

2

▼

Building a Life of Resonance

Believe it or not, it takes time and practice to learn how to breathe properly. In week 2 of this 10-week protocol, I'll guide you through the mechanics of proper breathing, but suffice it to say, most of us are doing it wrong. We tend to breathe into our chests when we should, in fact, be breathing into our lower abdomens. (This is how we're born breathing, but the stress of modern life, exacerbated by epidemic levels of poor posture, trains us out of it.) There's also an ideal inhale to exhale ratio that, when struck, maximizes our ability to reset and helps fortify our parasympathetic nervous system.

Throughout the next 10 weeks, I'll introduce you to multiple breathing-based strategies, including ones that have you connecting to various heart-based emotions, both negative and positive, on the inhales and exhales. For example, one method I teach clients involves the repeated practice of releasing sensations associated with pain, such as anger, fear, or disappointment, on the exhale, while monitoring their heart rate deceleration on a heart rate tracking device.

But before you can attempt that, you'll need to find your resonance breathing frequency—the rate that maximizes your heart rate oscillations, thereby gaining greater control over your autonomic nervous system and enabling you to nimbly navigate challenges.

The most universal resonance frequency for most individuals is 6 breaths per minute. Breathing at this rate activates resonance properties and induces high-amplitude oscillations in the heart rate at 0.1 Hz. (Individualized factors such as emotional sensitivity, physical fitness, or height can render the resonance frequency slightly higher or lower than 6 cycles per minute.) Clinical research shows that most individuals will locate their resonance between 4 and 7 breaths per minute, but over more than a decade and a half of practice, I have found that more than half of us fall within an even tighter range of 5 to 6.5 breaths per minute.

You might be thinking, "That's a really small range. What could possibly be the difference between taking six breaths a minute and seven?" The answer? It makes all the difference in the world! In one recent study, subjects were divided into three groups and asked to breathe at different rates for 15 minutes. The first group breathed at their resonance frequency while the second group breathed at 1 breath per minute higher than their resonance frequency; the third group sat quietly for the 15 minutes. Afterward, the group that breathed at their specific, determined resonance frequency reported an elevated mood, lower systolic blood pressure, and other coveted HRV-BFB outcomes.

Classic mind-body relaxation techniques like yoga and meditation can help you achieve a near-resonance state for the time that you're on your mat or cushion. But in order to embed that feeling deep within your physiology, you need to layer in the biofeedback training and breathe in a way that systematically exercises the baroreflex and strengthens vagal tone. Think of resonance breathing as a high-performance alternative to yoga and meditation.

THE VASCHILLOS

Drs. Evgeny and Bronya Vaschillo first discovered that resonance frequency amplifies heart oscillations back in the 1970s while working with Russian cosmonauts. Initially, they found that when the cosmonauts were shown a computer-generated sine wave pattern and asked to match their heart rate to the undulations, they were able to achieve large fluctuations in heart rate. What the Vaschillos found was that subjects typically showed the highest amplitude of heart rate oscillations within the range of ~0.076 to 0.107 Hertz (Hz). (Hertz measures frequency and 1 Hertz equals 1 oscillation per second). More specifically, subjects typically created maximum heart rate oscillations at ~0.1 Hz, achieved by breathing at a frequency of 6 breaths per minute.

The Vaschillos labeled the rates at which individuals produced the highest amplitude of heart rate and blood pressure as the individual's resonance frequency. Since then, it has successfully been used to treat an amalgamation of diseases and disorders, including but not limited to depression, anxiety, high blood pressure, asthma, irritable bowel syndrome, insomnia, and post-traumatic stress disorder.

RESONANCE BREATHING IRL

In an Italian study of 23 healthy adults, reciting the Ave Maria or the meditative mantra "om-mani-padme-om" slowed breathing to almost precisely 6 breath cycles per minute (0.1 Hz). The researchers concluded that recitation of either the prayer or the mantra exerted an effect similar to that of slow breathing, strengthening the baroreflex.

THE POWER OF RESONANCE

Breathing at your resonance frequency triggers an awe-inspiring and truly remarkable cascade: it strengthens the baroreflex, which helps rebalance the ANS and reduces cardiovascular reactivity. That, in turn, has a reverberating effect throughout the entire body.

- Systems and organs connected to the vagus nerve become stimulated. One such organ is your brain — and more specifically, your prefrontal lobe — giving you the capacity for greater control over your thoughts, the ability to inhibit impulses and urges, and greater attention to detail. Also, with increased frontal lobe activity, small stressors don't carry the same weight. You'll spend far less time replaying events in your mind and will be more likely to stay in the present.
- Diaphragmatic resonance breathing increases HRV, which reliably leads to improvement in chronic medical issues related to anxiety or ANS dysfunction, including depression, anxiety, headaches, high blood pressure, GI troubles, and more.
- You become more skilled at connecting with desired positive emotions on a physiological level, steering your cardiovascular response back to baseline more quickly in the heat of the moment.
- Stamina increases as a result of augmented blood and oxygen flow to muscles, enhancing athletic performance.
- The depth and rate of your breathing impact your brain rhythms in a manner known to improve overall emotional well-being, perhaps because boosting the amplitude of heart rate oscillations in turn spurs oscillatory activity in regions of the brain associated with emotion regulation.
- You may experience a newfound level of empathy. Many of my clients find they can more easily see things from another person's perspective. One client began viewing his mother, who had been abusive during his childhood, as injured and fighting to survive

during his youth. Instead of bitterness and resentment, his heart shifted to empathy, which he was able to carry with him as he met up with her for occasional visits.

This is just a tiny sampling of the psychological, physiological, and emotional benefits of resonance breathing. Throughout *Heart Breath Mind* I'll explore several more effects, including reducing blood pressure, easing headaches, defeating phobias, and more.

IF SLEEP IS A CONCERN FOR YOU . . .

One of my clients, William, was working as a biomedical engineer when he began experiencing insomnia. Falling asleep was sometimes difficult for him, but his main problem was waking up in the middle of the night, around 2 or 3 a.m., and not being able to get back to sleep. William had tried several approaches—cognitive therapies, hypnosis, blue light–blocking glasses—but each of these techniques moved the needle just a tiny bit. He told me that as he lay there, staring at the ceiling at 2 a.m., he felt like a prisoner of his own mind.

When William first came to see me, he was 29; a friend of his had referred him to me. We found his resonance frequency and embarked on the 10-week protocol in which he practiced resonance breathing for 20 minutes twice per day. In addition, William implemented resonance breathing during his middle-of-the-night wakeups until he was able to fall back asleep. After about 5 weeks, he began noticing himself drifting off a bit more easily and in less time during these awakenings.

Newly motivated, he began to include some smart new sleep hygiene habits, like reading for 30 minutes before bed (a paper book, not on a screen) and charging his phone in a room other than his bedroom to prevent mindless scrolling and checking his phone in the middle of the night. William and I worked together to implement a sleep routine, as well, including stretching and breathing prior to bed. William was also interested in biohacking, a millennial-popularized phenomenon that employs lifestyle changes to alter or "hack" into the body's maximum performance potential, and he seemed to appreciate the fact that with HRV-BFB, he could use his resonance breathing frequency to hack into and chip away at his insomnia. The awakenings happened less and less, evidence of his increased HRV kicking into gear overnight. Further, when William did experience occasional middle-of-the-night awakenings, he left the bed, practiced breathing at his resonance frequency, and was able to return to bed and fall asleep.

When my clients tell me what it's like to be in resonance, they say that their mind clears, their heart feels calm, their muscles relax, and their focus sharpens. It's a feeling reminiscent of the experience of relaxing on the beach, listening to the waves crash against the shore, or holding your newborn child for the first time. Part of our work together will be identifying those moments and learning to replicate the physiology associated with them so that you can begin to engage in resonance on demand as needed. By accessing resonance for specific performance challenges and situations, you can close the gap between your current and desired levels of performance.

DEVELOPING RESONANCE ACROSS MULTIPLE AREAS OF YOUR LIFE

So far, I have described the clinical definition of resonance, but after studying heart rhythms for more than a decade, I believe there is much more to resonance to be explored. An organic state of resonance can be achieved by aligning your behaviors with your innate motivations and desires. It's a holistic state in which your words, behaviors, relationships, and actions reflect the person you want to be — an alignment of the heart and mind. This is where the art of peak performance meets the science.

When you tap into your innate ability to use your heart rhythm pattern to shape and guide how you feel, think, and behave, you're rewiring your physiology — the same physiology you bring with you to work, to compete, to interact with your loved ones. You're not just upping your chances of nailing a presentation or becoming a better listener at work, you're evolving into a more passionate spouse or partner, a more patient, empathic parent. It's a physiological and cognitive reset.

If you give your best to this protocol, you may feel your heart open in a way that feels pure, rich, and relationship-enriching. I truly believe that resonance is more than 0.1 Hz in our heart. This frequency generated by the most powerful muscle in our body creates a system-wide optimization that retunes not only how we respond to stress but how we maximize our potential in every aspect of life, including health, relationships, cognitive control, and more. For this reason, I am honored and excited to be here to guide you through every step of this training and to cheer you on through this powerful journey.

IS STRESS AT HOME AFFECTING YOUR PERFORMANCE AT WORK?

Angela was the assistant coach of a women's college basketball team. Between interacting with players, scouting recruits, traveling with the team, analyzing game film, and more, she was under tremendous pressure. But her players felt a strong affinity for her, and she for them. They relied on her not just as a coach but as a mentor and friend.

Angela and her husband had recently lost a beloved family member, and she found herself becoming emotional on the job to the point where it was interfering with her ability to coach effectively. She admitted to me that she was skeptical of my protocol, but as a longtime fan of meditation, she opted to give it a try. Angela had difficulty sitting still during the breathing at first, in part because her muscle tension was so extreme. Once she saw how her muscle tension decreased after about 5 minutes of resonance breathing, she made terrific headway. Soon she found herself looking forward to her breathing sessions, which she felt were helping her to gain some control over her emotions.

By the end of our 10 weeks together, Angela felt that she could more tightly regulate her grief and other emotions on the job and had learned how to use resonance breathing to access a positive mood in fewer than 5 breaths. When she began incorporating her breathing immediately before games, she says, "I found myself interacting in a much more measured way with my players and fellow coaches. I could speak in a calmer, more confident manner, even during nerve-racking game moments, and could think more clearly about what the team needed to do to pull off a win. I feel like I process information more objectively. If there's a bad call or a player does something unexpected on the court, I can inhibit my reaction and quickly determine what needs to happen next with less effort." On the creative side of things, she developed more strategies for new plays as well as plans for how her team could use adversity to their advantage on the court. "The ideas," she said, "often come to me while I'm doing my breathing."

Overall, she reported improvement in her handling of stressful moments, more creative thinking, and an enhanced ability to bounce back from negative interactions in minutes instead of hours or days. "Everyone has 'on' days and 'off' days," she told me, "and now I understand that that is less a function of luck and more a function of being in the right state to create optimal performance. I'm more in the zone."

People benefit from HRV-BFB in so many extraordinary ways. There are the more generalized gains such as an enhanced baseline ability to manage stress and improvements in mood, memory, focus, and anxiety. And then there are more targeted, performance-oriented results: preparing for specific events, such as a presentation, sport competition, or test; facing phobias like fear of flying; preparing for a potentially sensitive conversation; and more.

Right about now, I'll bet you're thinking something along the lines of, "I've been breathing all of my life. How is this really going to help me?" In fact, that very question has been asked in my office countless times.

You're learning not just to strengthen your braking system but to become more flexible (able to amp up or calm down) in the way you act during stress and pressure. You will develop skills to prepare for challenge in advance, tackle stress in the moment like a warrior, and let go of stress that dampens your health and performance with precision and speed. The ability to control your heart rhythms provides beautifully transformative benefits in connecting, perceiving, and being able to navigate the diverse challenges of intimate relationships. Being able to control your stress response can help you feel more in control of your entire life.

Remember: "Inspire" means to motivate or encourage. It also means to *breathe*.

3

▼

How to Use This Book

Part II of this book contains your 10-week HRV-BFB training protocol. The first 4 weeks will focus on mastering the specific breathing techniques that put you in a state of resonance and rewire your body's spontaneous stress response. In weeks 4 through 8, you'll learn strategies for strengthening the parasympathetic nervous system and managing stress on demand. In weeks 9 and 10, you will learn how to use your resonance to optimize your interactions with others.

All of this will build on the resonance breathing techniques you acquire during week 1, which starts with determining your resonance frequency rate.

Before we begin, let's go over the key concepts behind HRV. Having a firm grasp on the following basic principles is essential before embarking on the protocol.

UNDERSTANDING HRV

We tend to imagine our heart beating at a steady, monotonous pace like a metronome. Most of us think it would look like this:

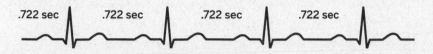

This illustration shows an unhealthy heart rate variability with constant 722-millisecond intervals between beats.

The reality, however, is that a healthy heartbeat is unexpectedly irregular. The time interval between beats changes, even when we are at rest. This variation in beat-to-beat intervals is called HRV.

Here's what it looks like on an EKG:

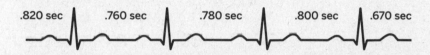

This illustration demonstrates a healthy heart rate variability with variation between beats.

Keep in mind that HRV is different from heart rate (HR). Your heart rate is an average of the number of times your heart beats in a given time period (usually 1 minute.) Generally speaking, a healthy individual's HR is low at rest and high during physical activity, exercise, or stress.

HRV reflects the specific changes in time between successive heartbeats. Each discrete time measurement is called an R-R interval (RRI), or interbeat interval, and happens so quickly that it needs to be measured in milliseconds. Your RRI is the distance between one R-spike and the next.

A low HRV, meaning less variability in the timing between heartbeats, is considered a sign that the body is under stress, either from exercise or physical activity, but also from psychological or emotional stressors. The stress need not be happening at the same time as HRV is being measured; people who hold on to their stress and have difficulty adapting to and recovering from stressors tend to have low HRV in general. Higher HRV, which reflects more variability or irregularity between heartbeats, indicates a flexible autonomic nervous system that easily and efficiently responds to both internal and external stressors. A person with high HRV can adapt and recover faster, and high HRV is considered a promising indicator of an athlete's ability to perform.

When you breathe at your resonance frequency (about 6 breaths per minute for most people), you'll induce high-amplitude oscillations in the heart rate at 0.1 Hz.

THE NEXT WAVE OF HRV TRAINING

While conducting HRV training in my office, I connect clients to electrodes that report heart rate data to a computer system. The system displays a representation of their HRV on a screen, similar to the images on page 33, and allows them to observe firsthand how resonance frequency breathing affects their HRV. Of course, not everyone has access to a certified biofeedback practitioner, so I've created a user-friendly plan for anyone who wants to benefit from this process at home on their own. The method I will describe relies on developing somatic awareness. You will work on acquiring the skills necessary to feel stress as it is occurring in your physiology and then release it. My goal for you is to learn to feel resonance even if you're not able to see it on a screen.

For this reason, I recommend recording your HRV at week 1, week 4, week 7, and week 10 of the training. During each of these weeks, you will measure and record your HRV on 4 separate days to establish a more reliable baseline. (I will provide instructions on how to do this in week 1.)

By using an app on your phone, you will learn to breathe at your resonance frequency rate to synchronize your breath with your heart rhythms and reach a state of resonance. And you'll be able to reap many of the benefits of HRV-BFB training while relying mostly on sensory rather than technological feedback. With practice, you will learn to put yourself in a state of resonance on demand.

THE EQUIPMENT

Depending on your time, budget, and comfort with technology, you will select either one or both of the measuring and recording options below. You will need this equipment in place before the first week so you have a baseline against which you can later assess your HRV gains in the fourth, seventh, and tenth weeks.

- Breath pacing apps (required)
- HRV sensors + app (optional)

Let's explore each of these in greater detail.

Breath Pacing Apps

Tools to pace your breathing are essential to the protocol. There are several breath pacers that you can download for your iOS and Android mobile devices, all varying in terms of sound, visuals, and breathing rates (a bar that moves up and down on the screen; a circle that expands and contracts in size; a dancing sunflower; the sound of ocean waves, etc.).

If you have a 4-second inhale, 6-second exhale resonance frequency, you will have plenty of options to choose from. However, not all breath pacers will allow you to set your inhale and exhale length. If you have a different resonance frequency, you'll need to select a pacer that allows you to customize the breathing to the decimal. Below are several commercial apps that can be tailored to your specific resonance frequency. I do not endorse any particular app. The apps below are all under $5 (at the time of this writing), and some are even free. I encourage you to explore these and other apps, conduct your own research, and find the most appropri-ate pacer *for you*.

Please keep the following criteria in mind — I've listed them in order of priority:

1. Select a pacer that allows you to breathe at your resonance frequency.
2. Choose the app that feels the most visually pleasing to you.

Breath Pacers
iOS

Elite HRV (includes the Heart Breath Mind program and soft geometric breathing guides)
Awesome Breathing (glowing circle)
Breathe2Relax (cylinder fills and empties)
Breath Pacer (expanding and contracting sunflower)
Breathe (up-and-down square, can set a daily reminder to breathe)

Android

Elite HRV (includes the Heart Breath Mind program and soft geometric breathing guides)
Paced Breathing (simple up and down)
Awesome Breathing (glowing circle)
Breathe2Relax (cylinder fills and empties)

HRV Sensors + Apps

HRV sensors typically come in one of three forms: a strap that wraps around the chest; a sensor that clips gently to your finger; or a camera on the back of a smartphone. There are pros and cons to each type of device.

Chest straps tend to be the most accurate because the sensors are affixed to the skin to detect electromagnetic signals close to the heart. The finger sensor device can be accurate and more comfortable to use, but it can be sensitive to cold hands or weaker circulation. It works best if you take a few deep breaths before starting to capture HRV. With most camera sensor apps, you place the pad of your index finger on your smartphone's camera, and your pulse is read. Many people enjoy the camera method for its ease and convenience, but accuracy varies between apps and phones, and it can be difficult to maintain the correct finger pressure and stillness required for accurate pulse detection.

The CorSense HRV Sensor (by Elite HRV) is a small, portable finger sensor that is designed specifically for HRV and, according to the company's CEO, produces comparable reliability to the chest strap sensor. This sensor can measure HRV for up to 4 hours at a time, with a standby battery life of 6+ months on a full charge, and can be used with the free Elite HRV app or any app set up to receive HRV sensor data, such as HRV4Training, SweetBeat HRV, or ithlete.

Two popular chest straps include:

Polar H7 Bluetooth Heart Rate Sensor for the Chest: This waterproof chest strap monitor seems to be the best and most accurate for use with the majority of the HRV apps available. It offers 200 hours of battery life, which is more than sufficient for most beginners.

Polar H10 Bluetooth Heart Rate Sensor for the Chest: Waterproof and offering 400 hours of battery life, the Polar H10 can be paired with a GoPro Hero5 compatibility camera to overlay your heart rate data onto recorded video. This can be useful for individuals who want to explore heart rate trends during specific moments of stress and competition.

Before purchasing an external sensor, make sure that the sensor is compatible with your chosen HRV app.

Only a small fraction of HRV apps allow you to measure your baseline HRV (e.g., for tracking at weeks 1, 4, 7, and 10) and also provide you with a continuous EKG for feedback. Below is a list of a few of the HRV apps that work well with HRV sensors like the CorSense or a chest strap. Please note that this list is not exhaustive and is reflective of the apps available at the time this book was written. For the most up-to-date list of HRV apps, please refer to my website at www.drleahlagos.com.

- Heart Breath Mind (elitehrv.com/hbm)
- HRV4Training (hrv4training.com)
- Sweetwater HRV (sweetwater.com)
- ithlete HRV (myithlete.com)

If you feel that the ease of having your measuring equipment literally at your fingertips will help you commit to your HRV measurements, you can use the Heart Breath Mind, HRV4Training, and ithlete HRV apps, which utilize the built-in camera sensor on your smartphone.

Alternatively, you can try a handheld device that also offers a desktop app for more detailed HRV measurements or a sensor that connects to a tablet:

- Emwave (heartmath.com)
- eVu TPS (thoughttechnology.com)*

Even in my clinical practice, I recommend that clients use only the breath pacer for daily home practice. In fact, the use of daily HRV tracking can detract from training, causing many of my clients to become overly focused on obtaining a specific result instead of remaining present in the process. I call this the paradox of letting go; the more frequently you track your outcome, the less adept you may become at developing the ability to release and reset. The irony here is that for some people, using technology to constantly evaluate HRV daily can cause anxiety.

Thus, I recommend only measuring your HRV during weeks 1, 4, 7,

---

* The eVu TPS is a sensor that monitors HRV, respiration, and hand temperature.

and 10. You will be calculating your weekly mean, or average, HRV each time. For each of these weeks, you'll collect data over the course of 4 days. (See page 224 for a tracking sheet.) I recommend doing this on Monday, Wednesday, Friday, and Sunday of each week, which will allow you to capture HRV fluctuations as they occur throughout the week. This will result in a more accurate, reliable mean.

I also suggest that you record your data first thing in the morning, immediately upon waking. Don't check e-mail first, or start to plan out your day, as stress can alter your measurements. When measuring your HRV, sit upright in bed or a chair, feet on the floor, back straight but relaxed.

Rick Harvey, PhD, an associate professor at San Francisco State University, describes each HRV measurement as a snapshot in time — you don't want to place too much emphasis on any individual measurement but rather should view the collection of them as you might a child's growth curve.

Your HRV is best regarded as data that you will track over time, Harvey says, and context matters greatly, so at this point simply make note of anything that might be affecting your HRV — lack of sleep, exercise, skipped or heavy meals — and then put your tracking device away until you get to week 4! If you choose to continue to monitor your HRV after the 10 weeks are up, you will begin to see patterns in the variables that may be affecting your data.

YOUR TECH ACTION PLAN

1. Choose your pacing/tracking method and obtain the necessary equipment.
2. Measure your HRV on Monday, Wednesday, Friday, and Sunday during weeks 1, 4, 7, and 10. This will enable you to calculate your weekly mean (average) HRV.
3. Take your HRV measurement immediately upon waking up in the morning. Reading your e-mail or starting to think about your work day might cause additional stress, thereby altering readings.

4. When you measure your HRV, I suggest sitting upright in your bed or a nearby chair. Your back should be straight but relaxed.

5. Make sure to note factors that may be impacting your HRV, including lack of sleep, jet lag, alcohol, illness, caffeine, or recent physical exercise.

6. Calculate your weekly mean HRV by adding all four HRV scores and dividing by four.

7. Practice breathing at your resonance frequency for two 20-minute sessions per day, using a breath pacer on your phone.

TWO DAILY BREATHING SESSIONS PER DAY

The goal of this program is to get you breathing for 20 minutes, twice a day, for 10 weeks. This is the protocol followed by my clients, whether they're Olympic athletes or weekend warriors, whether they work in a stressful office or work from home (that includes all the unpaid hours of parenting), and it's the protocol that yields the best results.

Over the course of the following weeks, I'll introduce new skills, such as letting go of stress, preparing for challenges in advance, and creating an ideal heart state on demand. Every week there will be an Action Plan —a sort of homework "prescription." It will always be based on a foundation of two 20-minute breathing sessions per day, the last segment of which will integrate the specific theme or skill presented in that week's chapter.

That means that every week, the final 5 minutes of your breathing sessions will vary. In week 2, for instance, the last 5 minutes will center on diaphragmatic breathing, also called belly breathing; in week 3, you'll spend those final 5 minutes connecting to a daily stressor on the inhale and releasing it on the exhale; by week 6, you'll end by practicing Emotional Pivoting, teaching yourself to shift from, say, irritation to love (when imagining interacting with family members), from a feeling of pressure to calmness (at work), or from fatigue to increased energy (at the end of a long and trying day).

Five minutes might seem short for techniques promising such powerful effects, but I promise you these 5 minutes are strategically placed for maximum benefit. The period immediately following resonance breathing is when your mind is most receptive to new ideas. That's because, with regular practice, 15 minutes of resonance breathing will put you into a kind of meditative state, characterized by an increase in alpha brain waves, a sign of relaxation. Once you're in resonance, your brain is essentially humming with evidence of parasympathetic dominance. Your subconscious becomes more permeable, allowing the week-specific technique you are practicing the chance to become hardwired.

MAKE THE COMMITMENT

People sometimes balk when they hear "20 minutes twice a day." Not everyone will feel as if they have the same amount of time for this practice. Life happens, and 40 combined minutes can feel like a major time commitment.

But 20 minutes twice a day is the most potent equation. Those combined 40 minutes a day are essential for finding resonance and rewiring your body's stress response. You will not obtain the full range of benefits described in this book by practicing for fewer than two 20-minute sessions per day; you won't develop the reflex that kicks in during moments of stress to optimize your functioning.

Think of it like strength training: Will you gain muscle mass if you start lifting weights for 5 or 10 minutes a day? Sure, a little. But bump that time up to 15 minutes twice a day, and you'll see significantly more progress. Twenty minutes twice a day? You're going to develop a reflex that automatically kicks in during stressful moments, allowing you to nimbly navigate whatever issue is at hand. I tell my clients to think about how their lives will change when they can let go of stress more quickly, recover in less time, and shift how they are feeling on demand. Most people begin to see results within the third or fourth week.

I had one client come to me having suffered from debilitating head-aches for years; she wanted to set a goal to eliminate the pain by the end of 10 weeks. She is happy to report that she was able to do so — in fact, now that she has her health back, she is using her resonance breathing to tackle additional goals for performance. I have also had clients come to me with a performance issue, but as we dive deep into their stressors, we find that they are experiencing a great deal of stress in their marriage or relationship. Many clients feel that this process helps improve their ability to perceive and connect with their partner throughout the training. I am amazed at how many people who start this process single are in the early stages of a new partnership by the tenth week of training. The time you spend breathing is an investment in your own potential. So, whatever brought you here, whatever made you pick up this book and give this program a chance, remember that the first step to optimizing your health and performing at your peak is to find 20 minutes two times a day for resonance breathing.

CAN'T COMMIT TO 20 MINUTES TWO TIMES A DAY?

I think that if we were all able to achieve resonance, we could change the world. But I appreciate that not everyone will want to start with such lofty ambitions. Even if you think that time constraints or personal preference will keep you from meeting the required 20 minutes twice a day, you can still benefit mightily from this book. You'll be able to learn new strategies for shifting your physiology on demand to control your emotions and even make gains in cognitive arenas, such as focus and positive self-talk. You will then be able to use these strategies to adjust how you respond to challenges and difficult situations. But to reap *all* the benefits, you need to commit to 20 minutes twice a day.

ON-BOARDING OPTION

To make things feel less daunting, you can begin with two 10- or 15-minute daily sessions for the first 2 weeks, and slowly start to add 5 minutes to each practice. Everyone should be at the two full 20-minute daily sessions by the third week of training. If you choose to proceed with this track, you will still be able to successfully rewire your body's stress response and gain the full roster of benefits.

TRAINING *DON'T*s

Don't multitask. Driving, watching TV, checking e-mail and social media, cooking — none of these are conducive to your daily breathing practice. Give yourself the gift of dedicated time and space to devote to your training. If an interruption occurs, like a baby crying or a pet needing to be walked, address it and return to your breathing.

Don't try to juggle HRV-BFB and meditation. I ask my regularly meditating clients to put their practice on hold during HRV training. You can come back to it after 10 weeks. For now, it's best if you focus on the HRV-BFB. Baroreflex-wise, it will fast-track what years of meditation can do.

Don't try to get all your breathing done in a single 40-minute session. Even the most seasoned resonance breathers might find 40 minutes a bit long. By dividing the total 40 minutes into two 20-minute sessions, you maximize your odds of staying on task and minimize the likelihood of fatigue or distraction.

Don't practice when you're tired. If you schedule your second breathing session at the end of a long, exhausting day, you will likely fall asleep. And while that sleep may feel rejuvenating, you'll miss out on the full 20 minutes needed to obtain the cognitive benefits.

TRAINING *DO*s

Find a place. Once you have committed to doing your breathing exercises, it's important to identify a place for your training. Think about your day: Where and when do you regularly have time for 20-minute breathing sessions and reviewing your goals? Where will you feel most comfortable and unself-conscious? Many of my clients do their training first thing in the morning and again just before they go to bed, but your best times and places to practice may be different. What matters is consistency. Once you determine the time and place that works best for you and begin to practice in it, it will serve as a reminder to do your breathing whenever you are there.

Add a reminder. Even with the best of intentions, we all get too busy or even forget a session or two. As you are building this new routine, it is important to add a reminder to yourself to do the training. The strongest cues or reminders are those built into existing routines. For example, if you make coffee at home each morning, you may say: "After I start the coffee maker, I will do my resonance breathing for 20 minutes." Similarly, in the evening, you may say: "After I put the kids to bed, I will do my breathing for 20 minutes." The key is that the reminder is consistent and built into each day. Regularly practicing in the same place will become its own reminder as well. If you don't have a consistent routine to build around, you can also try setting an alarm or scheduling your training in your calendar. This can be less effective, however, because it is harder to instill internal reminders in the body this way and a beeping phone is easier to ignore than a somatic instinct.

If you must skip a few days, dive back in as soon as possible. The foremost recommendation is to complete 10 consecutive weeks. That's the gold standard. But I understand that things do come up — life happens. If a situation comes along that is not compatible with your training, take the day or two you need to address it and then get back on track. (I would argue that continuing your twice-daily breathing will likely help you navigate your unexpected stressor, but sometimes it just won't seem feasible.) Try your best to not miss more than a few days in a row; missing more than a week will deprive you of the baro-reflex strengthening needed to maximize your benefits.

Turn all sounds off on your breathing pacer. Breathing pacers typically use sounds like ocean waves, chimes, or white noise to indicate inhales and exhales. They can be needlessly distracting. Just focus on the feeling of your breath. I also recommend turning off your ringer.

Track your progress on the Homework Tracking Notes. Beginning on page 223, you'll find papers that can be used to track your progress and collect data during various exercises. Consider this another form of valuable feedback for yourself.

PART II

▼

REWIRING THE STRESS RESPONSE

4

▼

Week 1:

Finding Your Resonance Frequency

Imagine a wine glass and a silver spoon sitting in front of you. You hold the glass in one hand, your fingers and thumb gently grasping its slender stem. With your other hand, you take the spoon and lightly tap the glass bowl. Do you hear that beautiful ping? That note reverberating from the glass to your ears? That is resonance.

Even though you're not made of glass, you can resonate. How? By identifying the precise slow breathing rate that elicits balance in your own unique autonomic nervous system. That's your resonance frequency — the state where your heart rate oscillations synchronize with your breath and your sympathetic and parasympathetic nervous systems align. When you breathe at this rate, your heart rate will go up a little more than usual when you inhale and slow down a little more quickly when you exhale. This amplification results in greater heart rate variability and, as we'll explore throughout this chapter, allows for increased control over your body's response to stress. Your mind unblocks, anxiety dissipates, muscle

tension reduces, and you feel alert and in the zone. When you're in resonance, you can access your own personal state of peak performance.

Getting there requires effort, but the rewards impact almost every
area of your life, including your health, relationships, confidence, and
ability to perform at your peak under pressure. Because resonance frequency breathing fortifies your baroreflex and increases your heart rate
variability, you're training an internal, system-wide, stress-releasing reflex to kick in without any conscious activation during moments of stress.
Here's what that looks like:

- An elite rower who learned to tame her prerace nerves
- A mother of four who reduced the severity and frequency of her
  chronic headaches
- An executive who overcame depression and increased end-of-
  the-day energy levels
- A medical doctor who shifted his communication style from crit-
  ical to empathic to more effectively lead his team
- And so much more

When you've identified the rate that comfortably brings you into a
clear, calm, and confident internal state, you have found your resonance
frequency.

TO BEGIN

You'll need to have one of the breathing pacers I described on page 36
downloaded to your phone or computer. Many people enjoy using an app
because you can set the pacer specifically to your individual frequency
and then follow the pacer as you practice. (No pacer? Follow the counting instructions in Exercise #1 and then skip to page 55.) If you're opting
to use a handheld device, please have that nearby.

Once you have your equipment prepared and ready to use, find a comfortable seated position with your back straight, feet flat on the ground,

legs bent at 90 degrees, and palms resting face-up on your thighs. Let's find your resonance frequency.

BREATHING EXERCISE #1: INHALE FOR 4, EXHALE FOR 6

The standard rate that works for most individuals is to inhale for 4 seconds and exhale for 6 seconds with no pause in between. This is a 10-second breath, or, technically speaking, a frequency of 0.1 Hz. Breathing at this rate will result in 6 breaths per minute. For context, most adults breathe at a rate of 12 breaths per minute.

The magic ratio here is 40:60 — you spend 40 percent of each breath inhaling and 60 percent exhaling.

Let's start by breathing at this rate for 2 minutes. Set your timer. Begin inhaling through your nose and exhaling through pursed lips, as if you are blowing on hot soup, trying to cool it. As you mentally count — 4 seconds in, 6 seconds out — focus on the sensation of air flowing in through your nose and out through your mouth. Really enjoy the next 2 minutes; it's probably been a long time since you slowed down and simply focused on your own breath. These 2 minutes are your first step toward finding resonance.

At the end, take stock of how you feel. Do you feel clearer, calmer, or more centered than you did before the exercise? Some people feel a pleasant tingling in their hands or feet. Many notice a decrease in anxiety and feel more alert or less "busy" in their brain. All these physiological improvements have their roots in the body's relaxation response, but there's also special magic in the act of counting. Counting is handled by the same area of the brain that's responsible for worrying. It's difficult to do both at the same time, so counting is exceptionally effective at crowding out stress, calming a busy brain, and enhancing focus.

BREATHING EXERCISE #2:
PERSONALIZE YOUR BREATHING RATE

Nearly everyone can cultivate resonance throughout their body at or around 6 breaths per minute as in Exercise 1 on page 51. You can breathe at this rate with no further experimentation and still get many of the benefits of this practice.

But being more precise yields an even greater payoff. My goal is to help you determine your personal resonance breathing rate as precisely as possible to truly maximize the benefits of this 10-week protocol.

Spend 2 minutes breathing at each of the following rates. (Choose a pacer app that can be set using highly specific frequencies such as these.) Between each one, take a moment to clear your mind and note how breathing at that rate felt compared to the other ones. If you are tracking your HRV with technology, look at the next page for additional instructions.

- 3.4 seconds to inhale, 5.2 seconds to exhale (7 breaths per minute)
- 3.7 seconds to inhale, 5.5 seconds to exhale (6.5 breaths per minute)
- 3.8 seconds to inhale, 5.8 seconds to exhale (6.2 breaths per minute)
- 4 seconds to inhale, 6 seconds to exhale (6 breaths per minute)
- 4.2 seconds to inhale, 6.2 seconds to exhale (5.7 breaths per minute)
- 4.4 seconds to inhale, 6.6 seconds to exhale (5.5 breaths per minute)
- 4.8 seconds to inhale, 7.2 seconds to exhale (5 breaths per minute)

Ask yourself how you feel after attempting each pace. There's no complicated introspection required — it's as simple as asking yourself which rate felt the most comfortable. This difference can be exquisitely subtle and is highly individualized, so I always reassure my clients that there's no pressure to rank every breathing frequency on a scale of 1 to 10 or to somehow pinpoint their levels of calm and stress levels after each one. Just ask yourself, "Which pace felt the most enjoyable and least effortful?" Write down your preferred rate. (See page 223 for a tracking sheet.)

Nine times out of 10, **the breathing rate that feels the most comfort-**

able is your resonance frequency. This is the breathing frequency that will stimulate your heart rate to produce maximum variability. If you were connected to biofeedback equipment, you would see your heart rate rising and falling in those gorgeous, undulating oscillations.

If you don't notice a discernible difference between one rate and the next or find it too difficult to track your breath to a fraction of a second, revert to the standard rate — 4 seconds in, 6 seconds out. For nearly everyone, this frequency will elicit resonance in the cardiovascular system and strengthen your ability to control your response to stress and pressure. If you have difficulty recognizing one particular sensation when breathing at the different frequencies, you are not alone. It's 100 percent acceptable to opt for the 4 seconds in, 6 seconds out pace. You can always fine-tune in the coming weeks.

FINDING YOUR FREQUENCY WITH HRV TECHNOLOGY

In Chapter 3, I mentioned that some of my clients choose to purchase instrumentation to measure their HRV. If you have access to these instruments, you can use them to establish your resonance frequency. While you don't need to use this sort of technology to determine your resonance frequency, it may be especially appealing to people who love all things tech or who crave the most precise data possible.

If you opt to utilize your HRV instrumentation, use your HRV sensor and the app on your phone and breathe at each of the rates on the previous page for 2 minutes while tracking your heart rate. (See page 224 for a tracking sheet.) Which of the rates felt the least effortful and produced the greatest heart rate oscillations on your equipment? Your RMSSD (root mean square of successive differences) is the clinical measure of HRV. (There are other measures of HRV, such as SDNN [standard deviation of time between heartbeats], but for the purpose of this protocol, we will measure HRV via RMSSD.) This measure is considered the most accurate reflection of the autonomic nervous system when tracking over the short term.

If you are in doubt or changing your breathing rate doesn't seem to produce much variation in your HRV, simply pick the breathing rate that feels easiest and least effortful. If one breathing rate produces the highest RMSSD but another breathing rate feels more comfortable, choose the breathing rate that feels the most comfortable.

ANY QUESTIONS?

"What if it feels like I'm running out of breath?"

Most, if not all, of these breathing paces should feel *good*. If either the inhalation or exhalation feels uncomfortably long or awkwardly short, you are *not* breathing at your resonance frequency. This week is all about experimenting with different rates to discover the perfect one for you. If you force yourself to take too large of an inhale, you will likely exhale too quickly to compensate. Many people try to focus on the depth of the inhale, but the key is a gentle inhale and a slow, easy exhale.

REMEMBER YOUR BASIC BREATHING TIPS

- Focus on a slow, gentle inhale through the nose and a slow exhale through a gently opened mouth. (The emphasis is slightly more on the exhale than on the inhale.)
- Breathe easily and comfortably. Do not try too hard. Note: If you notice symptoms of hyperventilation, such as dizziness, a fast heartbeat, or feeling like you can't catch your breath, try breathing less deeply.

RESONANCE FREQUENCIES IRL

Your resonance frequency is affected by many factors, including your gender, height, and overall cardiovascular health. Men generally have slower resonance frequencies than women; taller people tend to have slower resonance frequencies than their shorter counterparts. Why? Blood volume is a major predictor of resonance frequency—the bigger you are, the greater your blood volume, and the slower your resonance frequency.

THE POWER OF POSTURE

There's a reason teachers are always telling students to sit up straight: when we slouch or hunch over, we impair blood flow to the brain, clouding our thinking and making it more difficult to concentrate.

Sitting up straight and tall, on the other hand, has been shown to make it easier for people to engage in positive thinking and to access enjoyable thoughts and emotions. In one study, when college-age study subjects were asked to recall happy memories — spending time with friends, acing an exam, striving for success — it was physiologically easier for them to do so while sitting erect as opposed to slouching in a chair.

Here's why: Our mind connects slumping over with feeling powerless or defeated. When we slouch, we essentially give our brains permission to tap into helpless, hopeless, or depressing thoughts. Not an ideal frame of mind for starting a 10-week performance-enhancing program that aims to change your life for the better.

Slouching also inhibits the breathing process itself. Hunching over essentially robs all the organs and muscles within your core of the space they need to perform. Breathing suffers, and when you can't breathe properly, you perform at a suboptimal level across the board. Another study led by the same researcher even linked sitting tall with improved performance on a math exercise. Subjects who sat up straight as they attempted to mentally count down by sevens from a triple-digit number rated the challenge easier than those who slouched while subtracting.

As you're reading this book right now, stop right where you are and check in with your spine. Don't make any effort to improve your posture; the goal is to honestly assess your sitting position. Are you slouching? If somebody were viewing an X-ray of your body, would your vertebrae appear directly stacked on top of one another, or would they appear in more of a C-shaped curve? If it's the latter, don't criticize yourself; most adults slouch. But do use it as motivation to straighten your spine, sitting up as beautifully erect as possible.

Make sure you choose a comfortable chair that allows you to sit with a straight back, the vertebrae of your spine stacked neatly on top of one another. Your feet should be flat on the floor, legs uncrossed, knees at a 90-degree angle. Palms can rest face-up on your lap. This is your new performance posture.

ANY QUESTIONS?

"What do I do if my mind is wandering?"

Mind-wandering is a natural, common occurrence as you learn to shift from your head to your heart. I find that my clients who tend toward perfectionism tend to have the most trouble forgiving their wandering mind. Try not to judge yourself for it. For now, don't worry about attempting to control your thoughts or keep them from wandering. The point of week 1's exercise is not to stop your thinking mind but rather to tune in and try to feel what it is like to be in resonance. This is about relaxing into your resonance frequency. Simply enjoy the air as it comes in through your nose and flows out through your mouth. The key area of focus should be following along with the breath pacer to maintain your resonance rhythm and not constantly worrying if you are doing it perfectly. When you notice your mind drifting, gently bring your awareness back to your heart.

As you practice breathing at each rate, pay attention to the following signs that you are shifting into a state of resonance:

- Reduced anxiety
- Improved mood
- Enhanced focus
- Decreased muscle tension

A LIFE OF RESONANCE: SETTING GOALS

When clients come to my office, one of our first tasks is defining the objective of their training. Why did you pick up this book? What is your goal? Perhaps you want to improve your ability to stay calm when you lead team meetings. Maybe you want to reduce fatigue throughout your workday. If you're experiencing frequent awakenings throughout the night, your goal may be to fall back asleep within 10 minutes or less of waking.

Here are a few examples of goals that have been set — and achieved — by my clients:

Over 10 weeks I'd like to . . .

- Feel my heart rate calm before a performance event (speaking engagement, presentation, athletic performance, etc.)
- Reduce my frequency of panic attacks by a third
- Turn off my busy brain so I can fall asleep within minutes after getting up at night
- Be able to fall back asleep within 5 minutes of waking
- Reduce my frequency of headaches to once a week (or once a day, in severe cases)
- Lower my blood pressure to within a healthy range
- Recover in half the time after experiencing a stressful event
- Consume no more than two glasses of wine or two beers in a social setting per week
- Access flow on demand

When they practice for 20 minutes, twice a day for 10 weeks, many of my clients make significant progress toward their goals. You will, too. Some people feel so motivated by having accomplished their goals that they continue beyond 10 weeks of training to try for more. Watching my clients achieve and often exceed their goals is one of the most rewarding aspects of my job.

Ask yourself why you picked up this book. What goal did you hope it would help you achieve? Is there a specific problem or challenge you're hoping to solve? Are you hoping to reach a new level of performance at work or improve a relationship that is meaningful to you? Maybe you have a more general goal concerning stress. Take a moment to write down some of your aspirations (see Homework Tracking Notes, page 225).

Now, look at what you have written down, and explore how or why your body and mind might be preventing you from achieving it. Maybe you long for a close, loving relationship but find yourself emotionally shutting down after the first few dates. Maybe the stress of public speaking causes your heart to race and your back to sweat. Maybe you get overwhelmed with day-to-day tasks and find yourself lashing out at family members. One of my clients, a film actor, named his desire to perform on Broadway but was petrified of live audiences; another client wanted to begin dating again after a difficult divorce, but the wounds still felt too fresh. A hockey player came to me wanting to close the gap between how he performed in practice and how he competed at national-level tournaments. Whatever connections you uncover, take a moment to write them down. Try filling in the blanks:

"I want to _____. But when I try, _____ happens."

or

"I wish I could _____, but _____ keeps getting in my way."

GETTING S.M.A.R.T.R. ABOUT YOUR GOALS

You may be nodding your head at this commonplace suggestion — *yes, yes, set a goal, got it.* But it's time to upgrade the traditional goal-creation process so you can pursue your objectives with passion and purpose.

Most people who seek me out wish to improve their emotional control, manage stress, and perform at their peak under pressure and challenge. When working with clients to set their goals, I ask them to think about how they currently handle pressure and how they would like that to change over the next 10 weeks. If possible, we try to tie these goals to specific health and performance outcomes so they can circle back at the end of the 10 weeks and objectively evaluate their progress.

You've likely heard about S.M.A.R.T. goals: Specific. Measurable. Achievable. Relevant. Timely. One reason so many people fall through on their New Year's resolutions? Not setting S.M.A.R.T. goals. (Thirty percent of Americans give up on their New Year's resolutions after 2 weeks.) Kicking off the New Year saying "I want to be less stressed" or "I want to get in shape" is doomed to fail because generic goals like those lack every quality included in the S.M.A.R.T. acronym.

But tweak those same goals to fit the S.M.A.R.T. criteria and they become actionable. Instead of "getting in shape," how about "I'm going to jog or run for 20 minutes a day, 3 days a week"? "I want to be less stressed" transforms into "I'd like to learn how to lower my heart rate before speaking in front of a crowd."

When choosing your goals for the next 10 weeks, I encourage you to consider whether they can be realistically achieved within that time frame. Next, take a moment to consider ways to evaluate your progress over the next 10 weeks. One client, a CEO of a start-up company, was seeking help mitigating the stress he felt when reviewing profit and loss statements each month. He decided to track his stress levels on a scale of 1 (lowest) to 10 (most) stress while reviewing those statements over a few months. A professional tennis player who frequently failed to perform as well on game day as he did during practice chose to rank his anxiety before, halfway through, and at the end of each tournament to see what impact his HRV-BFB training was having on his ability to self-regulate. As you train, you too will monitor and evaluate changes in your performance. So, when pinpointing your goal, I want you to add a critical extra piece of criteria to the S.M.A.R.T. acronym. I want you to make your goal S.M.A.R.T.R.: Specific, Measurable, Achievable, Relevant, Timely, and Resonant.

Before moving on to the next section, write out your S.M.A.R.T.R. goals on page 225. You'll be able to track your progress by ranking your current level of achievement at weeks 1, 4, 7, and 10.

This is a dynamic process that interacts with your own biology, genetics, and lifestyle. You may experience benefits as early as the second week, but it's more common to experience changes starting at the third or fourth week. If you don't feel much change before the fourth week, don't be alarmed. Researchers who have studied why this process works suggest that the fourth week is when measurable physiological change occurs in the parasympathetic nervous system. Accordingly, you are likely to notice improvements in your mood, anxiety, and ability to let go after a month of this practice. Then, depending on your commitment to training, you will experience incremental weekly improvements in your mind and body.

Regardless of the goal you select, it must have one more important quality: it needs to resonate within you. Your goal must embody a change your body and mind have been craving—a transformation that infuses you with hope, that holds the power to change the way you experience life and drives you toward your peak health and performance.

Keep your goals close at hand; you'll be reviewing them once a day prior to your morning breathing exercise.

RESONANCE IRL

Certain words tend to have a resonance effect: *calm, competent, fearless, courageous, fierce, gratitude, magic*. Hearing these words tends to maximize people's HRV, almost as if they naturally align with our heart's desires. If there's a particular word you've always been drawn to, feel free to weave it into your goal.

Similarly, avoid words that are restrictive or limiting in nature, such as *no, not, don't, won't, can't.* Instead, focus on the positive aspects of what you want and what you will do. For example, with the CEO, I asked him to rethink his initial goal of *Eliminate the stress response,* and revise it so that it described the state he *wanted* to be in when reviewing profit and loss statements, not the state he wanted to avoid: *In 10 weeks, I will feel calm, confident, and in control when I review profit and loss statements.*

WHAT YOU'LL EXPERIENCE

You've taken the first step toward gaining control over your body's response to stress. I know what you may be thinking: *I'm just breathing.* But it's so much more than that. You're breathing the way nature intended but the stress of modern life has corrupted. You're strengthening your parasympathetic braking system. You're finding your resonance frequency, aligning with your goals in a way that echoes authentically within your body and mind. You're on your way to a higher-performing *you.* Change is about to happen.

HIGHLIGHT ON HEALTH: HEART HEALTH

There is a robust link between HRV and cardiac health. As we've discussed before, slow breathing increases your baroreflex sensitivity, and a stronger baroreflex leads to greater HRV (and vice versa). Individuals with stronger baroreflexes enjoy more regulated blood pressure levels than their fast- and shallow-breathing counterparts. As previously discussed, this has to do with the switch from sympathetic nervous system dominance to parasympathetic dominance.

HRV has also been shown to be a strong predictor of health outcomes after a heart attack as well as a strong indicator of whether an individual develops heart disease or high blood pressure at some point in the future. Research out of the decades-long, world-renowned Framingham Heart Study examined the ability of baseline HRV to predict risk of future cardiac events in individuals free from heart disease. Of all the participants who ultimately did experience an event, the majority occurred in those with the lowest HRVs. In fact, HRV was deemed a better predictor of future cardiac events than cholesterol, resting heart rate, or blood pressure.

High blood pressure (also called hypertension) is at epidemic levels in the United States—one in three Americans suffers from it—and the American Heart Association recommends deep breathing as a strategy for easing hypertension and preventing heart disease, right alongside eating veggies and quitting smoking.

Surprisingly enough, resonance breathing may actually help you avoid being misdiagnosed with hypertension. Up to 30 percent of people who are told they have high blood pressure actually suffer from white-coat hypertension, essentially doctor-related anxiety that ramps up one's blood pressure. A study in the aptly named journal *Blood Pressure* found that deep breathing for 30 seconds was enough to regulate blood pressure in a way that allowed health care providers to distinguish true hypertension from the white-coat variety.

Note: If you have a known heart condition, high blood pressure, diabetes, asthma, or another chronic health condition, speak to your health care provider before embarking on this program. *Heart Breath Mind* is not meant to be a substitute for treatment. That said, it may reduce symptoms enough that your doctor may decide to reduce your usual medication dosage. Record your experiences and share them with your doctor, reviewing your progress together.

ANY QUESTIONS?

"What do I do if I'm having difficulty sitting still?"

Initially, sitting and simply breathing for 20 minutes may feel fairly challenging. Many of my clients come back to me after the first week complaining that the time dragged by extremely slowly. That's because we live in a fast-paced, hypervigilant world, constantly checking our e-mails, looking at our watches, posting updates on social media. We think we're being lazy if we're not multitasking. Our attention and focus have become so fragmented that sitting in a chair and just breathing makes us feel unproductive, maybe even guilty.

It gets easier. Just as you grew up and began to easily ride in the car for longer periods of time, I promise that as you get closer to the fourth week of practice, you soon will have no problem making it through the full 20 minutes . . . especially as the benefits of persistent practice start manifesting in your daily life. Take this as an encouraging sign: when your practice time begins to feel like it's flying by, this is evidence of your sympathetic and parasympathetic nervous systems becoming aligned and your baroreflex growing stronger.

WEEK 1 ACTION PLAN

1. Measure your HRV four times this week, right after waking up. Mark your results on the homework tracking sheet on page 224.
2. Try breathing at the six recommended breathing rates, and determine the one that feels best to you. This is your resonance frequency. You'll know you've found it when your mind clears, your heart feels calm, and your muscles feel less tense. Again, mark your results on the homework tracking sheet on page 224.
3. Reflect on your goals and write them down, making sure they follow the S.M.A.R.T.R. criteria and that they resonate within *you*. Rank each goal on current level of achievement from 1 (lowest) to

10 (highest) using the space on your homework tracking sheet on page 225. You will have the chance to reflect on these again during weeks 4, 7, and 10.

4. Practice your resonance breathing for 20 minutes twice a day, reviewing your goals in the morning before your initial breathing session. After breathing, check in with your heart, brain, and body. Do you notice any shift in your mood, anxiety, focus, or tension in your body? If you need to start with 10 or 15 minutes twice daily and slowly ramp up over the next few weeks, that's perfectly fine.

5

▼

Week 2:

Using Your Breath to Increase Energy

The average person takes about 20,000 breaths a day. You'd think we would be pros at it by now. We're not.

The truth is, most adults breathe absolutely the wrong way—from our chests, not our bellies. The fallout? Relentless stress, sluggish energy levels, emotional dysregulation, a worsening of chronic health conditions . . . poor breathing technique impairs performance in essentially every area of life.

You deserve better.

A TALE OF 2 BREATHS

Many of us think the lungs play the most important role in breathing, but it's actually the diaphragm that is the star of the show. This is the point where most people ask, "What's a diaphragm?" Excellent question. It's a dome-shaped muscle that lives just below the lungs. Its main purpose is to drive breathing. As you inhale, the diaphragm wants to contract, forcing the lungs to expand and draw in air. As you exhale, the diaphragm is designed to relax, allowing the lungs to return to their resting state. Then the whole thing starts over again.

This is called diaphragmatic breathing (it also goes by *belly breathing* or *Buddha breathing*), and it's how the body was designed to function. Need proof? Watch a baby lying on her back as she snoozes for a minute or two. Her belly does all the work, puffing out and in like a soft balloon. Her lungs are working, of course, but they don't really move up and down. She may not yet know how to walk or talk, but she knows that her diaphragm is where all the action happens. (No baby around? Watch a dog or cat — they know the right way to breathe, too.)

But most of the adult population has trained itself to breathe without tapping into the diaphragm's immense power. We've become a nation of chest-breathers . . . and our mental and physical well-being is suffering as a result.

It can start in childhood, when we spend a huge chunk of our waking hours sitting behind a desk at school. Slouching is inevitable, and this sort of rounded posture causes the shoulders and rib cage to hunch forward and the lower back to contract, making it hard for our diaphragm to move in and out. The same phenomenon happens — probably to a greater degree, in fact — as we start using technology; smartphones, tablets, computers and laptops . . . these inventions have helped society grow by leaps and bounds, but they have also drawn our attention forward and down, whether we're squinting at small type on the computer or mindlessly scrolling through social media on our phone. Once again, our upper body becomes rounded, and the diaphragm can't do its job.

In response, we learn to breathe with our chests. The next time you're at a café, look around. You'll see customers hunched over, staring at their screens and lattes, their bellies still and their *chests* moving in and out. That tells you not only are they breathing inefficiently, but their bodies are operating in a sympathetic-dominated survival mode marked by anxiety and hypervigilance, neither of which is required or advantageous for studying for their medical school exam, writing a pre-meeting memo, or doing whatever brought them to the coffee shop in the first place.

It's worth noting that the lower lungs are loaded with parasympathetic nerve receptors that, when stimulated through belly breathing, help spread a sense of calm throughout the body and mind. When you chest breathe, those lovely lower-lung receptors go untouched. Chest breathing does, on the other hand, do a stellar job of triggering the *sympathetic* nerve receptors located in the upper part of the lungs. As a result, your fight-or-flight reaction gets switched on when it doesn't need to be . . . sometimes 24/7. You'll feel stressed, anxious, tired, and on edge while increasing your risk of a host of chronic diseases, including heart disease, depression, cancer, and more.

WHY THE WAY YOU BREATHE MATTERS

Oxygenated blood is your life force — every single cell of your body needs it to function. Every inhale carries energizing, oxygenated blood to your brain, organs, and muscles. When you ignore your diaphragm and use only your chest to breathe, the trillions of microscopic cells throughout your body do receive enough oxygen to function, yes. But you don't want to just function, do you?

You want to thrive.

With belly breathing, there's a dynamic at work called full oxygen exchange. The process is critical to powering you through your day, fueling your stamina, and maintaining a clear, focused mind.

Breath holding, on the other hand, restricts the lungs and, in turn, interrupts the flow of energizing oxygen.

There are two parts to this phenomenon, and when put into action, they yield truly phenomenal results.

Part 1: The Gentle, Slow Inhale

When you breathe from your belly, you are actually forcing your lungs to take in more air. This optimizes the amount of oxygen (O_2) traveling through your bloodstream to your muscles and organs, including the heart and the brain.

But that's not the full picture.

Part 2: The Longer, Slow Exhale

In order for that nourishing oxygen to get where it needs to go, it needs an assist from CO_2. As you may remember from middle school biology, when you breathe in oxygen, it helps your cells create energy. Carbon dioxide (CO_2) is formed as a byproduct. Some CO_2 must be exhaled, but your body actually needs some of it to help ferry O_2 throughout the body.

The key to the perfect exhale is *slowing down*. Many people new to belly breathing tend to inhale a huge amount of air, then end up exhaling too quickly because their body isn't yet used to this new style of respiration. Exhaling too quickly, though, causes you to expel too much CO_2. If you lose too much CO_2, your precious O_2 can't get where it needs to go. (This is called overbreathing, and it not only impedes delivery of oxygen to the brain by 30 to 60 percent, it can actually exacerbate feelings of anxiety, anger, or pain.) Keep things slow to take full advantage of the power of your exhale.

Breathing through a slightly opened mouth is an easy way to slow things down. Picture yourself blowing on a spoonful of hot soup, and you'll see what I mean.

With belly breathing, you'll learn to breathe in a way that not only stimulates all those calming lower lung parasympathetic receptors with each inhale but also strikes the ideal ratio of O_2 to CO_2 on the exhale.

DEEP BREATHING IRL

A large chunk of my clientele, from athletes to business executives, develop increased physical endurance after practicing belly breathing at their resonance frequency for approximately 2 months. A golfer on the PGA Tour reported increased stamina on holes where he had previously felt fatigued. Individuals in the workplace noticed their afternoon energy dip happened less and less.

After several athletes, from Olympians to NBA players, reported to me that their energy had started to ramp up around the seventh week of their HRV training, I began to research why. I reached out to Evgeny Vaschillo, the noted Russian scientist who first discovered the cardiovascular benefits of breathing at one's resonance frequency. Dr. Vaschillo suggested that breathing at resonance frequency through the mouth, coupled with belly breathing, created a second-wind effect. As a result, muscles that were previously depleted of oxygen were now being replenished. The effect was a feeling of increased energy during moments when these clients had previously experienced fatigue.

I personally experienced the physical endurance benefits of this style of breathing. For years, I was an avid 3-mile runner. After 7 weeks of training myself to breathe at resonance and with my belly, I experienced an unprecedented increase in my endurance. I no longer felt fatigued at the 3-mile mark. My muscles and body had more stamina. Following my twelfth week of breathing practice, I enrolled in and completed my first 10K.

BREATHING EXERCISE #3: BELLY BREATHING

Ready to give belly breathing a try? Psyched up to start slowing things down? Let's start right now.

Step 1: Begin by sitting in a comfortable chair. Place one hand on your belly. Breathe normally, as you do when you're reclining in your favorite armchair, listening to calming music. What happens to your hand as you inhale and exhale? For most people, their hand will more or less remain still. That's because modern life has trained us away from belly breathing.

Keeping that hand on your belly, place your other hand on your chest. Take some more slow, even breaths. Is the hand on your chest moving in and out or even up and down? If so, you're not alone . . . but you are breathing suboptimally. Your goal is to flip the script: you want the *belly* moving and the *chest* staying more or less still. I know it sounds counter-intuitive — *"You want my chest to stay still while I breathe?"* But, yes, that is precisely the goal for all the reasons I've discussed so far and more. Remember: your diaphragm is your main breathing muscle, and your diaphragm lives in your belly.

Step 2: Focus on breathing in slowly through your nose so that your stomach gently expands up and out against your hand. Let that belly go — really let it peek out. Your stomach should now be pressing gently against your hand. Some people feel self-conscious about really letting their stomach go and expand during this exercise, but you should go ahead and really let that belly release. The hand on your chest should remain still.

Step 3: Slowly exhale through a slightly open mouth. As you exhale, gently contract your stomach muscles as they move back toward your spine. You don't need to actively flex your muscles, like someone trying to make a six-pack emerge, just allow your belly to smoothly move in and out.

Take a few more breaths just like that. You want the hand on your belly gently moving out, away from your spine, as you breathe in through your nose, and gently moving back toward your spine as you release the air through your mouth. All the while, the hand on your upper chest remains as still as possible.

Next, set down this book and continue to breathe with one hand on your chest and the other on your belly for 5 minutes. Your belly should gently expand with every inhale, then contract toward the spine on the exhales. Your hands are all you need to tell you if you are or aren't breathing to maximize your energy.

BELLY BREATHING IRL

Many women wear slimming garments beneath their clothes—underwear, tights, or shirts with slimming panels that aim to smooth the tummy. (Men may feel similar pressure, thanks to labels like "beer belly" or "dad bod.") Your belly may appear flatter, but your breathing may suffer in the process—these garments are modern-day corsets! The abdomen and diaphragm are pushed unnaturally inward, hampering breathing. For the best results, I recommend not wearing anything that constricts your stomach.

THE BIRTH OF BREATH MASTERY

The art of mastering one's breath with the goal of improving health and wellness has been around for thousands of years. Long a mainstay of Eastern medicine—diaphragmatic breathing features heavily in meditation and yoga, where it's called pranayama—belly breathing hit the Western mainstream In 1975 when a book called *The Relaxation Response* was published. This book was the first to propose that the human body had the power to elicit a massive relaxation response—the opposite of the fight-or-flight phenomenon—through a combination of slow, deep breathing; reduced muscle tension; and meditation. It was written by Dr. Herbert Benson, now Distinguished Mind Body Medicine Professor of Medicine at Harvard Medical School, but at that point a young cardiologist who was met with incredulity by his Harvard colleagues for suggesting such a mind-body connection might even exist.

Dr. Benson's book was an immediate hit—within weeks, it had soared to the top of the *New York Times* bestseller list—and it served as a catalyst for more research and interest in deep breathing.

ANY QUESTIONS?

"Do I need to breathe at the same time each day for this training to work?"

No, you don't. If you're a morning person, you can look forward to practicing right after you wake up. If your day is jam-packed but you tend to have a lull in activity around 6 p.m., try it then. If you often find yourself lying in bed, tired but wired from a long, busy day, maybe bedtime is your optimal second practice window. Many people experiment with times, find one that works well, and ultimately end up choosing to breathe at approximately the same times every day.

The most critical point about the timing of breath training is setting time aside for your practices. You may want to make appointments in your phone or calendar to help maintain your practice for your breathing sessions. Within a few weeks, your body will begin to look forward to these sessions. After a few weeks of practice, your body will start to cue you that it's time for a breathing session without you having to set an alert on your phone or wristwatch.

Stay consistent, and you will soon be an expert at this belly-breathing thing!

"Can I practice while driving?"

No. This sort of paced breathing can make some people drowsy. Refrain from practicing your twice-a-day, 20-minute breathing while driving.

DO YOU FEEL STRESS UNRAVELING YOUR COMPOSURE BUT DON'T KNOW HOW TO STOP IT?

Elizabeth was a mother who experienced uncomfortable levels of stress while watching her gymnast son compete. She came to see me during a college eligibility year. If her son performed well over the following few months, he would likely earn an athletic scholarship to college. The stakes were higher than ever, and Elizabeth was feeling progressively worse before and during each of his meets. Her heart would pound in her chest, her breathing grew uncomfortably fast, and she felt as if she were on the verge of a panic attack right there in the gymnasium bleachers.

We talked about belly breathing, and I explained that she could use this tool to help remain calm before and during competitions. First, I asked her to pay special attention to her breathing in the hours leading up to her son's gymnastic competitions. Was she breathing from the chest or the abdomen? When she reported back, she told me she was shocked to realize how frequently she had been taking shallow, rapid breaths and her chest was doing all the heavy lifting.

Elizabeth began practicing belly breathing at the office, at home, and on the go, reminding herself to shift her attention to the movement of her abdomen whenever she felt anxious. She became increasingly masterful at noticing subtle elevations in her anxiety and then shifting to deep, diaphragmatic breathing. In about a month, she found herself able to sit and enjoy watching her son compete, focusing on the strength and athleticism of his moves rather than her own fear of witnessing a critical mistake. This is how Elizabeth found her own champion mind-set. "Before, I was always focused on the possibility of losing. When I made space in my belly to take deeper, fuller breaths, I felt an openness in my body and heart and greater control over my thoughts. I was no longer in a state of fear."

What You'll Experience

Belly breathing may feel unnatural to you, at least initially. Our tech-obsessed, flat-belly-focused culture has trained us to breathe from our chests. We are rewarded for stifling strong emotions — girls and women are expected to rein in anger; boys and men are exhorted not to cry — and when we hold back tears, stifle anger, or try to tiptoe through painful situations, we also breathe irregularly . . . or hold our breath altogether.

This week, you will likely experience a calming of the mind as you breathe — a wonderful indication that your brain is getting the oxygen it needs to produce energy for optimal health and performance. With consistent practice over the next 9 weeks, you will create a muscle memory in your heart that will prompt belly breathing to occur on its own during moments of stress. By rehearsing diaphragmatic breathing through consistent practice, my patients train their bodies to breathe this way all the time, so they are optimizing the mind and body during critical moments of stress and challenge. Expanding your abdomen as you inhale through the nose and then contracting it as you exhale through an open mouth becomes an ingrained habit, something you carry with you throughout your day everywhere you go, like your phone or keys. Every time you need a reset, you can tap into the power of your belly breathing and quickly bring yourself back to "that space," where you are clear, focused, and ready to conquer your next challenge.

Never forget that the way you breathe can directly improve your energy levels, revitalize your brain power, and potentially touch every aspect of your physical and emotional well-being. It's just that good.

Using Belly Breathing to Turn Off Your Busy Brain

Many of us tend to default to altered breath patterns — chest breathing, holding our breath, or even gasping — when we feel worried or get caught in a cycle of stressful thinking. This is a very common human response to negative emotions like tension, anxiety, fear, anger, and annoyance.

Throughout your day, you can tap into your new belly-breathing skills to help break up these negative or stressful thoughts. Gently shift your focus away from these thoughts and toward the movement of your abdomen as you breathe in and out. Whether you're waiting in a frustratingly long line at the grocery store, stuck in traffic, about to meet a potential new anchor client, or waiting for the starting whistle to blow before a race, acknowledge the worry you're feeling and focus on changing your breathing.

This doesn't mean that you dismiss the concern — you have every right to feel annoyed at the long line or nervous about an important meeting. But instead of allowing it to sap you of physical and mental energy, course correct in the moment and tap into your breathing to help improve your outlook and response. Try to acknowledge your thoughts by stepping back and noticing them, labeling them as "anxious" or "angry" or "racing mind." This will allow you to start to detach from them.

Slowly, try to fully return to the feeling of air moving in and out. Get curious about the motions of your belly: As you inhale, what does your abdomen feel like when expanding outward? Push it a little farther. Now, really let it hang out. What does it feel like to just let go? Notice your belly button and the way it leads your belly inward on the inhale. See if you can notice all the muscles in the abdomen working to help you contract. Moment by moment, refocus your mind on the movement of your abdomen. You are building up your mental muscles in an atmosphere of simplicity and openness. The goal is to create space between your negative thoughts, calming the busy chatter of the mind for longer and longer pulses of time.

To do this consistently is challenging. It takes practice, practice, and practice—mindful practice—to change. But with that practice, your body will begin to enjoy the feeling so much that when it anticipates these triggering circumstances, it will automatically shift into belly-breathing mode. Throughout these 10 weeks, you are training your mind, heart, and body to perform at their peak level of ability.

EXPERIENCE THE DIFFERENCE

Now that you're more familiar with belly breathing and the pleasurable feelings it creates, I want to move backward a bit and revert to how you were breathing before you began this chapter. I'm going to lead you through an exercise that will give you a clear sense of what chest breathing truly feels like for your body and the uncomfortable sensations it elicits. Doing this usually impacts people strongly enough that they quickly begin catching themselves in real time and shifting to belly breathing.

The exercise is based on an exquisitely simple yet effective study conducted by my colleague and dear friend Erik Peper, PhD, a professor of holistic health at San Francisco State University and a pioneer in the biofeedback field. It's designed to show the ramifications of poor breathing. Dr. Peper and another researcher trained 35 volunteers in slow belly breathing. The volunteers were then instructed to rein in their breathing, exhaling only about 70 percent of the air in their lungs with every exhale. After just 30 seconds of this subpar breathing, almost every subject reported a climb in unpleasant symptoms, including anxiety, dizziness, light-headedness, and neck and shoulder tension. Bringing themselves back to the slow belly breathing counteracted those symptoms, and stress levels returned to normal.

Give it a try: Take a few normal breaths, and then alter your breathing pattern so that you're exhaling only 70 percent of your previously inhaled air. (It might be easier to envision only three-quarters of the air in your lungs flowing out with every exhale.) If you need to stop because you feel light-headed, definitely do so. After 30 seconds of this, you'll probably feel not-so-great . . . and that's precisely the point.

Every exercise in this chapter is designed to show you, in real time, how good belly breathing can make you feel. With continued practice, you'll continue to increase your HRV and gain greater control of your emotions.

NIGHTTIME STRATEGIES

What do nuns have to do with restful sleep? A lot, surprisingly! Researchers at the University of Salzburg, Austria, and the University of California set out to see if daytime heart rate variability (HRV) was linked with healthy sleep. They monitored 29 healthy women over the course of 11 days, including assessing the quality of their slumber with various brain- and heart-monitoring equipment. In order to get an accurate baseline HRV for everyone, the subjects watched a movie about nuns living their daily lives — the content was so neutral, it was perfect for a calm, nonstressful bedtime flick.

The results? Subjects with a higher daytime HRV took less time to fall asleep, woke up fewer times during the night, and rated their sleep as feeling more restful than those with lower daytime HRVs.

Your heart depends on restful sleep for optimal performance, just as every other part of your body does. Compared with people who regularly log 7 hours of sleep per night, those who sleep just 1 hour less face a 6 percent increased risk of all-cause mortality (dying for any reason) and cardiovascular disease and a 5 percent increased risk of stroke. Just one night of poor sleep is enough to increase blood pressure, regardless of how fit or healthy you may be. In fact, in one study, hospitals reported a 24 percent jump in heart attack patients the Monday following the spring switch to Daylight Saving Time (the one where we "spring forward" and lose an hour of sleep). Those same hospitals also saw a 21 percent *reduction* in heart attack cases on the Tuesday following the fall time adjustment (the one where we "fall back" and gain an hour of rest).

Possible reasons for this include the fact that poor sleep causes fluctuations in levels of critical proteins and hormones—such as C-reactive protein and testosterone—that have both direct and indirect effects on heart health.

But let's be honest: most of us aren't missing only a night of solid slumber here or there; we're constantly skimping on sleep, building up our cumulative sleep deficit to the point of chronic fatigue. Study after study has linked this sort of habitual suboptimal sleep to a dominant sympathetic nervous system. That's why I want you to really dedicate yourself to polishing your sleep hygiene. Deep sleep increases HRV, and a lack of sleep, or interrupted sleep, is a main cause of drops in HRV.

TIPS FOR CATCHING THE BEST ZZZZS POSSIBLE

Build a cave. If you tend to sleep well in hotel rooms, you can thank those blackout curtains that turn even the sunniest of rooms into a cave. Light sends a signal to our brain that screams, "Time to wake up!"— that's why you may have heard it's a smart idea to throw your shades open as soon as you wake up. But light at night is a sleep saboteur. If outside light is seeping into your bedroom, invest in some blackout shades, and make sure they're large enough to cover all the glass on your windows, preferably extending past the glass to the window frame.

Unplug. Does your smartphone sleep on the nightstand, just inches from your face? You deserve a better bed buddy. By keeping your tech so close, you'll be tempted to check e-mails, social media, or even stock market prices in bed. Not only does this keep your mind active when it should be winding down, but the blue light emitted by phones, laptops, and tablets has been proven to disturb sleep patterns by delaying or preventing the release of melatonin, which is particularly disruptive to the brain's natural bedtime mechanism and can keep you up longer. If you must use your phone as an alarm clock, plug it in across the room, face down. Even better, purchase an analog alarm clock, turn it away from you or cover it with fabric (for many, the sight of glowing numbers and the hours visibly ticking by can create more stress), and park your phone in another room altogether. Remember to save your bed for sleeping, reading, and sex. Activities that your mind associates with being awake and alert, like talking on the phone, crafting a PowerPoint presentation, or ordering something online, don't belong in bed.

Keep things cool. Keep your thermostat set between 60 to 67 degrees Fahrenheit overnight. This is the temperature range known to optimize sleep. If that feels too chilly for drifting off, program your thermostat to drop down about an hour after your usual bedtime and to rise before you wake.

Get the sleep gear you need. Many manufacturers sell sheets and pajamas made from high-performance, sweat-wicking materials similar to what you might find in athletic gear. These are a smart idea for people who sleep hot. Especially hot sleepers should consider a mattress or mattress topper made with cooling technology. Mattresses made from foam or other materials that cradle the body can trap heat, leading to night sweats.

Skip the p.m. buzz. Consuming caffeine in the late afternoon and evening can leave you staring zombie-eyed at your ceiling later that night. That's because caffeine mimics an energizing brain compound called adenosine, telling your brain it's time to be awake. Large amounts of caffeine — the equivalent of more than 3 cups of coffee — can also reduce HRV.

Drift off with magnesium or melatonin. Magnesium is a mineral with calming, muscle-relaxing properties. Melatonin is a hormone produced by the body that helps govern the sleep-wake cycle. Both can be used to help you fall and/or stay asleep. Always discuss any supplement or sleep aid with your doctor before starting.

Don't exercise too late in the day. Regular physical exercise is a wonderful tool for enhancing sleep, but don't work out too close to bedtime. HRV is decreased by exercise, and you want to give it time to rebound before you climb into bed. When possible, schedule your workout earlier in the day or 3 hours before bedtime at the latest.

OPTIMIZATION STRATEGIES FOR BETTER SLEEP

Belly Breathing in Bed

If practicing your belly breathing while sitting up feels difficult or simply too foreign to you, you may want to try it lying down. Many of my patients have reported feeling more comfortable practicing for the first few days in a horizontal position.

Step 1: Lie flat on your back with your knees bent and your head resting on a pillow; you can do this on a bed, the floor, or a yoga mat. Tuck another pillow beneath your legs to help keep your lower back comfortable. Place one hand on your chest, right above your heart, and the other hand on your abdomen. This will allow you to focus on the feeling of your belly moving up and down and your chest staying still as you breathe.

Step 2: Breathe in slowly through your nose so that your stomach puffs up and out against your hand. Let that belly go — really let it peek out. Your stomach is now expanding gently out against your hand. The hand on your chest is remaining as still as possible.

Step 3: Next, as you exhale through pursed lips or a slightly open mouth, gently contract your stomach muscles as they drop down toward your spine. The hand on your upper chest remains as still as possible.

Repeat for the next 5 minutes. Take this time to get used to following the feeling of your belly expanding while inhaling through your nose and contracting as you exhale through your mouth. With a soft gaze, watch your abdomen rise and fall.

After about a week, breathing from the abdomen should feel a bit easier.

ANY QUESTIONS?

"Why am I so sleepy after my sessions?"

You may feel a bit sleepy after completing your breathing sessions. That's because we're still focusing solely on bringing down the sympathetic nervous system but aren't yet working to power up the parasympathetic nervous system. Your sympathetic nervous system is what causes you to feel on high alert, so it makes sense that as you begin slowing it down by mastering resonance breathing and belly breathing, you may feel a bit less amped up than usual. Not to worry; by week 4, your parasympathetic nervous system will start making serious gains. Not only will this postpractice sleepiness disappear, it will be replaced by heightened energy in later weeks. As your nervous system becomes more aligned and your braking system becomes stronger, you are going to feel more refreshed and invigorated.

LIFE-CHANGING WAYS BELLY BREATHING CAN ELEVATE YOUR HEALTH

Immunity and Aging

Research out of the Medical University of South Carolina revealed that just a single 20-minute session of a specific type of deep breathing was enough to increase saliva production. That might not sound exciting in and of itself, but saliva contains all sorts of microscopic goodies, from proteins that bind to and disable viruses and bacteria to tumor-suppressing genes that help prevent normal cells from turning cancerous. Study participants who performed the deep breathing exercises also had significantly lower levels of inflammatory markers in their saliva than did their counterparts who simply read for 20 minutes, as well as increased amounts of nerve growth factor (NGF) in their saliva. Salivary NGF has potent healing capabilities — the reason that wounds in the mouth heal faster than on the body is thought to be because they're coated in NGF. It also gets shuttled to the brain, where it may have powerful antiaging and possibly Alzheimer's-protective effects.

Sharper Focus

Easily distracted? Breathing deeply can get you back on track. This happens in many ways — here are just a few.

- During times of stress, our brains secrete noradrenaline, a hormone that quickens heart rate and ramps up blood pressure because the body thinks it needs to prepare for a battle or escape. Noradrenaline is also released, though in different amounts, during times of intense focus, curiosity, or passion, promoting the growth of new connections in the brain. Researchers at the Trinity College Institute of Neuroscience and the Global Brain Health Institute in Dublin, Ireland, found that slow, controlled, deep breathing helps the brain nail the noradrenaline "sweet spot," heightening attention and getting people laser focused.
- When researchers at Harvard, Yale, and the Massachusetts Institute of Technology scanned the brains of experienced meditators, they dis-

covered increased thickness in regions of the brain's cortex, or gray matter, related to focus and attention. Increased cortical thickness is suggestive of proficiency in an area; individuals who speak two languages have thicker cortexes in regions related to language; professional musicians have thicker cortexes in areas related to music. Now, this chapter isn't about meditation—it's about diaphragmatic breathing. But what's intriguing about this study is that breathing rate was used to determine how deeply in meditation the subjects were able to get; the slower the breathing rate, the deeper in meditation participants became . . . and the more pronounced their increase in gray matter. This discovery is especially promising considering our brains naturally thin with age, and yet the researchers noticed the thickening was more noticeable in older study subjects.

Fewer Symptoms of Irritable Bowel Syndrome (IBS)

The most common GI disorder in the United States, affecting more than 10 percent of the population, IBS afflicts its sufferers with abdominal pain, gas, bloating, constipation, and diarrhea. Nearly all people dealing with this sort of chronic belly discomfort will tend to tense their abdomen at all times, as if guarding themselves from a punch—a recipe for shallow chest breathing. Chest breathing is particularly disadvantageous for individuals with belly trouble, considering diaphragmatic breathing creates a gentle massage action that is felt by the stomach and intestines, helping to relieve pain, constipation, and more.

A case report published in the journal *Biofeedback* detailed the experience of a 21-year-old woman with severe IBS. Diagnosed in her teens, she suffered excessive weight loss and depression. Her doctor told her it was incurable and offered morphine as her consolation prize. Lying in her hospital bed one day, she started scrolling on her phone and happened upon a link to something called diaphragmatic breathing. She tried it immediately. "While practicing, she could feel her stomach and abdomen becoming warmer," the researchers wrote—a sign that she was switching from fight-or-flight mode to rest-and-digest and increasing blood flow throughout her body. She cried tears of joyful surprise. This was the first time she'd been pain-free in years. The authors report that the patient ultimately experienced a near-disappearance of IBS symptoms with continued practice.

WEEK 2 ACTION PLAN

1. Practice resonance breathing for 20 minutes twice per day. If you are still working up to 20-minute sessions, add 5 minutes more to your breathing practice, no matter what length it is now. You can do this! Keep your eyes on the prize: you are investing in a lifelong skill, building a reflex to manage stress, and giving your body a tool that it will soon crave.

2. For the final 5 minutes of each practice, place one hand over your heart and the other hand on your abdomen.

3. If you find that your thoughts are distracting you, note them as such — "Those are just thoughts" — and return to the feeling of movement in your belly. See if you can acknowledge the thoughts that appear in your mind but not engage with them, then bring yourself back to the movement of your belly.

4. Try to remember to observe your breathing pattern during the day. As you move throughout your day, break up negative or stressful thoughts by gently shifting your focus to the movement of the abdomen. The goal is to calm the busy chatter of the mind for longer and longer pulses of time. Belly breathing isn't like brushing your teeth — you don't do it just twice a day and forget about it. You need to take moments throughout the day to check in and see how things are going.

5. Follow the routines that you have established for quality sleep. There's a simple way to measure your success in this: Do you feel an increase in energy during the middle and/or end of the day? That's because you're recharging yourself with deeper, more refreshing sleep.

6

▼

Week 3:

Letting Go of Your Stress and

Expanding Your Emotional Range

After 8 years of medical school and specialized training in orthopedic surgery, Mark was in the final year of his residency. He had already been recruited by a highly respected group practice and was looking forward to the opportunity to help injured athletes rehabilitate and get back in their game.

Coming up on his final 6 months of residency, however, he began to suffer a sudden unexplainable tremor in his left hand as he performed operations. Mark was a lefty. Medical tests ruled out any nefarious medical conditions. This was stress doing what it loves to do best: hijack performance.

Mark came to me to explore the cause of his shaking and hopefully to find a treatment. He reported escalating levels of anxiety and self-doubt regarding his professional capabilities as he neared completion of his residency. Deep breathing techniques alone, like those at the heart of yoga and meditation, helped him relax while he was doing them, but the sense of composure evaporated once he entered the surgical suite. Despite Mark's strong academic and clinical track record, stress was undoing his countless hours of training and practice.

Mark's experience is a prime example of how proficient stress is at dysregulating the body and mind. By now I hope you understand why we must change from a paradigm of dealing with stress cognitively to dealing with it physiologically. Dealing with stress cognitively — trying to think it away — isn't enough. No matter how many times Mark told himself he was an excellent surgeon or reminded himself of his upcoming position with the prominent practice, it was no match for his sympathetic nervous system's ability to override his brain. Stress launches the body into fight-or-flight no matter what you do or don't think about. That's why mantras and cognitive reframing can work but typically only in the short term; they don't create a lasting imprint on your physiology.

If your mind is doing everything perfectly but your body is not cooperating? You. Will. Be. Stressed.

By learning to recognize and steer the stress response in your body, though, you have the power to manage your thoughts . . . but it must happen in that order. This is the focus of week 3: teaching the body how to let go of stress. I'm going to help you learn how to train your heart — the actual muscle — to let go of emotions that obstruct health and hinder peak performance.

LET IT GO? IT'S HARDER THAN IT SOUNDS.

So many of us spend our lives holding on to anxiety, anger, and negativity, constantly bracing ourselves for what's to come. Traumatic or stress-provoking events — be they as momentous as the death of a loved one or as seemingly inconsequential as a high-school breakup — can become physiologically stuck, growing into the fabric of our being and allowing their negative energy to idle long after the actual trauma has passed.

Letting go is a skill that must be developed. Training ourselves to let go of past hurts and disappointments is a crucial step toward breaking through physical, emotional, or professional plateaus; expanding your emotional range; and being able to experience life with a fresh perspective. When we don't let them go, negative emotions become ingrained in our sympathetic nervous system, locking us in a cycle of stress. Letting go doesn't mean you need to forget your past; it means you allow your body to fully process the stress response associated with negative experiences and emotions, then release it.

This week you'll learn how to add another layer of skill to your resonance breathing — one that teaches the heart, at a cellular level, how to let go of stress. The resulting combination teaches your body a new muscle pattern. When practiced frequently, this muscle pattern strengthens, increasing your resilience and your ability to release stress quickly and effectively. If fear had prevented you from showing emotion before, you'll notice yourself feeling less guarded. On an interpersonal level, you may now feel more engaged with those around you, starting to connect more deeply with family, friends, and colleagues. The strengthening of the parasympathetic braking system is what allows you to expand your emotional range and connect with your partner, friends, family, and even work colleagues on a more trusting and vulnerable level.

IDENTIFYING YOUR DAY-TO-DAY STRESSORS

Your first step is to identify three reoccurring stressors in your life. (Use the Homework Tracking Notes on page 226.) Most people have no trouble naming these, but in case you need a little inspiration, here are some examples that frequently arise with my clients.

- Time pressure
- Parenting or caregiving stress
- Work-related stress
- Conflict with partner/spouse
- Financial stress
- Personal or family health problems

Once you've named your stressors, I'd like you to pick the one that causes you the most strife on a day-to-day basis. Don't think too hard about it — the first thing that comes to your mind is usually the one creating the most stress in your body and mind and weighing most heavily on your heart.

EMBRACING YOUR STRESS

My next request might surprise you. I want you to connect to the feeling that underscores your stress: the frustration that lingers in your body when you leave a stressful meeting but have only 5 minutes to reset before another begins. The anxiety in your heart that you feel when your boss askes for honest feedback regarding a sticky work situation. The *What will they think of me?* angst that plagues so many of us as we prepare to deliver a presentation or speech in public. The self-doubt that keeps you from running your best race (if you're competitive) or from running at all (if you're just starting out). It might seem counterintuitive at first, but you need to experience it — to lean into and embrace the negative — in order to fully release it. This act of connecting to your daily or repeated stressors is a form of deliberate practice and will be a key feature of this week's at-home training.

This exercise should succeed in bringing your stress triggers — the ones that elicit such a strong response that your sympathetic nervous system enters (or becomes stuck in) fight-or-flight mode — to the forefront of your attention so you can start to recognize and manage them in real time. Tell me . . . did you notice any of the following common physiological reactions?

- Increased heart rate
- Chest breathing
- Racing mind
- Perspiration or clammy hands
- Muscle tension in your arms, shoulders, neck, back, legs, or face

With regular practice, you will learn to identify what it feels like in your body when you experience your most frustrating stressors. This is crucial for the next step in the process, which is integrating those disruptive feelings and sensations into the breath as a means of letting go of them.

BREATHING EXERCISE #4: RELEASE EMOTION THROUGH RESONANCE FREQUENCY BREATHING

Just as previous weeks have had you focusing on specific goals during the inhale and the exhale (counting to 4 on the inhale and 6 on the exhale; concentrating on your belly expanding on the inhale and softening on the exhale), week 3, too, has an inhale/exhale component.

The goal here is honing the ability to feel the stressor on the inhale and release the stressor during the exhale while breathing at your resonance frequency.

You want to imagine the stressor and try to re-create its emotional effects within your body — the unease, the anxiety, the frustration — as you slowly inhale. Your train was delayed underground and you spent your commute frantically but unsuccessfully trying to text your colleagues to let them know? *Feel* that irritation as you breathe in. Connect to it. Try to remember how annoyed, helpless, and on edge you felt.

And on the exhale? Let it go. Release the frustration; feel it escape through your mouth as you breathe out, like steam escaping when you crack a lid on a pot of boiling water.

Let's say you were recently caught in a miserable 45-minute traffic jam. You've been holding your breath, clenching your jaw and abdomen, squeezing the steering wheel. Maybe you even yelled or swore out loud. We've all been there. As you finally emerge from the gridlock, give yourself some time to recover and relax as you make your way to your destination. Once you've arrived, see if you can take a few minutes to try breathing away the stress of the traffic. Mentally bring yourself back to the jam and, as you inhale, experience the panicked breath holding and all-over muscle clenching. Then, as you exhale, release that stress from your body.

Here's what is happening inside your body: you are teaching your heart to feel stress . . . and let it go. If you were connected to my biofeedback equipment as you did this, you would see your heart rate accelerating on the inhale and decelerating by approximately the same magnitude on the exhale. Your body comes right back to where it began with every breath. That's the physiological effect of feeling and letting go.

Contrast that with what it would look like if you were a chronically stressed client hooked up to my equipment, breathing normally, with no pacing or purposeful re-creation of stress. The heart rate may accelerate on the inhale, but it would decelerate just a fraction of what it should on the exhale. In some situations, you may get stuck at the top of the inhale, plateauing instead of decelerating. That is an incomplete exhale, which prevents the braking of fight-or-flight response — the opposite of resilience.

You're teaching your heart to adopt a new muscle rhythm, one that can decelerate on the exhale as quickly and prominently as it can accelerate on the inhale. We're so used to just feeling, feeling, feeling, but we don't let those feelings go. Our autonomic nervous system settles into a state of disequilibrium as a result. Week 3 is when you cultivate the ability to feel deeply and then set those feelings free.

You may wonder whether purposefully focusing on negative emotions to the point where you physically feel the effects is, in fact, creating more stress. I assure you that we're not creating this stress; we're tapping into it. It's always there, in the heart, as is every other emotion you wish to access. Tapping into the feeling of stress on the inhale and the feeling of release on the exhale exercises the heart while providing chronic stimulation to the baroreflex so that quickly returning to baseline becomes a pattern without having to consciously activate it.

I truly believe that learning how to feel and let go is as crucial a lifelong skill as is learning how to read. It helps you navigate life in a whole new way, one full of energy, passion, fearlessness, and maximum performance.

Continue to access your chosen emotion on the inhales and release it on the exhales. This is you physically training your body to let go. In and out, in and out. Feeling and letting go, feeling and letting go. Just as you would do when attempting to build any other muscle in your body, you'll need hundreds of repetitions before embracing the stress and letting it go becomes as natural a process as your basic inhale and exhale.

What You'll Experience

As you gain proficiency in accessing these emotions and then releasing them, you become able to tap into this technique as stress arises during the day, breathing away negative emotions that may be hindering your performance. When you keep up with your practice, you will report a dampening of the stress response by the end of week 3. You will rebound more quickly and easily from negative day-to-day situations and, with time, become less likely to allow new or unexpected stressors to take up residence in your heart and nervous system.

Remember Mark, the orthopedic surgery resident with the trembling hand? During week 3 of his HRV training, we practiced breathing away the tremor, which he now recognized was a physical manifestation of his inner critic. He realized that the shaking represented his anxiety about moving forward careerwise. We discussed the importance of being able to let go of his "college" and "medical school" selves and visualize himself as a fully credentialed doctor. During his at-home practice, Mark imagined himself in surgery, the tremor beginning. He practiced connecting to that anxiety on the inhale and letting go of it on the exhale, releasing it into the air surrounding him as he pictured his hand steadying. Soon he also practiced this technique between surgeries. As he prepped for his next case, he would purposefully connect to any lingering anxiety from the prior procedure, then release it on the exhale.

In addition to this upgraded ability to let go of stress, you may also notice a subtle improvement in mood—an increased sense of connection to and engagement with colleagues, family, friends, and teammates;

more comfort with emotional vulnerability; and an overall enhanced sense of calm.

You may find it initially feels a bit strange to access an emotion and then let go of it so quickly. But with time and practice, this process will become easier and easier until it becomes second nature. Remember that persistent practice is the only way to build this skill. You must actually train the heart muscle to let go, just as you would train the muscles in your arm to perform a tennis serve. Through regular practice and repetition, your heart will learn to let go with greater potency and speed. It will feel softer, more open, and free.

A few other examples of clients successfully re-creating and releasing their stressors during week 3:

- A Broadway actor whose heart felt "like it was doing cartwheels" in his chest every time he performed an opening scene from the top of a 12-foot ladder. After practicing at home, he was able to take a few week 3 breaths from the top of that ladder and feel the fear, even with hundreds of eyes trained on him from the audience, and let it go.
- A professor interviewing for positions at universities across the country who perspired heavily if he felt a lack of connection with his interviewer. With practice, he learned how to identify the very beginnings of the perspiration and to begin breathing away the fear of negative evaluation.
- A teenaged athlete whose body would grow cold immediately before a game and whose color would drain from her face. She learned how to recognize and breathe away these symptoms of precompetitive anxiety the instant they began bubbling up inside her.

Remember: after being overwhelmed by something that has thrown us off kilter, whether a moment ago or decades ago, earth-shattering or mundane, our nervous system needs to be reset. Otherwise, the negative energy gets stuck in our bodies, and we lose the ability to fluctuate easily between states of different intensity. This stuck charge is prone to being triggered when we encounter events, people, or things that remind us of the unresolved earlier experience.

OPTIMIZATION STRATEGY: IMPLEMENTING THE POWER 10

The Power 10 is a tool you can use at any given moment to modulate your arousal and bring yourself back to your baseline. It works anytime, anywhere. I developed it with busy individuals in mind, many of whom need a tool to help them quickly reset after a stress has occurred. With the Power 10 method, you connect to the feeling of the stressor on the inhale and release it on the exhale for 10 consecutive breaths. This technique allows you to gain control of your autonomic nervous system in the moment, as the stressful event is taking place. (It can also be used immediately after a stressor has occurred.) My clients hold the Power 10 in high regard, as it helps them effectively release increased arousal exactly as stress is attempting to take over.

For Mark, the surgeon, we found that if he could refocus his attention to feeling the stress on the inhale and feeling the letting go on the exhale right then and there in the operating room as his hand started to tremble, the shaking decreased in severity. This was transformative for Mark. Over time, he felt increasingly confident in his ability to moderate his stress response; and as his confidence grew, the tremors reduced in severity, then frequency, and then slowly disappeared.

DOES STRESS ACCELERATE YOUR NERVOUS SYSTEM AND IMPAIR YOUR PERFORMANCE?

Sam was a razor-sharp CEO who had dedicated his career to helping the world's top investors generate higher returns. He grappled with multiple stressors every day, including managing employees, the company's growth, and investors' expectations. He was sharply focused at work but found it hard to move from meeting to meeting throughout the day without his stress accumulating.

But the success of Sam's business depended on his ability to stay objective and collected. Even a subtle overreaction could damage the financial advice he dispensed to colleagues and clients.

We began working together. In week 3, he practiced inhaling as he physiologically immersed himself in the stressors of work and exhaling as he released those feelings of stress. Sam commented to me that focusing on the movement of his abdomen in and out significantly helped him with this process. With every exhale, he mastered the art of letting go.

One day, after a session, he returned to his office in a state of resonance and, as he put it, felt an impenetrable sense of objectivity as he entered the lobby of his office building. But the moment he walked through the door, Sam was bombarded with news about an investment that had unraveled, causing him and his colleagues a significant financial loss. Normally, this sort of ambush would have put him on the defensive and loomed over him all day long. This time, he was prepared.

He led everyone to a conference room, discreetly practicing a Power 10 as they made their way there. That short walk was the perfect opportunity to take 10 slow breaths, inhaling the palpable stress and worry of his team, then releasing those feelings on the exhale.

"Look," he told his team in an effort to re-frame their perspective, "we don't need to overreact. Let's concentrate on the long-term outlook." Everyone in the room was surprised by Sam's measured, reassuring response. Instead of feeling disappointed or frustrated by the loss, he maintained his position on the investment — which, in fact, turned around and made a significant profit the next week. By staying calm and levelheaded in the face of panic, Sam was able to avoid fleeing an investment unnecessarily and could lead with confidence. Sam continues to practice Power 10 breathing before meetings to strengthen his objectivity and hone his ability to inhibit impulsivity throughout the day.

As you work on implementing Power 10s throughout your day to modulate your stress level, you'll eventually reach the point where you can shorten them to Power 5s or even Power 1s. Clients who have worked with me for more than a year are often able to let go of their stressor in fewer than 3 breaths.

MAPPING OUT YOUR POWER 10S

Like Sam, you can moderate your emotions in the moment. In fact, many of my clients create a schedule of specific times to insert Power 10s throughout their day, based on their body's reactions to previous experiences. This is called Mapping Out Your Power 10s. It isn't so much about preparing for stress as it is about moderating your stress in the moment or afterward, if it's lingering. You can anticipate when your trigger stressors are most likely to occur — 8 a.m. highway traffic; your Monday meeting with your boss; holiday dinners with extended family — and insert a Power 10 in the moments before. Think of it as a planned intervention.

Some questions to help you strategically Map Out Your Power 10s: Are there any repeated stressors in your morning routine where you feel out of resonance? Are there any repeated stressors in your evening routine where you feel out of resonance? What sorts of interpersonal interactions cause you stress? When could you use a Power 10 to calm yourself in a discussion with a partner, spouse, or family member? What sorts of professional interactions cause you stress? Are there specific work situations such as presenting at meetings or speaking to your boss or a work colleague that push you out of resonance? (Use the homework tracking sheet on page 227 for this exercise.)

HIGHLIGHT ON HEALTH: HEADACHES

HRV-BFB can be extremely effective in treating and preventing headaches. Migraine, tension headache, and related conditions are thought to be more common in individuals with autonomic nervous system dys-regulation. Headache sufferers often have lower HRV than their pain-free counterparts, which may be correlated with the increased inflammation and altered pain processing often at the root of these painful episodes. Several of my clients who suffer from chronic migraines have found my 10-week protocol to be more effective than medications they've used to reduce their headache frequency and duration.

Consider Nancy, a retired college professor who has battled headaches her entire life. When she came to me, she revealed that she'd been experiencing headaches every day for 40 years. Forty years! Nancy sought help from multiple neurologists and was prescribed antidepressant medication even though she wasn't depressed. She tried acupuncture, yoga, and dozens of other treatments. She also developed what she described as an addiction to over-the-counter pain relievers, inadvertently setting her up for even more discomfort, as using OTC pain relievers 10 or more days per month can cause rebound, or withdrawal, headaches.

Fortunately, one doctor eventually asked Nancy if she had ever tried biofeedback. Nancy arrived in my office with a skeptical look on her face that said, "For decades, everything else has failed me. You think breathing is going to work?" Thankfully, she gave me a chance.

After finding her resonance breathing pace and learning how to belly breathe, she began using her week 3 tools to breathe away her pain. She would focus on the sensation of the pain, connect to it on the inhale, and push it outside of her body on the exhale. I'd ask her to rate her pain on a scale of 1 to 4 before and after, and after about a week of dedicated practice, Nancy was able to reduce her pain by at least two integers with 5 minutes of breathing, representing a significant strengthening of her baroreflex. After 10 weeks, her headaches occurred with much less frequency and severity.

HEART CLEARING

One of my clients' biggest breakthroughs, by the end of the third week, relates to the letting go of destructive, deeply ingrained energy often associated with traumatic or unresolved emotional experiences. In my practice, I call this a Heart Clearing.

Trauma lives in our bodies as well as in our minds. Scientists have noted that when someone experiences trauma, he or she often undergoes an incomplete fight-or-flight response. People get stuck in that stressed state because their parasympathetic braking system is underactive and cannot stop it. This happens with all magnitudes of trauma — no one is immune to negative experiences, and those experiences become encoded in our circuitry. If you learned as a child that speaking in front of a group was dangerous because you were bullied, the idea of presenting at a board meeting might send you into a state of fight-or-flight. The circuit from your brain to your heart goes both ways: your thoughts influence your body state, and your body state influences your thoughts.

I call these triggers that become imprinted in your physiology and cause your body to react under specific circumstances ghost imprints. They are meant to protect you from re-experiencing a potential stressor but instead leave you in a state of fight-or-flight when such a state does not serve you.

When you identify your ghost imprints and strengthen your body's braking system, the overarousal from the traumatic experience is released, and you are able to let it go. For my clients, this release often happens during week 3.

You may experience this phenomenon as a feeling of sudden melancholy or even anger, which appears out of nowhere with no particular trigger or event. It can happen hours or minutes before or after a breathing session. Many of my clients report intermittent tears, which catch them by surprise as nothing, as far as they can tell, is causing them distress. But these emotional experiences live in your heart, and the unexpected feelings are a sign that your body is trying to discard this extra energy, purging it so that you can let go and operate at your peak.

This discharge of trauma, which I refer to as the Heart Clearing, is a truly significant event. The heart is freeing itself so that it can operate from a place of openness, vulnerability, and emotional freedom. Additionally, removing this trauma frees not only the heart but also the mind; my clients noticed a new lucidity to their thinking with an increased self-confidence. If the person is hooked up to biofeedback equipment in my office, I often see realignment between the survival system and the braking system after a Heart Clearing. The braking system grows stronger than the survival system. The individual is no longer operating with a trauma-infused imbalance in the body.

The frequent result is heightened creativity, increased intimacy, elevated overall performance, and a heart that is more able to experience (and recover from) a fuller, richer range of emotions.

DO YOU WANT TO BUILD EMPATHY AND ENHANCE YOUR RELATIONSHIPS?

Max was an ambitious, Ivy League–educated venture capitalist. He came to see me to increase his ability to stay cool and calm under pressure. At 34, Max was adept at sales and persuading others of his position, but he lacked the ability to perceive and empathically respond to the needs of his team members. Sometimes he operated too quickly and made decisions that didn't take others' needs or desires into account.

This was affecting his work as well as his marriage. Max wanted to be a loving and nurturing husband, but he couldn't hold back his anger, particularly when his wife's fear of heights and other phobias meant that the family had to make sacrifices, such as avoiding specific vacation spots.

During week 3, Max had a major breakthrough in which he felt an outpouring of grief, anxiety, and anger toward his mother, who had also suffered from anxiety. When Max was a child, he was unable to participate in many youth sports due to her fear that he would get hurt or permanently injure himself. During his Heart Clearing, Max realized how alive and vivid the anger he felt toward his mother still was, decades later.

In the following weeks, Max would report an uptick in loving interactions with his wife. His interactions at work also improved; he was able to begin shifting from seeing only his perspective to considering the perspectives of others. Breathing away stress was allowing him to pause his immediate reactions and more closely listen to other peoples' needs.

A FEW MORE NOTES ON HEART CLEARING

Anyone can experience Heart Clearing. Age, gender, height, socioeconomic status, education level, and physical health do not correlate in any way with the ability to expand your emotional range. However, Heart Clearing will occur only among individuals who are practicing 20 minutes of resonance breathing twice per day.

About 60 percent of my clients experience a Heart Clearing, generally toward the end of week 3 or 4. Typically, it happens only once during this process. Out of the hundreds of clients I've worked with in the last decade, I have seen only a few experience a Heart Clearing reoccurrence — and all of these were long-term clients who trained with me far beyond the 10 weeks.

As startling and emotional as the Heart Clearing can be, I urge you to view it with gratitude, appreciation, and wonder. Think of it this way: your heart, in its effort to protect you from uncontrollable hurt and pain from your past, has kept you from fully feeling these negative emotional memories. While this may have felt better in the short term, it also inhibited you from connecting deeply and authentically with others and even with yourself. With a Clearing, your heart is ridding itself of these obstructions so that it and you are no longer locked in the past. To reach a place of openness and freedom, you need to welcome the experience of the heart letting go; you need to trust that your body knows what it is doing.

Write about the experience. Allow your emotions to be fully present in your body. You want the Heart Clearing to be as deep and full as possible.

PRACTICAL STRATEGIES

It's not uncommon for people to encounter difficulties in re-creating, or imagining, their stressor on the inhale and letting go of the stressor on the exhale, especially if they have not spent time cultivating awareness of the body's internal state or if repressed emotions are at play. That's why the weeks are ordered in the sequence they are; once you complete weeks 1 and 2, you should be able to achieve the resonance and calm needed to attempt this emotional release. Even then, it's not unusual to still need a little assistance. Here are some tips.

How to Connect to the Stressor on the Inhale

First, make sure that you're isolating just one stressor per inhale and release. Trying to connect with the anxiety of parenting *and* the stress of finances, for instance, will be overwhelming. Distill down to the most troublesome one. You can concentrate on the other or others the next time that you practice.

As you try to lean into the stressor, ask yourself what it feels like in your heart. Does your heart feel heavy? Constricted? Afraid? Some clients find that focusing on their heart facilitates the connection needed on the inhale.

How to Let Go of the Stressor on the Exhale

Some people have no problem conjuring their stressor, but they encounter difficulty in releasing it. This may occur when the pace feels too quick or abrupt. The "muscle" required to feel and let go needs to be built up by repetition, which takes time and practice. Stay patient, keep up the good work—it will happen! It requires as much repetition and practice as possible.

Proper Fueling

Building a life of resonance also requires building other habits that improve your heart rate variability. Week by week, I work with my clients to start adding more healthy practices that will enhance their training and experiences. To start, I advise my clients to consider food as fuel and to fuel up at regular times throughout the day. A reliable, consistent schedule of breakfast, lunch, and dinner is interpreted by the body as a feeling of safety, while inconsistency in meal timing triggers uncertainty that puts us on high alert, reinforcing hypervigilance and sympathetic dominance.

In addition to following the basic tenets of a healthy diet—lots of produce, whole grains, beans and legumes, nuts and seeds, dairy, small amounts of animal-based protein if you enjoy it, limited servings of processed foods—try to stay hydrated. Even mild dehydration (around a 1 percent drop) has been linked with impaired executive functioning, a suite of emotional skills that help us manage time, focus, multitask, problem solve, and more. Dehydration can also lead to a reduction in cognitive flexibility. In a recent study, healthy, young, active women were asked to limit their fluid intake to just 6 ounces for a day before playing a complicated card game. They were then allowed to rehydrate and play the game. When dehydrated—by just a 1 percent drop—they made about 12 percent more errors.

Although many of my clients love their coffee, I do ask that they, and you, strive to limit caffeine intake during these 10 weeks. Large amounts of caffeine *reduce* heart rate variability, counteracting or even canceling out the HRV-increasing effects of your resonance frequency breathing. My recommendation is to consume 2 cups of coffee per day or less.

Even better, exchange your coffee for green tea or water. Like coffee, tea contains caffeine, a stimulant that works by disabling a sleep-inducing brain chemical called adenosine. But green tea contains less caffeine than coffee, so it's invigorating without feeling overly stimulating or causing jitters. At the same time, green tea has calming properties, perhaps due to an active compound called L-theanine, which increases production of various calming neurochemicals while lowering levels of excitatory, stress-producing brain chemicals. L-theanine has also been shown to increase HRV. Think of it as a gentler caffeine.

An additional perk: multiple studies suggest that a compound in green tea called epigallocatechin-3-gallate (EGCG) may increase brain connectivity and enhance working memory, making it the perfect beverage to drink throughout this 10-week journey.

ANY QUESTIONS?

"If I'm feeling a lot of stress on a particular day, should I breathe for longer than two 20-minute sessions?"

You can always keep breathing if you are enjoying the process — as long as you continue to commit to at least 20 minutes a session every day. I've found that when some clients extend the length of their practice on one day, they may be more likely to cut the length of their practice on another day when they're feeling rushed. Psychologically, when we give more than expected, we're more likely to cut corners on another day. We think, "Well, I logged 60 minutes yesterday; I can get away with just 20 today." But your body needs both 20-minute sessions every day for 10 weeks.

ANY QUESTIONS?

"My mind is wandering during the training. Can I add music?"

Not yet. For now, I'd like for you to focus on clearing your mind, nomadic as it may seem, during your breathing practice. Continue to use the strategies from week 2 for calming a busy brain (see page 56). I'll address the use of music and its ability to help shift your physiology for specific performance moments in Chapter 11.

WEEK 3 ACTION PLAN

1. Continue to dedicate 20 minutes twice a day to your resonance breathing sessions. (If you opted to start at 10 or 15 minutes per session, you should now be up to 20.)
2. For the final 5 minutes of each session, practice connecting to your daily or repeated stressor on the inhale and releasing it on the exhale.
3. Explore using one or more Power 10s (10 consecutive breaths in which you connect with the stressor on the inhale and release it from your body on the exhale) during your day to manage stress. This is called Mapping Out Your Power 10s. It may help to keep your homework tracking sheet handy throughout the day.
4. Pay attention to your nutrition, fueling up on a regular, reliable basis and hydrating smartly with limited caffeine.
5. Should you unexpectedly experience a Heart Clearing, remain calm, and try to approach it with positivity and gratitude. You're moving closer and closer to your goals.

A PEEK AHEAD

Don't forget to measure and record your HRV next week, during week 4.

7

▼

Week 4:

Healing the Broken Parts

The incomplete fight-or-flight response theory has its roots in decades of research conducted by noted psychologist Peter Levine, PhD, an expert on stress and trauma. After spending time observing various wild animals in their natural habitats, Levine gathered evidence indicating that these creatures have an innate ability to recover quickly and completely from stressful events. In his book *Waking the Tiger: Healing Trauma,* he gives the example of a herd of deer grazing in a clearing when a twig snaps. "Instantly," he writes, "the deer are alert — ready to flee into the forest. If cornered, they may fight. Each animal becomes still. Muscles tensed . . . another stimulus sends the animals back into the state of alertness and extreme vigilance (hypervigilance)." But seconds later, after determining that no true threat was present, the deer returned to grazing, caring for their fawns, and warming themselves in the sun. In doing this, they discharge the energy that has just flooded their nervous systems.

These deer, Levine says, have done what we, as humans, seem to have extreme difficulty accomplishing: they entered a state of sympathetic dominance — their brain's way of protecting them — then fully regained balance, allowing their parasympathetic systems to not just brake but to recover. Animals, then, have the ability to seamlessly shift between states of calm alertness and heightened vigilance. A threat occurs; they respond by either fighting, fleeing, or freezing; and then their nervous system returns to baseline.

FIGHT, FLIGHT . . . OR FREEZE?

In the 1990s, psychophysiologist Stephen Porges, PhD, proposed a model called the polyvagal theory, which added the freezing element into the list of innate stress responses. Polyvagal theory contends that when a living being senses imminent danger and is unable to use mobilization strategies (flight or fight), it will immobilize, or freeze, in an effort to survive. This is why snakes being held in glass boxes at a zoo or pet store always seem to stay in one position; they sense that they're being watched by a predator but are unable to fight or flee, so they come to a complete standstill. Turtles pull themselves inside their shells. A mouse that's been snatched by a cat plays dead. In the case of us humans, freezing could theoretically help in a life-or-death situation by convincing an assailant that we're dead, prompting him to leave. But we've maladapted to stress in such a way that our nervous system now thinks freezing is an advantageous choice in far more benign situations, like before taking to the podium to deliver a presentation.

As for us humans? Many of us are not quite as resilient. We experience all types of trauma and, depending on our unique blend of physiology, emotional sensitivity, and past experience, we respond by fighting, fleeing, or freezing. But unlike animals, we lack the innate ability to immediately return to baseline following upsetting events.

Why? We can blame a little thing called *emotions*. Levine explains that our highly evolved brain, with all of its thinking and feeling, interferes with the physiological stress recovery process, and we don't fully discharge the energy created during the fight, flight, or freeze process. We may become extremely upset when we miss our train or are running late, panic when asked a question by our supervisor at a team meeting, or struggle to discuss a contentious issue with a loved one without it escalating into an argument.

So, we experience heightened stress states of varying magnitude that become encoded in our circuitry. Fragments of energy are stored like time capsules in our autonomic nervous systems. We become physiologically stuck, our bodies no longer able to fluctuate easily between states of varying intensity. The charge embedded in our system becomes retriggered when we encounter people, things, and events that remind us of the earlier experience, and we assume a state of hypervigilance.

In this way, emotionally turbulent experiences or tragedies continue to inflict emotional, psychological, spiritual, and even physiological pain. We tend not to be like those deer that perceive a threat, respond, and recover. We cannot deftly move from possibly being attacked to enjoying the warm sun on our skin. Instead, we remain on high alert or play dead like the snake. Put simply, our reactions are shaped by life experiences that have become encoded in our physiological responses.

HEALING THE BROKEN PARTS

The word *trauma* may sound scary, I know. But you don't have to have experienced a major catastrophic life event, like losing a parent at a young age or being the victim of a crime, in order to have experienced a trauma. By trauma, I mean a stressor that impacted you deeply enough to imprint itself on your physiology. In my work, I've observed multiple major themes for these experiences including but not limited to:

- *Negative self-talk.* A client who may be battling a demeaning inner monologue may have internalized the voice of a critical parent or other authority figure.
- *Scarcity.* If a client grew up in fear of not having enough love, money, or food, he or she may internalize a sense of scarcity, rather than operate from an abundance mind-set that believes in opportunity.
- *Perfectionism or fear of disappointing others.* This theme can stem from growing up in environments where receiving parental validation feels extremely important, as if one needed to perform well or exceed expectations to earn the parents' attention.
- *A need for control.* Excessive amounts of change (anything from moving several times to watching one's parents get divorced) or repeated traumas can leave a physiological imprint resulting in a sense of a lack of control.

These ghost imprints live in our bodies more than our minds. They are triggers that are imprinted in your physiology and cause your body to react under specific circumstances in ways that do not serve you.

During week 3, we worked on identifying your day-to-day stressors — feeling constantly pressed for time; stress related to work, finances, parenting, or caring for older parents; romantic conflict — and training your body to feel them and then let go. We also discussed how your body may bring up previous experiences that caused stress in an attempt to realign your autonomic nervous system. This week, it's time to lean into the process of letting go. It's time to exorcise those repeating themes and thoughts that gnaw at your heart and mind, your ghosts.

A NEW STRATEGY FOR HEALING A BROKEN HEART AND MOVING FORWARD

Meg, a dynamic thinker and leader in psychology, came to me to release the pain of a love that didn't last. "When my relationship with my live-in boyfriend ended," she said, "my heart felt irreparably torn." Meg wondered whether loving anyone was worth the potential heartache. At the same time, she had begun to question if she was lovable. She tried traditional therapy for months and confided in me that "the talking helped me to make sense of what had happened but didn't reduce the sensation of grief, the heartache that was literally eating me up inside." In the 2 months following the breakup, Meg had lost nearly 15 pounds from her already-slim figure. She opened our initial conversation by disclosing that she hadn't been able to eat for weeks. "I think I'm trying to replace this gnawing pain in my heart with the feeling of hunger."

Meg's intense melancholy and anxiety were palpable. During our first breathing session, I asked her to describe what the pain felt like in her heart. Meg described her pain as an intense sadness, as if she had just experienced a death, along with fury that she had given so much to someone who didn't offer the same level of affection and commitment back to her. She ultimately singled out the melancholy as the sensation she most wished to eradicate. So we began by having her focus on the melancholy on the inhale, releasing it on the exhale. Later we progressed to focusing on her anger on the inhale and exhale.

Immediately following our first session, Meg remarked that she felt freer and calmer. Inspired, she began breathing for two daily sessions of approximately 20 minutes. On some days, when the pain felt intolerable, she would breathe for up to six 20-minute sessions per day. "The breathing became the only time when I felt that I was in control of the pain rather than the heartache being in control of me," she explained. "The more control I had over my breath and how my heart was reacting, the more confidence I gained in my own innate strength and ability to move forward."

Three weeks into the breathing, Meg was feeling much better in her day-to-day life. Her mood had started to improve. One day, though, she called me to ask about an unusual outpouring of emotions. "Out of no-where today, I started crying," she said. Initially, she assumed she had seen or heard something that subconsciously reminded her of the breakup. But as she allowed the tears to flow and tuned into the experience, she realized that her sorrow was coming from a deeper place. She experi-enced vivid memories of her 12-year-old self desperately trying to con-nect with her mother. Due to an ailing relationship with Meg's father, her mother was inattentive to Meg's needs. As a result, Meg had internalized her mother's love as deficient, or scarce. It sent the message to young Meg that "I must not be lovable." Meg had found her ghost!

Meg's ghost wasn't her ex or the breakup. Her ghost originated, as is the case with many of my clients, from a traumatic experience in her earlier years. Her sudden flood of emotions was a purging of old, stuck, physiological arousal. Week by week, as Meg's autonomic nervous system strengthened, the childhood energy sought to release itself. Because she knew what to expect, Meg had not been afraid of this; she had, in fact, welcomed her tears. As a result, she was able to successfully clear her en-ergy and felt a sense of comfort and relief. Within days, she was able to eat meals again and began steadily improving her dietary habits. She contin-ued her breathing practice for 20 weeks, supplementing it with increased daily exercise. She reported that her anxiety had decreased, and she no longer felt depressed. During her last week of training with me, Meg was able to reset her heart and begin dating someone new.

When you identify your ghost imprints and strengthen your body's braking system, the overarousal from traumatic experience is often re-leased, and you become increasingly able to let it go. For one person, this may result in enhanced creativity. Another individual might notice greater intimacy with a partner. Yet another may notice his or her heart feeling more able to experience (and recover from) a full range of emo-tions. These are a few of the results that seem to occur most often for my clients, but different people may experience different results.

BREATHING EXERCISE #5: LETTING GO OF DEEPLY HELD TRIGGERS AND BELIEFS

To physiologically release deep pain, you need to repeatedly identify the physiological sensation that accompanies the pain, exhaling it as you decelerate your heart rate. Through repetition and practice, you decelerate your heart more quickly and effortlessly to expedite your recovery. You may need to practice this hundreds of times. Don't let that scare you. Depending on your rate of breathing, you'll log approximately 30 repetitions in your final 5 minutes of breathing alone.

Similar to week 3, you'll again endeavor to feel your ghost imprint on the inhale and release it during the exhale. This time, the stressor should be something deeper and possibly darker than the annoyance you feel when you forget again to purchase everything on your grocery list or the sour stomach you feel before receiving medical test results. To identify this stressor, this ghost imprint, a little introspection is needed.

Step 1: When in your life have you felt a sense of disappointment, frustration, anxiety, or anger that lasted for weeks, months, or more? When you read my list of common ghost themes (negative self-talk; scarcity; perfectionism; fear of loss of control), which one first resonated with you? Alternatively, perhaps you have a ghost imprint that's unique to your personal experience in childhood and young adulthood. I often ask my clients, "Which experiences from your past still hold beachfront property in your mind?" The goal is, of course, to protect that prime mental space and reserve it for experiences that incite resonance, such as remembering the love you had for your childhood dog or the appreciation that you feel for a close friend.

Step 2: Next, try to recall the sensations you felt in your body during the actual stressor. For instance, how did it feel when you couldn't obtain your mother's approval even when trying your best? How did your heart feel when you were teased by a classmate? What was it like to be in your body when you had no control over the death of a loved one? Try to connect with the pain or the memory of how the experience felt *in your heart*. Really try to *feel* it without getting stuck in your thoughts or your memories. Your heart remembers. Do you feel a tightness there . . . the feeling of a heartstring being tugged . . . a jittery sense of anxiety in the center of your chest . . . a crushing heaviness . . . or something else?

After spending a few minutes immersing yourself like this, take a moment to jot down as many adjectives as you can that describe the way your heart felt during that experience. Feel free to use a pen and paper or your phone.

Step 3: *(Pacer needed, set to your resonance frequency.)* Now that you have explored the sensation, practice connecting to the pain. Invite it to feel present in your heart on your inhale. Then, as you exhale through an open mouth, imagine directing the stress outside of your body. A critical feature of the week 4 exhale is to add some gentle pressure; imagine you're blowing out two candles on a cake. Not 20 candles! Just two. This helps target the energy imbalance in the autonomic nervous system. The slope of the heart rate deceleration on the exhale is correlated with how quickly you can bring your heart rate back to baseline, translating into an improved ability to let go of deeply held stressors from our pasts and work through themes that often impair our ability to perform at our peak, such as perfectionism or need for control.

This is the process you'll repeat for the last 5 minutes of each breathing practice.

Remember that this is not a thinking activity. It is an exercise designed to reconnect with your ghost imprints and help you start to loosen their grip on your physiology.

BREATHING EXERCISE #6: CATCHING AND RELEASING YOUR GHOSTS

Every day, you are bombarded by stress. The kids want your attention. The phone is ringing. You're preparing for a company presentation at work. The dog needs a walk. Oh . . . and it's snowing outside. You get the idea. The feeling and letting-go techniques that you learned last week are effective for helping you reduce just these kinds of everyday stressors.

Yet without realizing it, most of us are simultaneously tackling a more complex and enduring type of stress that emanates from our past. In order to optimize our ability to manage stress, we need to be aware of the personal and deep-seated themes that underscore our emotional reactions — our ghosts — that cause us to behave in inefficient, often wildly ineffective ways, and address them at their emotional core — the heart.

The first step is becoming aware of historic triggers, like when Meg uncovered her root fear of being unlovable, and acknowledging how they manifest throughout your days in multiple domains. As you begin to identify your ghosts and recognize their prevalence, it's time to practice releasing their stuck energy from your physiology to create lasting change.

Here are some tips to guide you through catching and releasing your ghosts.

Reflect on your day. Using a notebook or a file on your computer or phone, track your reactions to stress for 3 days. Every night, think back on your day and write down any reactions you recall having to the myriad stressors that surely occurred. (Just don't do this right before bedtime, as it can be arousing.) Evaluate the magnitude of each reaction on a scale of 1 (not stressful) to 10 (extremely stressful). Try to approach this with curiosity rather than judgment.

Evaluate it. After 3 days, review your notes. What themes jump out at you? Themes of scarcity? Of self-doubt? A sense of time slipping away? A fear of being unlovable? Some clients may realize that they're often trying to please others before considering their own feelings or needs. Pay especially close attention to any experiences that elicited a ranking of 7 or higher — a ghost from your past may be lingering there.

Exorcise them. For the rest of the week (the next 4 days), practice recognizing your ghosts as they occur and breathing through them. When you do, practice connecting to the ghost on the inhale and releasing it on the exhale. Once again, focus on the exhale, breathing out two imaginary candles to optimize the deceleration of the heart rate in letting go. If you own a heart rate monitor such as a Fitbit, Apple Watch, or other wearable heart rate tracker, they don't let you see beat to beat changes in your heart rate. But they are sensitive enough to detect decelerations in heart rate. Try looking away from your device (to help mentally detach yourself) and take 5 breaths, feeling the stressor on the inhale and releasing it on the exhale. Now look at your heart rate monitor. Were you able to practice decelerating your heart rate by 2 beats or more?

CHASING GHOSTS WITH HRV TECHNOLOGY

If you opted to use an app that monitors heart rate variability while breathing, you might enjoy using it here to help catch and release your ghosts. You can use this equipment to track your cardiovascular responses in the moment. You'll need to be sitting down to ensure accurate tracking. You can begin by tracking your heart rate as you practice letting go of deeply held triggers. First, identify how many beats your heart rate accelerates by on the inhale. Then, practice letting go of your ghost on the exhale while monitoring the magnitude of your heart rate deceleration. Was there a difference in the number of beats that your heartbeat increased versus decreased? Your challenge is to approximate the deceleration of your heart on the exhale to the acceleration of the inhale, all while breathing in your ghost stressor and releasing it. An incomplete exhale or a stuck nervous system will resist a full deceleration on the exhale, perhaps plateauing at or near the crest of each heartbeat.

IS A GHOST IMPRINT HOLDING YOU BACK IN YOUR RELATIONSHIP?

Andrew, a manager with a soft-spoken demeanor and beautiful soul, came to me in his 30s. He was seeking help in romantic relationships. Andrew dated, but things rarely progressed past the first date. He had a great deal of difficulty sharing his heart with others, particularly women. Instead of being open and vulnerable, he watched what he said and failed to reveal his true self. He found himself holding back in conversations, shutting down if his date asked him about anything personal.

As we began the work of identifying his ghosts, Andrew revealed that he grew up in an extended family living in a small, crowded apartment. The adults there always seemed on edge, and if a young Andrew spoke when they were in a particularly bad mood, they would berate him or sometimes even hit him. The message that became embedded in his heart was that he should censor himself or else his safety could be endangered. Andrew stopped freely speaking his mind and learned to mute his emotions as a form of self-defense. This shift happened on a physiological level—not a conscious, cognitive level—and now, decades later, he was here in my office, still fearful of being punished for expressing himself. The idea of making himself vulnerable by speaking up in a potential relationship with a woman triggered a fight-or-flight response.

Together, we developed a protocol. Whenever Andrew felt himself being triggered (by a personal question, for instance), he stopped and attempted to identify the trigger. This was the cognitive piece. Once he knew why it was happening, he worked to shift his physiological response, taking 10 breaths, focusing on the pain of his childhood fear on the inhalation and letting go on the exhalation. He would also move his body by stretching his arms or performing gentle yoga movements during his at-home resonance breathing sessions. This helped to release pent-up energy and ultimately let go both cognitively and physiologically.

What You'll Experience

We can learn and grow from upsetting events, but that doesn't mean we have to allow their ghosts to linger in perpetuity. Through this week's potent pairing of resonance breathing and physiologic arousal and release, you are practicing letting go of the fears and traumas embedded deep in your physiology while training your ability to engage and relax more deeply. By strengthening your baroreflex, you are learning to let go more quickly and cultivate a state of resonance when you encounter obstacles great or small. Don't worry if this takes you more time to master. We have several weeks ahead to build on this skill. This is just the start.

Clients with chronic health issues related to anxiety or autonomic dysfunction often report an easing of their symptoms during week 4, so long as they are adhering to the two 20-minute sessions per day of training. Conditions like panic attacks, IBS, headaches, and insomnia often start to reduce in severity this week.

This is an exciting week, as you will be experiencing some notable changes in your outlook. You may feel slightly more positive, your energy levels should be picking up, and you may feel less anxious about life's daily surprises. Most amazing of all, you may start to feel less irritated by small stressors and more able to reduce your reaction to those deeply ingrained stressors stemming from your past.

Exorcising ghosts, though, is serious work, and reactions like that which Meg described are not at all uncommon. We all have experiences that become imprinted on our physiologies, and while our mind may forget them, our body never does. As long as the body holds on to these experiences, we will continue to periodically revisit the pain whenever new experiences trigger the emotional memory. But by releasing some of that negative, stuck energy, we can help ourselves overcome the immobilization caused by repeated trauma.

For many of my clients, the release of these trapped emotions paves the way toward the ability to take on greater emotional risks. For instance, so many of us are scared to truly love someone with all of our hearts, as there's an inherent risk of devastation involved should the relationship end. But with greater emotional flexibility, you may become more willing and able to take smart, well-thought-out risks. With the new confidence that you can calm yourself through your breathing, you know that even if you were to experience loss and pain, you would survive.

You may also release a ghost holding on to resentment you had for someone and discover a sense of empathy or forgiveness instead. When

Max, the venture capitalist from last chapter, felt his disappointment and anger toward his mother release, he was able to express himself more intimately with his wife in a whole new way. I've termed this type of response physiological forgiveness.

It's up to you how you respond to the gradual releasing of this old energetic charge — you are in control. You may decide to let the tears stream and stream. Journaling can be cathartic for many people. Some people want to be alone; others crave the comfort of close friends or family. Grant yourself permission to explore the magnitude of your emotion, its shape, depth, and weight.

Note: If you experience a Heart Clearing that is especially upsetting, don't be afraid to reach out to a mental health professional for extra support.

Flow

You might also feel as if your breathing sessions are passing by more quickly than in previous weeks. This is a very positive sign — congratulations! When you first began this process, you may have felt antsy or stared at the clock. By this week, though, you may catch yourself easily focusing on the breathing pacer moving on your screen. Twenty minutes may feel like 10. All these signs indicate that your parasympathetic nervous system is fortifying, putting you in greater autonomic balance. Your twice-daily 20-minute breathing practices are beginning to strengthen your baroreflex, reducing your overall blood pressure. This state of complete immersion in an activity, according to positive psychologist Mihaly Csikszentmihalyi, is a mental state known as flow.

Those key moments in your life when you performed at your very top level, giving 100 percent of your attention and effort, and everything else, including your sense of time, seemed to fall away? That was flow, too. If you've ever watched a basketball player enter the zone, sinking every shot with apparent ease, you've seen it in action. If you've delivered a presentation that felt utterly on point, with an engaged audience and a sense of confidence and composure that feels like you can do no wrong, you've felt it.

Flow happens outside the peak performance world, too: when you meet up with a friend you haven't seen in ages and 2 hours fly by in the blink of an eye, or when you watch a long but truly engaging movie or play without any fidgeting or watch-checking. While flow is a mental state and resonance is a physiological state, you may be able to access flow more quickly when you elicit a state of resonance.

Highlight on Health:
Weight Management and Disordered Eating

Ghost imprints can manifest in unhealthy behaviors, such as overeating and disordered eating. You can use your resonance breathing to curb these behaviors and, when paired with evidenced-based psychotherapy, eventually overcome them.

If food cravings are bothersome for you, beginning to derail your health goals, or are part of a more dangerous eating pattern such as bingeing and purging, you may find relief with a mindful breathing technique called urge surfing (sometimes called riding the urge or surfing the craving). Originally developed by G. Alan Marlatt, PhD, a leader in the field of addiction psychology, it's been used for years to help people tolerate, or "ride out," their impulses.

Cravings and urges aren't just in our minds; they produce physical sensations. They may manifest as a quickened heart rate, muscle tension, increased salivation, or feelings of hunger even when you're not hungry or even are already full. Urge surfing is a specific way of approaching these cravings, which tend to arrive like rolling waves, with a building of intensity, a peak, and, finally, a crash. It's a highly effective approach for resisting unhealthy cravings or urges rather than giving in to them. With practice, those urges will lessen in frequency and intensity.

How to Surf the Urge

When the first stirrings of a craving hit, try to view the feeling as an early warning signal and a reminder to pause and breathe. First, get curious about the craving: Where is it coming from? Your brain? Your stomach? Your tongue? Take a moment to actually feel that tension in your heart.

Once you've identified it, begin resonance breathing. On the inhale, embrace the craving, the desire that it brings. Feel the tension as you breathe in through your nose. Exhale the urgency you feel to give in, reassuring yourself that you have the power to surf this urge. You are stronger than your urge.

Then, like a surfer, ride the craving. Visualize yourself as an actual surfer, paddling as the wave takes off, popping up as you begin to pick up speed, then crouching down on your board and riding the wave all the way in. Even if you've never done it, surfing is a fairly easy activity to visualize, and because so many senses are involved—the cool feel of the water, the taste of the salt, the bright sun—you can become fully immersed, distracting yourself from the urge in the process.

Connect to the craving, feeling it in your heart on the inhale, then breathe it out for at least 10 breaths. You're following the craving like a wave, keeping your eyes trained on the shore as you ride toward the coastline.

ANY QUESTIONS?

"I read about a breath pacer that alerts me of my resonance frequency breathing through sounds—I don't even need to look at it. Can I try that?"

Many years ago, a company sent me CDs to distribute to clients that contained sounds to alert the listener when to inhale and exhale at their resonance frequency. After distributing these CDs to my clients, however, I found that at around week 7, their HRV training stopped producing the cognitive changes typically seen by that point. Upon further reflection, I realized that the music was diluting the protocol's effects by depriving the brain of the stimulation offered by visually tracking a pacer. When you follow along with your pacer, watching your heart oscillations rise and fall, you stimulate the prefrontal lobe, the area responsible for attention, focus, and executive function. This helps you stay keyed in to the subtle physiological changes occurring during your resonance breathing.

In my experience, listening to music, while it is relaxing, doesn't offer the same benefits. Auditory processing doesn't provide the same prefrontal lobe stimulation as visual processing does and, therefore, it doesn't yield the same cognitive and physiological benefits. For this reason, I highly recommend keeping your eyes open during your breathing practice and using a pacer on your cell phone to guide your breathing.

WEEK 4 ACTION PLAN

1. Remeasure your HRV using your equipment this week. (Refer to page 36 for a refresher. Mark your results on the homework tracking sheet on page 228.) If you have continued your practice of breathing for 20 minutes twice a day, has your HRV increased slightly? Progress! Seeing your HRV rise is incredibly motivating — evidence that your hard work is paying off. If you don't yet see the increase, keep in mind that some people manifest their benefits at different times than others. Keep enjoying the process.

2. Track down your ghosts. Use the guide provided in this chapter to uncover your deep-seated struggles and recognize their common triggers. For those who are using technology, are you able to use your slowed exhales to decelerate your heart rate following a stressor?

3. Continue to manage intermittent stressors throughout the day with Power 10 breathing and by catching and releasing your ghosts.

4. Continue your twice-a-day, 20-minute resonance breathing sessions.

   a. During your first session of each day, spend the last 5 minutes of your breathing practice connecting with one of your ghosts. Practice feeling the deep source of stress on the inhale and releasing it from your body on the exhale.

b. During your second session of each day, spend the last 5 minutes connecting with the stressors from the day in order to feel them and let them go with each breath.

A PEEK AHEAD

In weeks 5, 6, and 7, as you continue to strengthen your ability to navigate challenges, you will start to experience the cognitive benefits of this training, including sharpened focus and the ability to screen out negative thoughts. You will also embark on the process of training your heart to automatically shift and adapt during times of stress, including when preparing for a challenge, during the challenge, and afterward. Being able to recover quickly from a stressor and return to a state of confidence and flow is a hallmark of peak performance, and we're about to work together to train this ability in you.

8

▼

Week 5:

Preparing for Challenge

If you were a dancer, swimmer, or sprinter, you would train specific muscles to activate automatically during a routine or race. Your heart is a muscle, too, and with enough practice, you can train your heart rhythms to remember how to respond in moments of stress. Your heart knows how to feel stress and hold on to it. Now you are going to teach it how to feel that stress and automatically let it go. The technique you're about to learn builds on all your work so far, allowing you to create a shift in your heart rhythms that will facilitate you reaching your peak level of performance. It's called performing a Heart Shift.

I developed the Heart Shifting technique using feedback from clients who were stressed about major upcoming performance events. They needed something potent enough to help them optimize their physiology *before* their challenging feat even began. So, with their input, I created a method to teach their hearts to shift from an undesired state to a state of peak performance, all in advance of an anticipated event.

This training technique involves 15 consecutive breaths taken at your resonance frequency. The breaths are performed in three sets of 5 breaths each.

- The first 5 breaths (clearing the heart) are designed to help your autonomic nervous system release negative emotion.
- The second 5 breaths (clearing the mind) employ mindfulness to calm your mind.
- The third 5 breaths (shifting the heart) connect you to your ideal performance state.

Over and over, I've watched as clients have used this 15-breath technique to prepare in advance for challenge. They've employed it the night before and morning of a major event or competition to mobilize themselves and to chip away at long-term phobias and fears.

PRIME OPPORTUNITIES FOR HEART SHIFTING

- Delivering a major presentation
- Speaking with a loved one about a sensitive topic
- Preparing for a competitive sporting event
- Taking a test
- Facing a phobia, such as fear of flying or heights
- And more

THE HEART REMEMBERS

Your heart has a memory, one that's been molded and shaped over the years by your stress response. Through this exercise, you will learn how to teach your heart in advance how you want it to react during moments of stress. The technique can be used for a multitude of performance applications, from race day to overcoming flight phobias. To maximize its power, you'll want to practice it the night before as well as the morning of your competition or performance event. That's because, in my practice, I have observed that the heart will remember the new pattern of responding for up to 12 hours after you practice it. Thus, if you have a competition or a meeting at 9 a.m. the next day, you will need to practice the Heart Shift after 9 p.m. the evening before the event.

The goal of this exercise is to teach the heart to sustain a resonance heart rhythm during times of stress. It is a piece of the program that my clients consistently report as having the greatest impact on their lives, because it helps them to train the heart how to respond in advance of an anticipated stressor.

BREATHING EXERCISE #7: TRAINING YOUR HEART RHYTHMS

Pick a specific performance event that you have coming up. Once you've identified the event you wish to prepare for, find a quiet, comfortable space in which to sit. You should have your pacer app open and ready to use. Remember, Heart Shifting is practiced in advance of an event, including the night before and morning of. Heart Shifting during an actual competitive event is not recommended as it can distract you from the task at hand. You're now ready to practice Heart Shifting.

Step 1. Clear the Heart

I'd like you to take 5 breaths at your resonance frequency. (Use your pacer to match your inhale and exhale to your resonance frequency.) These first 5 breaths are intended to release negative emotions from your autonomic nervous system. On the inhale, connect to and experience your negative emotion — stress, anger, frustration, fear. What does the emotion feel like in your heart? Crushing and heavy? Anxious and fearful? Lonely?

On the exhale, focus on releasing that emotion from your heart by exhaling through your mouth and directing it out of your body. Remember, this is not a cognitive exercise; it is a physiological exercise, with you aiming to connect to the way that your heart feels on the inhale without engaging your thinking mind.

Step 2. Clear the Mind

For the second set of 5 breaths, focus on the crisp, fresh air on the inhale and the feeling of letting go on the exhale. This mindfulness-training activity requires you to narrow your focus to the sensations of your breath and, thereby, reduce the chatter of your busy brain.

Step 3. Shift the Heart

During the third set of 5 breaths, connect to your ideal performance state on the inhale, and let go of any negative emotions on the exhale. Think about what you want to feel like during your performance, and practice experiencing that heart state on the inhale. Do you want to feel excited? Perhaps calm and composed? What physiological state will be most conducive to your peak performance? Equally important, practice releasing any negative emotions on the exhale. In the absence of any negative emotions, you can also focus on the feeling of letting go on the exhale.

OVERCOMING GAME DAY NERVES

Shelly was an experienced runner, well liked by her college teammates and admired by her younger fans. Yet her internal state told a different story. Despite having practice times that would qualify her for the Olympics, the night before a race, Shelly's nerves caused her to experience a pounding heartbeat and clammy hands, the latter indicating a lack of blood flow to the periphery of her body, caused by autonomic system imbalance. The day of the actual competition, her mind was overwhelmed with catastrophizing thoughts — primarily self-doubt about her ability to perform under pressure and anxiety.

Along with meeting once weekly with me and practicing her breathing 20 minutes twice per day at home, she focused on Heart Shifting the night before and the morning of each race, including the Olympic trials, shifting from feeling anxiety to being a cool and calm competitor. She would select the imprint that she considered the most likely to inhibit her performance, such as her tendency to negatively compare herself to her fellow female competitors, then identify the ideal state she wanted to cultivate. Her protocol looked like this:

Step 1: Focusing on the feeling of doubt on the inhale, then letting go of the doubt on the exhale, for 5 breaths (clear the heart).

Step 2: Mindfully breathing, focusing on the inhale and the exhale, for 5 breaths (clear the mind).

Step 3: Imagining calm and confidence on the inhale, then letting go of doubt on the exhale (boost the heart).

The goal was to teach her body a new pattern for managing stress. At the end of the 15 breaths, she had created a new rhythm for responding that would activate during her performance moment. If she fell into an old pattern of doubt, her heart knew exactly what to do. That year, Shelly closed the gap between her practice and competition performances. She posted qualifying times that earned her a spot on Team USA. Shelly had worked on many aspects of her training, including HRV training, but noted that being in control of how her heart responded to specific moments of stress was a critical aspect for her to reduce her anxiety and perform at her peak.

What You'll Experience

By this week, you may be increasingly able to identify when you are in and out of resonance, a highly valuable skill that doubles as evidence that this program truly is working for you. During week 1, you learned the basics of resonance and found your resonance breathing frequency, but it's during week 5 that my clients become more familiar with the feeling of resonance and discover their dominant resonance symptom, a feeling or sensation that stands out when they're in resonance. The most common dominant resonance symptom is usually described as having "a clear mind," followed by "a calm heart," reduced muscle tension, enhanced focus, or another bodily signal that sends you the message "You are in resonance."

Still having trouble pinning it down? My clients have also described resonance as feeling any of the following sensations in the mind, heart, and body.

- Focused
- Objective
- Optimistic
- Sharp
- Clear
- Crisp
- Creative
- Flexible
- Free
- Devoted
- At peace
- Open
- Empathic
- Strong
- Confident
- Courageous
- Invincible
- Connected
- Calm
- Collected
- In balance
- Aligned with my mind
- Primed to perform

- Tingling (this is due to increased blood flow to the periphery of your body — a common sign of being in resonance)

These changes may be subtle. If you can't discern them quite yet, don't give up. The more you practice, the better you will get at picking up on your body's signs of being in resonance.

PHOTOS, MUSIC, MANTRAS, MOVEMENT: ADDITIONAL LAYERS TO SHIFT YOUR PHYSIOLOGY

Clearly, I'm passionate about resonance breathing's ability to shift physiology. But I'm also a fan of incorporating other simple, accessible strategies to promote, enhance, and maintain resonance. This is where photos, music, mantras, and movement come in. Some people scroll through pictures of nature to feel calm. Another client found that stretching between meetings helped his body release anxiety and relax. I myself have a picture of my daughters and husband on the background of my smartwatch, so that whenever I glance at the time (and am likely feeling rushed), I am flooded by feelings of love. All these layers help to shift your physiology and amplify resonance throughout your life.

If you build in these other activities, systematically, following your breathing, you can expedite how quickly you can achieve your desired performance state. The best part is, these layers are fun, and they're already part of the fabric of your everyday life.

Clients and I work together before their anticipated challenge to plan how they will respond to specific stressors. If you know particular stressors negatively influence your ability to perform at your level of ability, you need a plan. How will you let go of the stress as quickly as possible?

When Michael, a 16-year-old national-level tennis player, came to me, he was looking for tools to close the gap between how he played in practice and how he performed in competition. He discussed his difficulty regaining his composure and ability to perform at his level of skill after a referee issued a call that Michael perceived as bad or wrong. Given that this occurred during approximately one of every three games, Michael needed a way to optimize his response to this expected stressor. Instead of getting upset and losing focus and control over his plays, he needed to be able to feel his anger and then let it go.

That's right. He needed to be able to connect to the negative emotion right there on the court (as opposed to pretending that it never happened or trying to instantly feel confident) and then release it. Connecting to the negative was critical. I often tell my clients that it's healthy to feel negative emotions or stress; their job is just to feel it and let it go as quickly as possible.

To ensure the stress didn't linger, we created a protocol for Michael. The routine we developed consisted of 2 resonance breaths, whereby he connected to his anger and released it on the exhale, followed by a quick left-right shuffle of his feet and the silent mantra "Loose arms, fast feet." The shuffle was a rhythmic, 10-second movement consisting of shuffling 5 seconds to the left and 5 seconds to the right; we chose this specifically because Michael's resonance frequency was 10 breaths per minute, and research shows we can elicit resonance through movement at the same rate as our resonance frequency. The "loose arms, fast feet" mantra helped him focus on his process instead of the outcome, which helped him feel energized and ready to compete.

In times of high stress, you want to be able to employ a multitude of tools to shift your physiology in real time. To turn your goals into reality, reach for your favorite HRV strategies, in addition to breathing, to achieve these physiological outcomes.

OPTIMIZATION STRATEGY: HEART SHIFTING GHOSTS

Last week, we practiced connecting to your ghosts and feeling that deep source of stress on the inhale, then releasing it from your body on the exhale. That prepared you for this next step: using Heart Shifting to condition your nervous system in advance to feel the desired state that letting go will surely bring. To do this, practice Heart Shifting for the last 3 minutes of your daily breathing practices.

Step 1: Clear the heart. On the first set of 5 breaths, focus on the stressor that you'd like to let go, such as the need for control or perfection, and release it through your mouth on the exhale.

Step 2: Clear the mind. Next, focus on the crisp and fresh air on the inhale and the feeling of the air leaving the mouth on the exhale for the second set of 5 breaths.

Step 3: Shift the heart. Finally, connect with the desired state, such as calm and confidence, on the inhale and the letting go of the ghost state on the exhale for the last 5 breaths.

Each time you do this, you initiate a transformative physiological process that allows you to shift the heart toward your desired state. This Heart Shifting technique is particularly helpful for stressors that just don't seem to get unstuck even with the prior breathing-away training techniques.

HIGHLIGHT ON HEALTH: PHOBIAS

Heart Shifting has also been helpful for clients with phobias, even ones that have ruled their lives for decades.

My client Alex had a phobia about flying. She would begin feeling panic two nights before any airplane travel. This wasn't mild anxiety; Alex would develop a migraine, her stomach would become upset, and she'd feel frozen, as if her body couldn't move. At one point, she quit flying altogether, taking trains to visit friends and family, even if it meant an extra 10 hours of travel, and avoiding business travel altogether. Alex spent years trying many different interventions, including acupuncture, hypnotherapy, meditation, and cognitive behavioral therapy, all with little relief.

When Alex came to me, we chose her airplane-related migraines as the symptom most in need of tackling. For the first several weeks, we focused on breathing away the headaches on the exhale, and she did, in fact, report a reduction in their severity during the fourth week. At week 5, she asked me if I could prepare her for an upcoming trip, and I suggested we try Heart Shifting to teach her heart how she wanted it to perform the two nights prior to her flight and the day of. Our protocol looked different each night, but we used the 5-5-5 breathing technique to help shift her anticipated stressful response to an ideal state as follows:

Two nights before the flight, Alex began feeling anticipatory anxiety about not being able to sleep the night before the flight — she was anxious about the upcoming anxiety. Her goal was to prepare her body to be able to sleep. During her Heart Shift breathing exercise, she focused on shifting from anxiety to calm.

The night prior to the flight, Alex began fearing the possible migraines and other somatic symptoms that often began as she boarded the flight. Her goal was to prepare her body to let go of the night-before-flight fear and instead feel confident in her abilities to board the next-day flight. During her Heart Shift breathing exercise, she focused on shifting from a state of fear to a calm and confident self.

The morning of the flight, Alex felt mounting anxiety about boarding the plane. She was concerned she would feel a lack of control and an increasing sense of panic on the flight. Her goal was to board the flight and reach her destination feeling composed and in control. During her Heart Shift breathing exercise, she focused on shifting from panic to a feeling of control.

Though she was still mildly anxious, Alex boarded a plane for the first time in 10 years. She was able to sleep the two nights before travel, as well. She developed a small migraine while boarding the plane but said it was manageable, and she was able to prevent it from increasing in severity by using resonance breathing on the jet bridge.

To help her navigate the flight itself, Alex and I developed an in-flight protocol that included an assortment of anxiety-management tools.

- Belly breathing to anchor her attention and amplify her resonance.
- Scrolling through a folder of preselected pictures on her phone that sparked feelings of joy: a summer swimming trip in Niagara Falls; her toddler dancing in the living room; a recent surprise 40th birthday celebration her husband had thrown for her.
- Reciting positive mantras in her mind ("I've done this before. I can do it again. I'm in control.").
- Connecting with the person next to her on the flight or reaching out to an attendant with simple small talk or a request for assistance, if needed.

In our session following her airplane travel, Alex revealed that, to her surprise, she had needed to dip into this in-flight tool kit only once, after a moment of turbulence. She noted that she was able to reduce her anxiety, return to baseline, and even shift into a state of resonance after using the anxiety-management tools. (She didn't need to reach out to anyone to manage her emotions in-flight.) This was a huge success for Alex! Further, as she regained control of her ability to fly, she gained confidence in her ability to take on other risks, such as speaking in public, that she had been avoiding.

ANY QUESTIONS?

"How do I feel a memory rather than cognitively thinking about it?"

The goal of Heart Shifting is to reconnect with a sensation or feeling that occurred during a specific experience—a physiological memory in the heart. Many people, however, try to access this memory by re-creating the cognitive memory in which an emotion such as being calm or happy occurred. This is a very normal inclination, but it won't trigger your autonomic nervous system to discharge a negative physiological memory from your heart. To re-create the heart experience, focus on how your heart felt during a particular moment. For practice, I often ask

my clients to consider when they felt enormous amounts of love, gratitude, or magic in their lives. Choose a loved one, and bring yourself back
to the moment when you two first truly connected with each other. How
did your heart feel right in that moment? Did you feel trusting? Optimistic? Relaxed? Hopeful? Rejuvenated? What from your heart was telling
you that this was someone you wanted to get to know? The secret is
to connect to the feeling first in your heart, then see where that feeling
takes you in your mind. Allow the body to feel the memory first. If your
mind starts to take over and tries to conjure up memories of the experience that you have stored in your brain, remind yourself to gently refocus on the heart.

WEEK 5 ACTION PLAN

1. Continue your twice-a-day, 20-minute resonance breathing sessions. Heart Shift for the last 3 minutes of every breathing practice. You can choose to shift from a negative state to a positive
   state, or you can choose to let go of a deeply embedded ghost
   theme, such as the need for control, and shifting toward your as-
   piration state, such as a sense of calm confidence. (Yes, this is
   slightly different than the previous weeks, when you've spent the
   final 5 minutes practicing that week's particular technique. But
   15 resonance breaths take, on average, about 3 minutes.)
2. Use the Heart Shift the night before and morning of a known
   stressor, such as an important meeting, a presentation or speech,
   an athletic competition, or facing a phobia. Or, use the Heart
   Shift immediately following an external stressor that is difficult
   for you to let go. For instance, if someone made a comment that
   irritated you, practice the Heart Shift to let go of the irritation
   and boost your focus on a calm, confident you.
3. Practice Heart Shifting your ghosts and/or adding music, photos,
   or mantras to boost your HRV practice.

9

▼

Week 6:

Mastering the Emotional Pivot

THE PHYSIOLOGY OF RESILIENCE

Ultramarathoner Courtney Dauwalter routinely runs more than 100 miles at a time. In 2017, she completed the Moab 240, a 238-mile race through Utah backcountry, in 2 days, 9 hours, and 59 minutes, besting the next fastest competitor (a man) by 10 hours. In 2018, she ran 279.2 miles in Big's Backyard Ultra, in which runners must complete a 4.16667-mile loop every hour, with the last person standing the winner.

Courtney Dauwalter knows pain.

Sometimes she hallucinates. (Hello, leopard lounging in a hammock.)

She gets sidelined by a "feisty stomach" or a hip that simply stops working.

Still, she keeps coming back for more.

I asked the 35-year-old athletic phenom about the secret to her physical and mental resilience.

"Staying positive, talking to myself, and continuing to focus on forward motion are some of the ways I push through," she told me. "I often repeat to myself, 'You're fine. This is fine,' as a way to keep myself from panicking and to remind myself that I have been in this sort of situation before and it will be okay if I just keep pushing forward."

Oh, and she had T-shirts made featuring a leopard in a hammock.

The one thing in life that we can expect with superb reliability is stress. Yet most of us lack specific strategies to navigate stressful events and are unable to deftly pivot from a negative to a positive internal state before responding to the situation at hand. Such a skill set can be defined as resilience: the ability to recover from adversity and persevere to meet our goals.

Just as physical resilience is required to bounce back from an injury, we need emotional or psychological resilience to recover from what the mind perceives as stressors. This capacity to successfully work through hardship is considered a predictor of overall well-being. Psychological resilience is also necessary to reduce or prevent unproductive stress responses, such as anxiety, annoyance, frustration, and impatience.

Greater resting HRV is associated with an increased ability to remain positive and confident during adversity — a hallmark of resilience and absolutely crucial for the ability to Emotionally Pivot by shifting your emotions on demand. Positive emotions such as love, gratitude, and awe broaden people's attention and thinking and trigger upward spirals toward greater well-being in the future. It sounds implausible, but when researchers surveyed more than 150,000 individuals from 142 countries, they found that positive emotions had more of an influence on health than homelessness, hunger, or feeling unsafe.

Think about that for a moment. Positive emotions are powerful enough to help counteract the health effects of poverty, lack of food, or worse.

Research tells us that individuals who can cultivate positive emotions at will also show faster cardiovascular recovery following a stressful experience and, as a result, are able to return their nervous system to baseline more quickly and easily. When positive emotions are in short supply, however, you can get stuck. You lose your emotional flexibility and become myopic in your negative thinking process. Your heart rhythm is erratic and demonstrates decreased variability.

This week, I present a system for identifying and accessing positive experiences in the heart to fuel psychological resilience. This training will help you nimbly navigate challenges at work, in interpersonal and romantic relationships, in sports, and at home. The goal of this process is to teach you to connect to memories through your heart instead of your body and, as a result, cultivate a positive internal state on demand. In my practice, I call this Heart Pivoting. You'll practice connecting to a positive memory during times of stress so you can successfully pivot away from anxiety, fear, and anger and toward the positive emotion of your choice.

HEART PIVOTING: TRAINING YOURSELF TO PIVOT FROM A NEGATIVE TO A POSITIVE EMOTIONAL STATE

Mastering the art and science of Emotional Pivoting is ideally approached in four stages: physiological recall, increasing accessibility, bridging the gap, and pivoting with the heart.

Before we begin, let's take a moment to discuss the concept of nonjudgment. I'll soon be asking you to explore your emotions with a nonjudgmental attitude. If you've ever tried meditating and found your mind wandering away, you likely chastised yourself for it, thinking, "I can't do meditation! My mind keeps drifting off." But if you were to study with a meditation instructor, one of the first lessons you'd learn is that mind wandering is not a bad thing. It's simply something that happens, even to the most practiced of meditators, and should not be regarded with scorn or shame. You simply observe it for what it is — "Oh, there goes my mind, drifting off a bit" — and gently return your attention to the present. This is a hallmark of Buddhist ethical principles, and some might argue that the success of meditation lies in this ability to regard one's mind wandering with neutral objectivity. With practice, that skill eventually carries over into the everyday, helping you remain calm and silencing your inner critic.

During Heart Pivoting, the state of nonjudgment cultivates openness, wonder, and curiosity as emotional memories are invited and embraced. It leads to freedom to explore a range of emotions from highly positive to uncomfortably difficult. Somatic experiencing, or the ability to physiologically connect to memories of emotional events stored in the body, is founded upon such regulation of attention and lack of self-judgment. All too often, negative self-talk obstructs our ability to access positive emotional states or impedes our ability to shift into a desired physiological state. As you move through the Heart Pivot exercise, try to keep this spirit of nonjudgment top of mind.

Let's now explore each stage, step by step.

STEP 1: PHYSIOLOGICAL RECALL

Begin by remembering times in your life in which you felt love, gratitude, or awe. Perhaps you remember being flooded with genuine bliss and love on a celebratory occasion like a surprise birthday party, high school graduation, your wedding day, or when holding your child in your arms for the first time. Maybe you felt incredibly grateful when your spouse supported you during an important project, a coach offered you a position on their team, or a physical therapist helped teach you to walk again after an intensive surgery. Or you were struck with awe when looking at a lush, green landscape or traveling with your family to a beautiful beach or mountain.

The goal of this stage is to identify at least three memories that triggered physiological sensations in your heart at the time of the experience. Try to let go of the cognitive experience of the emotion, and shift your focus to the physiological sensation of the emotion in your heart. Did your heart feel full and happy? Clear and free? Strong and invincible?

Perhaps you felt warmth, a tingly excitement, or a feeling of hope. I call this enjoyable sensation a heart imprint. In the next step, you will be connecting with this Imprint, your heart's memory of a positive experience, during the inhale of your resonance breath.

If love, gratitude, and awe are not emotional experiences that resonate with you, don't worry, there are plenty of other heart imprints with which to experiment. For instance, one of my clients preferred to focus on the infinite sense of possibility he felt in his heart when sitting on his roof deck looking at the stars in the sky. Composure and confidence are two other qualities to which my clients often respond favorably. What matters most is that you are selecting experiences that created strong positive feelings when they first occurred. Write these down in the Homework section on page 232.

STEP 2: INCREASING ACCESSIBILITY

Once you've identified three specific instances that produce positive physical sensations in your heart, you are now ready to set up a practice strategy to increase the accessibility of these imprints so that you can connect to them anytime, anywhere. Choose only one heart imprint to focus on for the time being—for instance, love, gratitude, or courage. Begin your resonance breathing, connecting to your chosen imprint on the inhale and releasing stress on the exhale. (This is what you'll ultimately be doing for the final 5 minutes of each 20-minute breathing practice this week.)

STEP 3: BRIDGING THE GAP

Next, try activating the heart imprint in neutral situations, like while riding the train, standing in line for groceries, or waiting on hold on the phone. Practicing in familiar, unemotional environments like these will act as a bridge to helping you activate your heart imprint in stressful situations. See if you're able to boost your mood by focusing on your heart imprint on the inhale and letting go of stress on the exhale in approximately 10 breaths. If so, that's evidence of your resilience building. This step takes practice, so don't worry if it feels difficult or unnatural at first.

STEP 4: PIVOTING WITH THE HEART

Once you're able to shift from a neutral mood to a positive one, you are ready to dig a bit deeper. It's one thing to practice Heart Pivoting in the comfort and safety of your home. It is far more challenging to successfully do so in real time, as you are experiencing a negative internal state. This fourth step involves attempting to pivot from a negative to a positive emotional state to meet the demands of a specific moment.

Identify your favorite, go-to heart imprint. Many people have one or two heart imprints that they feel are the best for shifting to a positive state in the shortest amount of time. Most often it is love for their child or pet, the joy they felt on their wedding day, or a peak inspiring moment in their lives.

As stress occurs, try to connect to your heart imprint on the inhale, and let go of the negative emotion you're experiencing (or a state that isn't helping you to achieve your desired performance) on the exhale. Try to stay nonjudgmental as you do so. Feeling irritated during a tense conversation with a partner or colleague, for example, or fighting fatigue toward the end of a long day, are very normal responses; don't scold yourself for them. Rather, during these times of conflict, see if you can pivot from irritation to love. At work, challenge yourself to pivot from a feeling of pressure to calmness. At the end of the day, can you pivot from fatigue to increased energy?

The next time you find yourself in an emotionally charged situation, see if you can change your internal charge.

1. Connect to your heart imprint on the inhale to boost your HRV.
2. Release the negative emotions on the exhale.
3. Repeat until you feel in resonance.

What You'll Experience

With time and practice, repeatedly connecting to one of your heart imprints on your inhales will allow you to shift out of your undesired internal state and into resonance more quickly than traditional resonance frequency breathing alone. It will also extend the period in which you feel resonance. As you become more adept at accessing your heart imprints, your body will reflexively start to shift you into resonance during times of stress, as opposed to lingering in stress for an extended period.

You'll notice that you have the ability to more tightly regulate your emotions. You'll no longer run on automatic pilot and react out of self-defense or without conscious thought. You're now better able to screen out negative thoughts and minimize negative emotions — resentment, anger, jealousy — that have low utility in achieving your desired outcome. At the same time, you'll likely notice an uptick in sensing positive emotions in your heart — love, gratitude, wonder — that will help you reach your goals.

This is a game changer for many people because it allows them to engage more deeply in emotions that lead to a desired outcome. You are acquiring the ability to *choose* your response to various experiences, relationships, and performance challenges as opposed to letting your response choose you.

Why This Is Happening

Connecting with your heart imprint on the inhale amplifies your heart rate increase, advancing you to a positive internal state more quickly than regular resonance breathing alone. Activating that positive state allows your cardiovascular response to return to baseline more quickly in the heat of the moment. You're recovering faster, physiologically speaking, from stress.

University of North Carolina psychologists Barbara Frederickson, PhD, and Bethany Kok, PhD, demonstrated this beautifully when they asked 52 adults to track their positive emotions — awe, gratitude, joy —

for 9 weeks. They found that the higher a subject's HRV was at the beginning, the easier and more quickly he or she could experience positive feelings over the next 9 weeks.

You'll also likely notice improvements in executive functioning. When the heart rhythm pattern is erratic and disordered, the corresponding pattern of neural signals traveling from the heart to the brain inhibits higher cognitive functioning. This impedes the ability to think clearly, remember, learn, reason, and make effective decisions. In contrast, the steadier and more ordered the pattern of signals from the heart to the brain, the more enhanced your executive and overall cognitive functioning become.

THE POWER OF HEART PIVOTING

Brent was a 37-year-old COO of a Fortune 500 company and was seeking assistance in flexibly responding to work stressors. Concern about living up to his own expectations of peak performance by his 40th birthday was impacting his ability to let go of stress and negative emotion. All of this impacted his ability to access flow. He was stuck in a stifling state of contraction, muscles clenched, mind focusing on tangential aspects of work instead of the big picture, and his confidence diminished by fears of not being perfect. He wanted to be able to effortlessly express his ideas with conviction when speaking to his staff; to calmly engage with employees during company discussions; and then, during afternoon board meetings, be able to offer a thoughtful, composed summary of his organization's performance.

Our goal was to help Brent learn to quickly pivot between emotional states during his resonance breathing sessions, knowing that that skill would eventually carry over into stressful times at work. Throughout our first few weeks together, we began exploring his memories, both negative and positive, of stress at work, along with any corresponding physiological sensations. I encouraged him to do this with a nonjudgmental attitude.

During week 4, we determined that his ghost imprint was the pressure to have achieved a certain level of success by age 40, and in week 6, we homed in on the positive emotions, like a sense of calm composure, that Brent wished he could experience at work. To help him anchor these emotions, I asked him to describe a time in his life in which he felt love, gratitude, or awe. His response was immediate: spending time in nature—diving in the Great Barrier Reef or skiing on the slopes of Aspen. I could see his demeanor visibly improve when he spoke about those experiences; he lit up. Pinpointing his heart imprint helped him tap into the positive emotions he wished to feel during times of crisis at work: peaceful, calm, self-assured.

Brent began practicing resonance breathing, pairing his heart imprint with the inhale and letting go of his self-imposed pressures about success with the exhale. He practiced this at home for the last 5 minutes of twice-daily sessions as well as during moments of anxiety. He also began being able to access his heart imprint to shift out of negative thinking and worry during his workdays. Ultimately, Brent planned to connect with his heart imprint during moments of stress at work. With a plan for how to pivot emotions during critical moments of doubt and anxiety, Brent reported that he was able to lead his afternoon board meetings with authority and engage more deeply with his team during moments of pressure.

CONTROLLING YOUR HEART RHYTHMS TO GET UNSTUCK

Lauren has been a principal dancer with a globally acclaimed dance company for 21 years. She lived for the way dancing made her feel: blissfully alive and free. As a professional dancer, she felt grateful to be entrusted with the role of transporting others to a place of magic and wonder.

After decades of performing, though, the beloved career that brought her such joy and fulfillment was becoming tainted by intense demands and extreme levels of competition and criticism (including an inner bully that had begun narrating her faults during performances). Lauren started shaking in certain positions onstage and found it surprisingly difficult to perform movements that she had performed hundreds if not thousands of times before. She began taking antianxiety medications to calm her nerves, and while she had some success using affirmations and positive imagery, she reported an enduring sense of "my mind fighting my body. I wanted to evolve more in my dancing, to feel even more free onstage, more empowered, yet still open and vulnerable . . . but I'd begun to feel as if my mental self-critic was bullying me, interfering with my ability to perform at my peak and robbing my performing experience of the fulfillment I craved. My nerves were sabotaging me."

As a dancer, Lauren had a deep faith in her body's wisdom, and she needed and wanted to be able to trust it again.

She practiced her resonance breathing twice a day for 20 minutes. In my office, we used biofeedback equipment to watch her heart rate and breathing begin to shift, becoming functions she could direct and control. We identified some of her heart imprints, the strongest of which turned out to be her childhood love of dancing—the freedom and joy she felt from movement. Lauren began Heart Pivoting before going on stage, connecting to the intense sense of pride and fulfillment she imagined a young Lauren would have felt. She also practiced Heart Pivoting during performances, connecting to her passion for dance on the inhale and exhaling away her nerves and inner critic. With time, she began to feel the nervous anxiety morph into a tingling excitement, almost like a physical connectedness to her heart and her art. It was as if Lauren unlocked an old energy that could now flood her body.

With much hard work and dedication, Lauren was able to access her childhood love for dance and recall it on demand to help her feel freer and more connected to her body. She no longer needed medication, either, as her baseline level of anxiety was lower, and she could control fleeting negative emotions through her breath.

OPTIMIZATION STRATEGY: PERFORMING MINI HEART PIVOTS THROUGHOUT YOUR DAY

Mini Heart Pivots, performed throughout your day, are an excellent means of coping with stress. These are done in addition to your two 20-minute resonance breathing sessions. I have clients start by performing 10 Mini Heart Pivots three times a day. That means that three times a day, they take 10 strategic breaths, connecting to a positive emotion on the inhale and releasing a negative emotion or state on the exhale. Toggling between imprints is recommended. You can match your Heart Pivot to the emotional need of that specific time of day. You might try pivoting with a sense of gratitude in the morning (to help frame the day ahead); with courage or perseverance in the afternoon (to combat the 3 p.m. slump); and with a sense of calm in the evening (to wind down).

It's incredible to witness how powerful this simple tool can be. I've had clients reduce antianxiety and antidepressant medications following weeks of this practice. (See Highlight on Health, below, for more on this.) You are resetting your body three times a day to optimize HRV along with your ability to flexibly let go of the negative and embrace the positive.

HIGHLIGHT ON HEALTH: DEPRESSION

Heart health and mental health are inextricably linked. Look no further than the so-called broken heart syndrome, the increased likelihood of a husband or wife experiencing a cardiac event, even a fatal heart attack, following a partner's death. HRV plays a role here. Research shows that in the 3 months following a partner's death, widows, now at the apex of their grief, have lower HRV and higher rates of inflammatory markers in the blood compared with their non-bereaved counterparts.

When it comes to depression, the link with HRV may occur in two directions. A dysregulated autonomic nervous system may influence one's risk of depression, and having depression may dysregulate the nervous system. New research published in *JAMA Psychiatry* finds that the former pathway may be stronger, suggesting that cultivating a higher HRV may offer some protection against depression. This doesn't mean that having a high HRV eliminates the possibility of depression; it just means that we can view low HRV as a risk factor for depression, similar to social isolation or a family history of mental health issues.

Additionally, recent neurocardiology studies have revealed that the heart is capable of secreting feel-good chemicals like dopamine, oxytocin, and norepinephrine, all of which help to counteract feelings of depression. For years, the prevailing consensus has been that these powerful compounds were released only by the brain; the notion that the heart can produce these neurochemicals is exciting on many levels. This suggests that strengthening the heart through HRV-strengthening practices could possibly yield mild antidepressive effects. Considering the prevalence of depression — more than 17 million US adults have experienced at least one episode of major depression, and millions more live with the disorder in varying degrees of severity — making relatively small adjustments like improving HRV has the potential to yield promising results.

ANY QUESTIONS?

"The positive memory that I used to connect with no longer evokes any change in my body. What do I do now?"

Ahh, it sounds like you've been locking into the same experience to shift your internal state for too long and your body needs a refresh. It's normal for a memory to start to feel stale after repetitive practice or to produce less of a physiological change than when you started. For some people, this can even be startling: Why can't I tap into the love of my wedding day or the joy I felt holding my child for the first time?

Rest assured, this is not a cause for concern; you haven't exhausted your happy memory! Your body simply needs a fresh set of experiences to focus on. Frequent rehearsal of the same memory reduces its potency. To resolve this, you can focus on expanding the range of emotional memories in which you have felt awe, joy, wonder, gratitude, love, peace, or forgiveness. Jot down at least three experiences for each of these emotional states. When a memory feels stale or is not producing the same shift in your body's response, you can connect to another experience on your list. I recommend identifying a new heart imprint every 2 to 3 months to continue to expand your emotional management repertoire.

WEEK 6 ACTION PLAN

1. Write down at least three instances in your life when you have felt tremendous love, gratitude, or awe. These are your heart imprints. (Use the homework tracking sheet on page 232.) How did you know that you felt this way? What was happening in your heart during each of these instances? Pairing this feeling with your inhale will increase the amplitude of your heart rate.
2. Continue your twice-a-day, 20-minute breathing sessions. Spend the last 5 minutes of your practice connecting to one of your heart imprints on the inhale and letting go of stress on the exhale. This is called Heart Pivoting.
3. Practice pivoting your emotional state during the day. When you notice yourself in a state that weighs you down or inhibits your ability to perform at your peak, connect to a heart imprint on the inhale and let go of the negative state on the exhale. Repeat this practice for 10 consecutive breaths or until you achieve resonance.

A PEEK AHEAD

Don't forget to measure and record your HRV next week, during week 7.

10

▼

Week 7:

Cultivating Resonance Under Fire

Imagine being a police officer. You are a member of an inherently stressful, often dangerous profession. Your job is to repeatedly enter unfamiliar situations where oftentimes the only information you have is that a threat is present and somebody's safety is on the line. Your job environment is often marked by menacing conditions: darkness, surprising noises, erratic individuals. Vulnerability and unpredictability are woven into the fabric of your uniform.

These stressors impact your job in particularly risky ways. When in a state of fight-or-flight, your body experiences a host of sensory distortions. As blood is shunted to your larger muscle groups (to aid in chasing or subduing a suspect, for instance), your vision can become compromised by up to 70 percent, peripheral vision in particular. This does not bode well for detecting movement around you, nor does it facilitate accurate shooting. With so much blood flow fueling your running and other gross motor functions, your fine motor skills, such as those required by your hands to safely maneuver a weapon or handcuffs, suffer. Compounding matters, the flow of blood and oxygen to the prefrontal cortex (an area of the brain tasked with retaining information and storing memories) is reduced. This can potentially interfere with your ability to call up the proper tactical protocol with the lightning speed required.

Curious about whether biofeedback could help police officers regulate their autonomic nervous systems, Canadian and Finnish researchers devised a research protocol in which SWAT team members were randomly assigned to receive or not receive stress exposure training (SET), which uses imagined exposure to stressors as well as controlled exposure to real stressors to train people to perform optimally under suboptimal conditions. In this study, the SET included being taught techniques such as visualization and biofeedback, mental rehearsal of stressful scenarios, and coaching to enhance sensory perception and controlled breathing.

After 3 days of SET, subjects were asked to engage in staged-but-realistic critical incident scenarios, such as responding to a murder in a known drug house occupied by potentially armed men (to guarantee the most lifelike details possible, the actors were trained police officers themselves, intimately familiar with how a drug addict or gang member would respond to a SWAT member coming through the door). A second scenario took place in a huge warehouse, this one filled with scenes such as men fighting at the end of a darkened hallway, a person behind a door quickly raising a weapon, a hostage crisis, and being approached from the side by a man with a radio in his hand, asking "What happened here?" immediately afterward.

Study coauthors Judith Andersen, PhD, and Harri Gustafsberg, PhD, found that those in the SET group demonstrated "significantly enhanced situational awareness, overall performance, and made a greater number of correct use of force (shoot/no shoot) decisions." SET improved the officers' ability to notice potential threats in their environment, manually overriding stress's negative impact on peripheral vision and recall. And because subjects had their HRV monitored throughout the study, the authors were able to observe that officers in the stress exposure training group experienced a lower maximum heart rate throughout the test scenarios and recovered more quickly afterward, compared with subjects in the control group. All of this, Andersen and Gustafsberg reported, translated into officers appearing capable of maintaining their individual optimal state associated with enhanced performance, along with "potential lifesaving decisions for police and the civilians they are working with."

Besides giving you a newfound respect for officers of the law, this example illustrates the profound impact stress can have on a human being.

Cultivating Resonance Under Fire Training is a heart-based approach to stress exposure training, teaching you how to perform optimally under suboptimal conditions such as the following:

- A celebrated musician who couldn't read negative reviews of his performances without feeling like a failure. In my office — a safe, controlled setting — I would have him read such reviews aloud, monitoring his rising heart rate on my biofeedback equipment. He would then practice reducing his state of arousal with 10 breaths, then 5 breaths, then 3 breaths; he was essentially training himself to let go in shorter durations.
- A professional baseball player who struggled to maintain his composure during games when crowd members heckled him. We used an audio recorder to capture some of these sounds during actual games then replayed them in my office, challenging him to try to slow his heart rate and apply his braking system.
- A tennis player preparing for her first US Open. She had never played in front of a crowd as large as this and never on television. In my office, we watched videotapes of her competing in front of her largest crowd as she was connected to biofeedback equipment. (That game had felt especially stressful to her because of the crowd size.) As she watched, her physiology responded — a spike in heart rate, increased muscle tension — as if she were actually playing, and she attempted to stay in resonance while watching.
- A hedge fund manager having aversive reactions to minute-by-minute changes in the stock market. He knew how imperative it was to remain calm and composed during market volatility —

you can't let your stress obscure your objectivity and decision making. We practiced achieving resonance while viewing his profit and loss statements.

The objective of Cultivating Resonance Under Fire is to reduce cardiovascular reactivity to a specific stressor. Over time, that reduced reactivity manifests as a better ability to tolerate that stressor when it appears throughout the day, when peak performance is essential.

UNDERSTANDING THE PHYSIOLOGY OF STRESS

In order to learn how to let go of stress, it's advantageous to have a basic understanding of how it works in the body. Here's a quick recap of what we've discussed so far.

When we detect a change in the environment that commands our attention, our body releases a precisely choreographed cascade of hormones designed to prepare us for a reaction. Our breathing and heart rate quicken. We may feel our muscles tense in preparation to fight or flee. Our body is shifting to a sympathetic-dominant state in order to prepare us for survival. This ramping up is normal and a signal of a healthy, functioning nervous system.

So, the truth is, not all stress is bad. If some sort of imminent danger truly exists, such as an oncoming car or the smell of smoke, you want these physiological changes to kick in automatically and without hesitation. This is called acute stress.

But as we know, humans aren't always successful when it comes to processing and fully releasing our acute stress. Unlike the deer who hears the crunch of a twig nearby, goes into alert mode, decides no threat is present, and fully discharges that energy from its nervous system, we struggle to return to homeostasis. Perpetually stressful work or home environments don't help matters. So, the brain acts as if threats are omnipresent. Cortisol and adrenaline continue to churn. The sympathetic nervous system remains stuck in "On" mode. This is chronic stress.

But stressors are a part of life. Drama arises at work. Relationships aren't 100 percent happy all the time. Traffic will always exist. We cannot prevent or avoid these stressors no matter how annoying, frustrating, or unpleasant they may be. But what we can do is manage our response. The objective is not to eliminate stress but to notice the arousal, embrace it, and then let go of it.

Stanford psychologist Kelly McGonigal, PhD, has been instrumental in popularizing this theory with her TED Talk "How to Make Stress Your Friend," which has been viewed more than 20 million times, and her book, *The Upside of Stress: Why Stress Is Good for You and How to Get Good at It*. Stress, McGonigal says, is most likely to cause harm when it feels out of your control, against your will, or devoid of meaning. This sort of mentality, this judging of our stress, has been shown to prompt people to adopt detrimental coping skills such as procrastinating, using alcohol or other substances, catastrophizing, and more. But when people find a way to view their stress in a positive light, perhaps by locating meaning in it or by seeking out friends for support, they ultimately turn to healthier, more productive ways of coping, reducing stress's overall toll on their life.

McGonigal also points out that, as part of that well-orchestrated cascade of hormones released in times of stress, a stress-recovery hormone called DHEA makes an appearance. DHEA is a steroid that increases neuroplasticity, which is the brain's ability to form new neural connections, learn new information, and reorganize existing memories. Put another way, DHEA helps your brain grow from challenging situations.

McGonigal's take on stress is instrumental for understanding how and why Cultivating Resonance Under Fire Training works. Embracing our stress response helps us act on it in a healthier, more productive way. When we Cultivate Resonance Under Fire, we have the chance to experience our stressors in a controlled environment that allows us to feel safe and is more maneuverable than real life. It's akin to strength training for the nervous system. Every time you practice it, you get stronger and stronger, and the next time that stressor comes along in real life, you're more able to embrace it and let it go.

The objective here is to reduce your cardiovascular response to a specific stressor that negatively impacts your ability to perform at your peak in relationships, health, work, sports, or life. It's been used successfully with the military, emergency responders, elite athletes, law enforcement, and more. It will still help reduce your cardiovascular reactivity against stress, but it can be done in a less clinical setting and is well suited to peak performance goals.

MAKING STRESS YOUR FRIEND

The first step involves selecting a specific stressor you consider particularly dysregulating. We all have external stressors that compromise our ability to perform at our peak. While some are relatively universal — many of us tend to be triggered by time pressure, noise, or certain individuals in our lives — I'd like you to create your own personal list. Be creative, and generate a personalized list that feels authentic to your needs. Consider as many stressors as possible — those at work, home, during your daily commute, while out and about — that cause you to feel tense, anxious, or just a general sense of heightened arousal. If possible, write this list of stressors on a piece of paper (you can use the workbook pages beginning on page 234) or on your phone so you can access it throughout the week. Here are some stressor examples to help you start thinking.

- Traffic noise
- Reviewing one's budget or daily P&L
- Watching the news or an emotional event
- Hearing cheers or jeers from a crowd
- Receiving negative feedback

Don't choose a stressor that is overly upsetting, such as a past trauma. This is not a clinical intervention; it's an optimization strategy to target performance. If you have a clinical condition, consult your health professional.

These stressors are about to become your new "friends." As McGonigal suggests, your mission will be to lean into your stress and befriend it in order to rob it of its damaging prowess.

Now, choose one stressor on which to focus. Which one seems to regularly chip away at your energy or decrease your ability to perform a desired task or activity?

The second preparatory step centers on identifying your most empowering breathing tool for managing stress. By this point you've learned several techniques:

- Quieting the mind by focusing on the inhale and exhale (or, alternatively, counting the seconds of your inhale and exhale). (Weeks 1 and 2)
- Breathing away your stress by feeling the stressor on the inhale and letting it go on the exhale. (Week 3)
- Connecting to the physiological sensation that accompanies your ghost (past pain) on the inhale and releasing it on the exhale. (Week 4)
- Preparing for stress in advance by practicing the Heart Shift, which involves 15 consecutive breaths to communicate to your heart how you want to respond in the moment. (Week 5)
- Improving your HRV by pairing positive emotions on the inhale with exhaling negative emotions. (Week 6)

Choose the breathing technique that feels the most powerful and accessible to you. Which one helps you achieve resonance in the shortest time possible? There is no right choice. As I have emphasized in previous chapters, this is a very personalized process wherein your preferences and dispositions will shape which techniques are most effective for you. While you may prefer calming your mind by counting the seconds of your breath during stressful moments, another person may feel that 10 Heart Pivots are more powerful in quickly achieving a desired state. Choose the technique that you find most enjoyable; this will be the technique you use here to buffer your response to stress.

CULTIVATING RESONANCE UNDER FIRE

Now that you've selected your stressor and breathing technique, it's time to practice Cultivating Resonance while being exposed to the stressor. You will practice this during the final minutes of your twice-a-day breathing sessions. It can take place in two forms: imaginal and *in vivo*. As the name suggests, the imaginal phase involves imagining the impact of an actual physical stressor like noise, time, or seeing a person who causes you stress; *in vivo* is Latin for "within the living" and means you'll be exposing yourself to the actual stressor.

Before you begin, rank your current level of stress on a scale of 1 to 10, with 1 being the lowest and 10 the highest. Then choose which form of exposure is most useful, and practice it for the last 5 minutes of each breathing session this week.

Imaginal Exposure (approximately 5 minutes)

1. Spend 2 minutes imagining or discussing the emotional impact of your chosen stressor. Doing this will increase your sympathetic activity.
2. Next, practice your preferred breathing method for 3 minutes. If you chose Heart Pivoting, try connecting to a positive emotional state, such as calm and confidence, on the inhale, and exhale away any negative emotions, for 10 consecutive breaths. If you're breathing away stress, feel the stressor on the inhale and let it go on the exhale. Take 15 breaths: 5 to clear the heart, 5 to clear the mind, and 5 to connect you to your ideal performance state.
3. Check in with yourself. Are you in resonance? Rate your current stress level. Were you able to reduce your stress response by at least two integers within 10 breaths?

If you haven't yet elicited resonance, continue your breathing for another 10 or 15 breaths (depending on your technique). If you still aren't in resonance, try a different breathing technique that you have learned through this training.

In Vivo Exposure (approximately 5 minutes)

1. View, listen, or otherwise expose yourself to your chosen stressor for 2 minutes.
2. As you continue to be exposed to the stressor, practice your preferred form of breathing.
3. Check in with yourself. Do you feel resonance? Were you able to reduce your stress level? How quickly can you access resonance while being exposed to stress?

SUCCESS STORY: JOSEPHINE

Josephine was a 42-year-old partner in a law firm. She worked with a fellow attorney who was extremely bright and capable, but his voice was grating to her. She found it difficult to stay focused in their conversations because his voice was so dysregulating, creating physiological anxiety in her body.

We began with imaginal exposure. She would imagine hearing him speak in a meeting or in her office. I encouraged her to feel the anxiety of hearing him speak and then release it. She practiced this repeatedly.

Once she was able to breathe away her feelings of anxiety, we began a graduated *in vivo* exposure; she had a photo of him from the internet, and she would look at the photo, recalling the feelings of irritation she felt while listening to him speak. After 2 minutes, she focused on her breath to achieve resonance while viewing that photo. On some days, we even practiced experimenting with pairing positive emotions, like gratitude and respect, on inhale (Heart Pivoting). After that, I asked her to practice the technique while in meetings with him. Not only did this make it more tolerable for Josephine to be around this lawyer, but after a few weeks, her psychological perception of him changed along with her physiological adaptation. She was surprised to admit that she even began to find him quite likeable.

What You'll Experience

Learning to elicit resonance during a particular stressor dampens your cardiovascular reactivity. By decreasing your physiological arousal, you are helping mitigate the extent to which external circumstances can interfere with your innate abilities. Every time you practice, picture yourself chipping away at the stressor's ability to highjack your autonomic nervous system. Many clients report feeling less stressed by their chosen stressor after practicing this training twice a day for 10 days (Cultivating Resonance Under Fire practiced for the last 5 minutes of each 20-minute breathing practice).

This week you may also see improvements in cognitive functioning as well: greater focus and organization, an enhanced ability to screen out unwanted thoughts, and more cognitive flexibility. This could be due to increased blood flow to the prefrontal cortex. Among the many skills housed under the executive functioning umbrella, that ability to screen out unwanted thoughts is particularly noteworthy. As HRV increases executive functioning, it also increases our ability to ignore intrusive thoughts, impulses, and urges just like a screen door lets in fresh air but keeps out bugs. A client I once worked with came up with a delightful analogy. Before this training, he said, "It was like I had a pack of squirrels running around in my brain, and I was chasing them, trying to get them to leave." Once he was able to tame his cardiovascular reactivity, he learned how to stop chasing those squirrels and just ignore them instead. When you're not chasing the squirrels, you can make better, smarter, more productive decisions quickly and under pressure.

STRESS IRL

Fun stress? It exists. There's a somewhat enjoyable type of stress called eustress, which happens when we get that burst of stress hormones—cortisol and adrenaline, specifically—in response to an event we perceive as pleasurable though still somewhat scary or nerve-racking. (Think of a first kiss; traveling to an unfamiliar but exciting city or country; signing your name on a mortgage for a new home; or the slow *click-click-click* of a climbing roller coaster.) Our brain perceives these short bursts of stress hormones in a positive way. In fact, they boost our brain functioning in the moment, sharpening our focus and making us feel more alive.

OPTIMIZATION STRATEGIES FOR WHEN STRESS IS AT ITS PEAK

Below, you'll find four additional strategies, all of them intended for use when preparing for times of peak stress such as midterm exams, earnings season, tax deadlines, competitive events, etc. If you know you are going to experience a period (2 or more days) of heightened stress, you need to be proactive about inserting these tools into your calendar. The first, Game Day Moments, tackles the cognitive piece of stress. The second, Power Pivots, is physiological. The third and fourth, which involve sleep and biofeedback, respectively, impact both.

Game Day Moments

Once a day, I'd like for you to practice cultivating resonance to a stressor that pops up: a distracting noise in your environment; distressing news on the TV; a box of doughnuts on your coworker's desk; seeing a photo of a person who stirs up negative emotions within you. When you notice the stressor, use it to pump yourself up instead of running from it. Think: "This is what I've been practicing for. This is my Olympic moment. Today is my day. I've got this." Then lean into the stressor, using your preferred breathing technique (see page 151), and see if you can reduce your level of stress. Were you able to achieve resonance just now while being exposed to your stressor?

Use Your Power Pivots

Three times a day, shore up your cardiovascular reactivity with 5 Heart Pivots. This is a shorter but still powerful version of Mini Heart Pivots. When your stressor appears, connect to your heart imprint on the inhale to boost your HRV, and release the negative emotions on the exhale. Doing so will help you generate as many feel-good neurotransmitters as possible, tempering anxiety and decreasing the physiological impact stress has on you. My clients also report that Power Pivots throughout the day help them obtain better and often deeper sleep at night.

The Sleep Factor

Sleep is the single most important arbiter of your ability to manage a stressor at your peak. Sleep deprivation is also linked with high blood pressure, diabetes, poor memory, food cravings, and weight gain. And you accumulate sleep debt with each passing night. Most adults need 8 hours a night, so subtracting just 1 hour of sleep per night every day for a week is the equivalent to missing an entire night of sleep.

To help get yourself in bed at a decent time, create an enjoyable, calming bedtime routine that you follow every night. Children love bedtime routines for their soothing, reliable nature, and you will, too. Putting away all technology is definitely the first step toward giving your brain the break it needs to feel drowsy. A warm bath can facilitate sleep, too. Even though it initially raises your body temperature slightly, when you get out of the tub and towel off, your body temp drops, signaling your brain that it's time to sleep. (Make sure to give yourself about an hour between the end of the bath and your intended bedtime to allow for this temperature dip.) Other components worth weaving into your bedtime routine: sipping warm caffeine-free tea; rocking in a chair; listening to soft music; lowering your thermostat; and cuddling with your partner.

Speaking of partners, if you share your bed with another person, consider making a sleep agreement. Talk about ways you can make sleep more restorative for both of you. This might include taking steps to account for snoring (ear plugs, sound machine), temperature differences (separate blankets), and differing bedtimes. If a night owl partner can't be persuaded to turn the lights off when you do, maybe he or she can take care of all bedtime preparations, such as brushing teeth, setting up pillows, etc., ahead of time, then slip into bed as quietly as possible. Sleeping apart on occasion is fine, too, and can even be beneficial if it helps you get better rest.

DISABLE YOUR STRESS BY BEFRIENDING IT

Casey was a publicist in his mid-30s who had a history of becoming overly emotional and self-critical when clients left his firm to try someplace new. Even though such a practice is fairly common within the public relations industry, he couldn't help but take it personally, and the ensuing negative self-talk was enough to cause crippling stomachaches.

Our first step was to discuss the stressor, and the feelings of embarrassment it provoked, for 1 minute. Doing this raised Casey's sympathetic dominance. Next, he practiced Heart Pivoting, his favorite breathing technique, connecting to calm and confidence on the inhale and letting go of his fear of failure on the exhale. Casey was highly adept at eliciting resonance, so I wasn't surprised to see his baseline heart rate decelerate by 10 beats through this exercise.

Then, we brought up an e-mail Casey had recently received from a client, announcing she was taking her business elsewhere. The e-mail was displayed on a computer screen. He stared at it for a minute, reading it and increasing his arousal, which manifested as a steep increase in heart rate. I asked him to Heart Pivot; could he generate positive emotions within 10 breaths? Could he decrease his heart rate by at least 10 beats as he did in the imaginal exposure exercise? To do this, he practiced accessing his feelings of love for his wife while staring at the letter.

It was during this week, week 7, that Casey began noticing a reduction in the severity of his stomach issues. By week 10, they had reduced in frequency as well. The ability to control his emotional state on demand began carrying over into other aspects of his life, too. With his expanded sense of confidence, he began bringing on new clients. His ability to manage fear not only elevated his confidence but also, according to Casey, helped him form relationships more quickly and then deepen them.

ANY QUESTIONS?

"Will this training automatically transfer to other stressors or types of stress?"

Cultivating Resonance Under Fire training is for task-specific stressors —the publicist needed help parting with clients; the tennis player needed help performing in front of large crowds. With time, practice, and dedication, you may begin to notice the effects transferring to general stressors, but they likely will not transfer to other specific stressors that have not been trained. But feel free to tackle new stressors over time. Once you're able to achieve resonance in 10 breaths or less, you can try to defeat another stressor.

Remember: The goal here isn't to *never* feel stress. The objective is to help you decrease your reactivity and then let go more quickly when exposed to specific stressors.

Video-Enhanced Biofeedback

If you have access to biofeedback equipment, you can conduct an enlightening experiment by tracking your HRV as you watch a video of yourself, particularly if that video shows you delivering a less-than-stellar performance. As you watch yourself, your physiology will mimic the stress response you likely experienced as it was happening in real time, as if you were reliving it. (This same phenomenon helps to explain why a hardcore sports fan reacts to a favorite team's loss with such emotion, as if he or she is the actual player.)

To get started, pay attention to your heart rate as you watch the video.

(You'll likely end up watching the video multiple times.) You can track the heart rate changes via a mobile heart rate tracking device; you can get fancy and track all your physiology including muscle tension and brain responses using biofeedback equipment; or you can simply be aware of when your heart speeds up while watching your video. Notice when your heart rate accelerates, and write down these moments. Then go back and practice generating resonance right at or before those moments. For instance, if you are a volleyball player and you're watching a video of yourself about to spike the ball, practice Heart Pivoting—accessing your heart imprint on the inhale and breathing out the stress on the exhale—for 3 breaths just before you raise your arm to spike it. Or perhaps you practice breathing away stress as you see yourself manage an uncomfortable public silence during a meant-to-be-humorous anecdote in your speech. As with the techniques previously discussed, the objective is to train your physiology to elicit resonance during anticipated stressors, training your nervous system in a way that will benefit your future performance.

ANY QUESTIONS?

"I usually drift off easily, but I wake up in the middle of the night and can't fall back asleep."

When you find yourself staring at the ceiling at 2 a.m., remember you're not alone: middle-of-the-night awakenings with trouble returning to sleep are among the most common symptoms of insomnia. Establish a "what to do if I wake up and can't sleep" routine. Ten minutes of resonance breathing is a great foundation for your middle-of-the-night protocol, and other activities can be layered in. As stress increases, add to your collection of tools to reduce your sympathetic nervous system activity. Here are some ideas to get you started on your way back to sleep in order of how I recommend approaching them.

If you're tossing and turning for more than 15 minutes, get up; you don't want to associate your bed with a place of unrest. You're better off leaving your bedroom entirely and starting your middle-of-the-night-wake-up protocol on the couch.

Read something not work related until drowsy.

Listen to calming music.

Turn on a show that makes you smile. It's important to choose something happy and light and that conveys a feeling of playfulness to your body—nothing violent or engine-revving. Laughter is calming and increases parasympathetic activity.

Don't psych yourself out. Your mind may be spiraling with thoughts about potentially feeling groggy for tomorrow's team meeting, but staring at the clock and obsessing over what-ifs will prevent your autonomic nervous system from resetting, cementing those what-ifs into reality. Let me reassure you that even on nights when it feels like you've barely netted any sleep, you are getting some. More likely than not, you're drifting off for bits of time here and there without realizing it. Try to let go of your catastrophic thinking and sense of urgency, and keep reminding yourself that, yes, you are getting some rest.

HIGHLIGHT ON HEALTH:
PREVENTING PTSD BY INCREASING HRV?

Between 7 and 9 percent of Americans will experience post-traumatic stress disorder (PTSD) at some point in their lives. The numbers are even higher for veterans—between 15 and 19 percent will develop PTSD at some point. Those numbers are high, to be sure. But, unfortunate as it may be, people live through frightening or violent situations all the time. What renders those 7 to 9 percent of individuals more susceptible to developing this disorder, characterized by haunting, often relentless symptoms like flashbacks, nightmares, hypervigilance, insomnia, intrusive thoughts, angry outbursts, and more? If an entire military unit is exposed to the same stressors and experiences, why doesn't everyone experience the same consequences? What makes some more susceptible than others?

Science's ability to predict vulnerability to PTSD is fairly limited, but the US government is actively investigating the relationship between heart rate variability and PTSD. Autonomic nervous system dysregulation is considered a hallmark feature of PTSD. In one study of 459 male veterans who are twins, those with current PTSD had a 49 percent lower HRV than their PTSD-free brothers. As the official Military Health System website puts it, "In simpler terms, a person with PTSD in a state of chronic stress is like an engine that is idling too high for too long — after a while the engine will stop performing properly."

Newer research suggests that lower predeployment HRV is associated with increased risk of PTSD postdeployment. In other words, the relationship between HRV and PTSD has a bit of a chicken-and-egg quality to it. This represents an intriguing area for further investigation. HRV-based interventions aimed at improving autonomic nervous system function may hold promise for the prevention as well as the treatment of PTSD.

WEEK 7 ACTION PLAN

1. Remeasure your HRV. Review your goals (refer to the homework tracking notes on page 236) and evaluate your current level of achievement.
2. List your main everyday stressors, and choose the one you most wish you could change.
3. Pick your favorite breathing technique.
4. Continue your twice-a-day, 20-minute breathing sessions. Spend the last 5 minutes of your practice on Cultivating Resonance Under Fire Training (imaginal exposure or *in vivo* exposure).
5. Experiment with the additional optimization strategies: Game Day Moments, Power Pivots, sleep, and video-enhanced feedback.

11

▼

Week 8:

Imprinting the Physiology of Success

Neuroscience researchers at Ohio University wanted to investigate just how deep the link ran between the nervous system and muscle strength. They recruited healthy volunteers who each agreed to have one wrist wrapped in a surgical cast from the fingertips to just below the elbow for 4 weeks. One group of volunteers was assigned to perform regular mental imagery exercises, spending 11 minutes, 5 days a week, imagining they were flexing their arm muscles. They weren't allowed to actually flex or contract the muscle, mind you — in fact, equipment capable of measuring muscle response to brain signals confirmed that muscle activation did not occur. But they did have to *think about* strengthening those casted muscles. A control group did not perform any mental imagery.

When the casts were removed a month later, those volunteers who mentally exercised their arms lost only half the amount of strength as did the group who was immobilized but did not do the imagery training.

Visualization is a prized tool used by peak performers to help train and condition their brains and bodies to perform at their optimal level of skill and ability. And it works; when you visualize, or imagine, yourself running your fastest mile or nailing a key presentation, you stimulate many of the same brain regions as you would if you were physically performing that same movement, or sequence of movements, in real time.

After the 1984 Olympics, researchers discovered that Olympians who had incorporated visualization techniques into their training, such as mentally rehearsing their desired performance, positively influenced their performance at the Games. Since then, further studies have uncovered similar findings, linking mental imagery with everything from improved speed to greater pass accuracy in volleyball to high jumpers being able to clear the bar more easily.

A prevailing theory is that visualization of specific movements forms new neural patterns in the brain, which then facilitate and enhance neuromuscular functioning. The effect is so powerful and so deeply embedded that even athletes with visual impairments can use it to improve their performance.

VISUALIZING WITH YOUR HEART

Imagine opening a jar of pickles and deeply inhaling the scent of the pungent, briny liquid. Now mentally take a sip of it. Your mouth is likely watering, correct? That's because with enough training (or in this case, a lifetime of pickle tasting), your body learns how it is expected to respond to certain stimuli.

Just as your brain does not always easily distinguish between what is happening in your mind and what's happening in your body, you can train your heart to equate a future desired state of success or performance with reality. If you can practice a future emotional state in your heart before it has actually happened, you can reduce or avoid the immobilization that often occurs during times of stress. It's the heart-centered version of mind over matter.

This week, I'll guide you through a series of unique visualization exercises based on how you wish to experience life in various arenas. It's about experiencing (not just picturing) yourself performing at your absolute peak during an important upcoming event: effortlessly completing a task at work, standing at a podium confidently giving a compelling presentation, preparing to address a family member about a serious health concern but wanting to do so with compassion and empathy. You won't just be imagining; you'll be feeling your inevitable success in your heart and imprinting it there for the future. This is about grabbing your future flow state — the one you know you'll experience once you achieve your goal — and bringing it into the here and now to optimize your heart. Clients who perform this training in my office demonstrate increases in HRV and the ability to elicit resonance. The results are truly remarkable. You will learn how to minimize uncertainty or anxiety and physiologically capture and experience your success

BREATHING EXERCISE #8: IMPRINTING THE PHYSIOLOGY OF SUCCESS

Step 1: What is a specific goal that you wish to achieve in the next month? Areas to consider: career/professional life, family life, social life, physical health, or a romantic relationship. Write down your goal in as much detail as possible. (Use page 237.) A few examples created by my clients include:

- To speak lovingly and compassionately to my spouse during times of stress
- To generate at least 5 innovative ideas for our portfolio in the upcoming year
- To run my first marathon
- To take greater risks in speaking my mind during team meetings

Step 2: Now, try to switch off your outcome-focused brain and tune into your heart. Dive deep. What emotions will flood your heart after you have achieved your goal? What do you feel? A few examples, corresponding to the sample goals listed in Step 1, include:

- Connection, safety, trust
- Energy, enthusiasm, creativity
- Pride, relief, accomplishment
- Confidence, clarity, drive

Write down the three emotions you will experience following the achievement of your desired goal using page 237. These are your imprints. Your cognitive brain may try to keep you in your head, telling you, "Those heart-based emotions are silly and impossible to achieve." Ignore it and just write. Let go of what sounds right or perfect. Ask yourself again, "What will my heart feel like after I have achieved this goal?" Really, just write and leave the thinking for another time. You've got this.

Step 3: Once you have defined your three imprints, take some time to sit with each of them. One at a time, allow each emotion to just sit there in your heart like an actual person pulling up a chair to the dinner table. Explore the energy of the emotion and get to know it. Note how it feels to sit next to this emotion and just be with it. You can spend 10 seconds doing this, 1 minute, whatever feels comfortable. Then, invite the next one and then the next one.

Your goal is to let your heart come alive. You are pulling your future physiological state, the way you will feel after achieving your goal, into the now. From a physiological perspective, you are defining how you want to feel and providing your body with a direct, specific sense of certainty.

POTENTIAL CHALLENGE

As mentioned in Step 2, your brain may try to interfere with your Heart Visualization; it's called cognitive resistance, and it's a normal occurrence. When we feel uncertain or anxious, as one might when trying a new technique like this, our mind tends to introduce doubt. But that uncertainty and trepidation can also compromise the encoding of our visualization. Research by psychophysiologist Stephen Porges, PhD, notes that a feeling of safety optimizes our neural circuitry and, therefore, sets the stage for performance optimization. (More on that in week 10.) The ability to experience what your body will feel like after you achieve your desired goal is, in part, so powerful because it instills a sense of safety in the body. You are preparing and reassuring your body, telling it what to expect and how it will feel. As a result, the anxious uncertainty is reduced or even dissolved.

The breakthrough comes when you really click into understanding that you can train your heart to feel your future physiological state before you have even achieved your goal. Move your heart to how you want your future self to feel, and your mind and the rest of your body will follow.

LOOKING TO THE FUTURE
TO OPTIMIZE THE PRESENT

Seth had recently moved across the country to begin a new job in sales. He had found a condo, met some new friends, and was beginning to cultivate a network of business relationships in his new city. When I asked what he envisioned for himself in the next 3 months, he spoke about a desire to feel inspired. He yearned to find a network of friends and colleagues that shared his interests and motivated one another to embrace new perspectives and challenges. In order to make this happen, Seth felt he would need to act with authenticity, vulnerability, and courage when meeting new people. But this intimidated him. He had dealt with social anxiety in the past and tended to worry about what others thought of him. How, he wondered, would he move outside of his comfort zone and initiate plans on his own?

Instead of focusing on the internal states that he believed he must embrace in order to create this network of business and life associates, he and I imagined what it would feel like *after* he achieved this goal—*after* the connections were made and the friendships were formed. The ultimate reward, he believed, would be an all-enveloping sense of connection, drive, inspiration, and shared passion. For the last few minutes of his daily breathing sessions, Seth practiced experiencing this future heart state. He did this for a few weeks.

To his surprise, he felt a significant lowering of social anxiety. He felt more confident "putting myself on the line," as he described it, reaching out to those he felt a connection with and suggesting they make plans. Instead of feeling like he had to wait for inspiring people to arrive in his life, he started seeking them out. He credited this new sense of liberation and eagerness to his ability to elicit his future heart state, as if he had already achieved his goal. To date, he has built a small group of three to five people with whom he regularly spends time and is looking forward to deeper bonds in the future.

What You'll Experience

You will experience a reduction of stress symptoms such as anxiety, doubt, and fear. The sense of immobilization, constriction, uncertainty, or defeat you might typically feel in the heat of an upsetting moment can dissipate with regular practice of this exercise. The more you practice your heart imprints, the more they will transfer into a dynamic state for responding to the world. Just like learning to ride a bicycle involves lots of practice until one day something just clicks, imprinting for the inevitability of success requires practice, practice, practice, but you'll soon be able to transfer your imprints into a baseline level of responding, where you feel these emotions more frequently without significant conscious thought. It will not inoculate you against every type of stress, but it will give you a stronger buffer and greater resilience during times of challenge. Repetition is how you encode these imprints as your new patterns for responding from the heart. If you feel it, if you practice it, it will come.

The rate of learning and acquisition is different and unique for each person. Yet, with enough rehearsal, you'll be able to ride the bike without monitoring every little thought or physical movement. The more you do it, the more you will see change occurring without your conscious intervention. So do try to connect to these future heart states as needed during the day, whenever you find yourself questioning your path or falling out of resonance. This exercise is especially useful for managing spikes in anxiety or doubt during the day.

OPTIMIZATION STRATEGY: HEART VISUALIZATION FOR COMPETITIVE MOMENTS

This is a more targeted, multipronged take on imprinting the physiology of success. It involves visualizing your heart state at the beginning, middle, and end of an upcoming performance event, such as a race, match, presentation, or conference. During any such performance, it's natural to toggle between various states of stress or pressure, so it makes sense that, when preparing, you become fluent in alternating between different intended heart states, each one specifically chosen to counteract the corresponding stress. The more that you practice, the more adept you will become at switching back and forth between emotions so that you can create the physiological state that will best serve you at different yet equally weighty moments.

Here's an example: my client Demi was an outdoor track and field champ, specializing in the 1600m (mile), who had recently found herself struggling to break free from the pack right around 400m, as she started her second lap on the track. We started planning how she wanted — and needed — to feel at that moment. I asked her to tune into her heart and tell me what emotion she imagined feeling there. She said she had a vision of herself as a 7-year-old, when she was just beginning to dabble in running. She imagined her 7-year-old self watching her adult self run, feeling proud and in awe. So, using Heart Visualizations for competitive moments, she planned to start her race with a feeling of her younger self flooding her heart. At 800m (the beginning of the third lap), she switched to a sensation of perseverance and grit. And for the final 400m, Demi strategically chose anger and fury to drive her home. At the end of her season, she e-mailed me to say that the practice of visualizing her heart experience "gave me a sense of structure that I didn't realize I needed. I am now more confident when I run because I know exactly what I want to feel and when."

CREATING A RESONANCE PLAYLIST: USING MUSIC TO AMPLIFY THE PHYSIOLOGICAL EXPERIENCE

Listening to, singing, or playing music is one of the most common ways of amplifying your HRV and eliciting resonance for longer periods of time. This makes sense because music has its own frequencies. The frequencies of certain songs can help shift your internal rhythms in a way that effortlessly propels you into resonance. For some people, specific songs may trigger resonance because the pace of the music matches their own heart frequency. For others, strong emotional associations with a particular song are enough to impart an effect. In other words, instead of a ghost imprint, songs can leave positive physiological imprints.

Dr. Paul Lehrer studied Buddhist chants and hymns that people have been using for centuries to put themselves in a trance. Most of them consist of 10-second beats, which we know is the most common resonance frequency breathing rate. And certain modern songs can have similar effects. This is one element that many people pick up on intuitively; we're naturally drawn to songs that engender resonance within us, and we're just as likely to turn off music that stresses our nervous systems.

By this point in the protocol you should be able to tell right away if a certain song helps shift you into resonance by paying attention to your physiological state and your markers of resonance. These are the songs you automatically put on during the workday when you need an energy boost, the ones you turn to for powering you through a workout, or the ones that help you relax and unwind. When UK researchers asked subjects to walk a quarter-mile at their own pace while listening to a podcast about cities, "Happy" by Pharrell Williams, or no sound at all, those who listened to music were found to have enjoyed their workout 28 percent more than those who walked in silence and 13 percent more than the podcast listeners. Enjoyable music, the study concluded, has the potential to "elicit a more positive emotional state."

This homework assignment, then, is an especially fun one. Create a resonance playlist. By pairing a song or songs to your Heart Mapping routine, you may be able to amplify your HRV, which my clients have reported allows them to more quickly encode and recall future heart states.

You can even create multiple playlists to help you tap into specific emotional states. You might have one playlist to put on when you need extra energy and another for when you want to channel a cool, calm position. There's no single algorithm. What songs invigorate you?

IF MUSIC MOVES YOU, USE IT TO YOUR ADVANTAGE

At 19 years old, Spence was already a nationally ranked tennis player. He was a committed athlete who trained at least 3 hours a day and was equally conscientious in the classroom, where he was a straight-A student. He was also a huge music fan, hip-hop and pop in particular. We were working together on a weak spot of his: his heart rate tended to speed up during matches because of his tendency to try so hard. This often resulted in Spence giving up a point due to a forced error.

We embarked on resonance breathing, with Spence focusing on the way he wanted his heart to feel — calm, confident, and light — as he walked onto the court. In my office, he would practice generating each of these emotions to help his body encode the heart state. Once the biofeedback equipment began to verify that he was able to elicit resonance during his Heart Visualization, we started playing the song "Clocks" by Coldplay, a song that he felt always put him into flow. Adding this additional layer into the Heart Mapping protocol helped amplify his state of calm and confidence, and with each replay, he felt his desired state for performance intensify.

Spence continued practicing at home, finishing his twice-a-day, 20-minute breathing sessions with 5 minutes of Coldplay-enhanced Heart Visualizations. About 2 weeks later, he reported that "Clocks" had taken on an almost Pavlovian quality — when he played it, he felt calm and free and less focused on the outcome. Spence began playing "Clocks" on his rides to tournaments and on his iPod as he walked onto the court. As he developed an increasing ability to cue his physiology, he became more confident and composed during matches. Spence also reduced his number of forced errors on the court. Spence told me that he attributed these enhancements to feeling less constricted in his body and more able to flexibly perform at his peak under pressure.

MUSICAL RESONANCE IRL

Researchers have postulated that maternal heartbeat may serve as our initial introduction to "music." That same heartbeat that enveloped and calmed us during 9 months of development continues to soothe us after we're born. Bleary-eyed parents of babies who refuse to sleep anywhere but on someone's chest can attest to that. In fact, we know that most mothers cradle and rock their infants on their left, regardless of whether mom is left- or right-handed, most likely an evolutionary adaptation designed to keep baby's ear near mama's heart.

ANY QUESTIONS?

"I'm just not that moved by music. What other cues can I use to amplify my emotional response or enhance the imprinting process?"

That's okay. Some people respond strongly to specific types of music, but you may be someone who uses different sensory modalities to access positive physiological imprints. Smell is a common one. Like music, a smell can evoke a state of resonance or dissonance, depending on its association in your heart. Surely, you've had a memory come rushing back just by experiencing a smell, whether it was your grandmother's chicken soup simmering on the stove or the fragrance your ex used to wear. And I'll bet that memory didn't just flood your mind; you felt it in your heart, too. You may associate the scent of freshly cut grass or soothing lavender oil with a specific heart state such as love or calmness. Using these scents can help you fall into resonance more quickly. I've had clients ask me for the brand of essential oil diffuser I use in my office. They implicitly associate it with a time of growth and awareness in their life, so they purchase one to keep at home or work to remind their heart of how far they've come and to continue catalyzing and crystallizing their experience.

You can also experiment with visual amplifiers, which involve looking at inspiring pictures or images. I once worked with a scientist who found that gazing at a particular image of outer space, which he associated with possibility and experimentation, helped him when brainstorming lists of research questions. Instead of playing a particular song, you use your image to help you encode and access your flow state.

HIGHLIGHT ON HEALTH: COMPETITIVE OR PREPERFORMANCE ANXIETY

Even the most seasoned professionals can feel anxious before a major event — the ultimate fear is typically underperforming. The phenomenon of a high-stress situation producing declines in performance is known as choking under pressure, and it's a perfect, albeit ill-timed, example of the powerful grip stress has on our behavior. One widely held cognitive theory posits that, compared to low-pressure situations like practice or rehearsal, higher stakes impact our working memory, perhaps by allowing worries and ruminations to take up precious space. (Working memory plays a role in how we process, utilize, and remember information on a day-to-day basis and is needed for task execution.)

On the physiological side of the equation is Julian Thayer's neurovisceral theory, which helped cement the link between HRV and the prefrontal cortex. Neurovisceral theory suggests that immobilization may result from an overstimulated sympathetic and understimulated para-sympathetic nervous system that siphons oxygen away from the prefrontal cortex, impairing working memory. Clearly, this puts one's working memory at a disadvantage. The result? An entrepreneur about to pitch his new business venture to investors draws a blank as he's introduced; a college junior performs unusually poorly on his GMAT; an actress forgets her acceptance speech at an awards ceremony; or, in the case of one rifle shooter at the 2004 Olympics in Athens, the final shot needed to earn a gold medal hits the bull's eye . . . of the opponent's target.

Recent research found that baseline HRV level predicted working memory performance under high-pressure circumstances, suggesting that HRV training can be used to prevent the choking-under-pressure phenomenon. And it's true: I've seen evidence of this in my own practice.

When I began working with a university golf team, several players revealed that as they progressed further and further with their HRV biofeedback training, they not only improved their driving distance and putting performance, but they were also feeling more tuned in and awake in class. Many claimed they'd seen improvements in their academic performance.

I was inspired by these results and also curious. I wanted to understand what was happening physiologically to produce so many changes across multiple domains, from sport to health to school. Was there a change in their physiology that we could identify? As we embarked on our second school year together, I used mobile biofeedback monitoring to monitor their HRV during several sessions of virtual reality golf practice. My colleagues and I found that their heart rates were spiking just before hitting the golf ball—a normal physiological reaction—but instead of returning to baseline afterward, their heart rates remained elevated. In some players, it continued to rise. In other words, they weren't recovering—their sympathetic nervous systems were stuck in the "On" position.

After the next 10 weeks of HRV-BFB training, there was a shift in how the golfers' hearts reacted before and after the shot. We found that their heart rates were accelerating before shots, but the incline was less steep than the previous year, indicating less cardiovascular reactivity. Even more promising, after the shot, their heart rates returned to baseline and stayed there until their next shot. What really excited me about this: before I was able to reveal their HRV results to them, several of the golfers had told me they'd been feeling less triggered by relationship stressors and less flustered by academic demands. In other words, they were experiencing the ability to bring themselves back to baseline in their day-to-day lives without realizing it was a direct reflection of their internal state. Their heart patterns told a story, which mirrored what the golfers relayed to me: they could let go.

WEEK 8 ACTION PLAN

1. Identify your three future emotional states that you will experience after achieving your desired goal. (Record them on the homework tracking sheet on page 237.)
2. Continue to practice resonance breathing for 20 minutes twice per day. For the final 5 minutes of each practice, practice Heart Visualization, attempting to feel the future emotional state you wish to feel on the inhale and letting go of anything negative on the exhale.
3. Connect to your imprints throughout the day to help reduce the intermittent anxiety or resistance that comes up when you feel uncertain about being able to achieve your goal.
4. Prepare for upcoming performance events with the beginning/middle/end Heart Visualization approach.
5. To encode your emotions and recall them more quickly in the moment, layer in music during any of these steps.

12

▼

Week 9:

Using Your Heart Rhythms to

Strengthen Your Relationships

At some point you've likely subconsciously synchronized your physiology with another person. Friends and strangers alike tend to fall in stride with each other while walking. We often yawn when we see someone else yawn, even if we're not tired. Whether we're aware of it or not, our heart rates synchronize with other people's, too. This sort of physiological coordination happens quite often particularly when we're near a person we care for or to whom we feel attached. If you've ever wondered why the heart has become a ubiquitous symbol for love, consider these examples.

- When two people in love are put in a room together, their heartbeats synchronize, and they begin breathing at the same intervals.
- Being touched by someone you love when you are in pain has the power to ease your discomfort by syncing your heart rates with each other.

- As two people sleep together, their heart rhythms interact significantly enough to allow authors of a 2019 study to conclude that
  sharing a bed with one's partner "connect[s] both co-sleepers'
  cardiac systems."
- When a mother gazes into the eyes of her 3-month-old infant,
  their heart rhythms can sync in less than 1 second.

Over the past 8 weeks, you've learned about the heart's incredibly
vast array of physiological capabilities: letting go of past hurt, breaking
through performance plateaus, optimizing the autonomic nervous system. This week, you will discover how the principles of *Heart Breath
Mind* can be used to enhance your relationships, create more durable
bonds, and allow you to exercise greater emotional control during moments of pressure or conflict. This applies to all manner of relationships:
romantic and sexual, familial, with friends or colleagues or teammates,
and more. It is possible to infuse the potency of resonance into your relationships and, as with so many things related to human connection, it all
starts with the heart.

HOW ESTIMATING HEART RATE
DEVELOPS EMPATHY

It's not just that our heartbeats shape and influence our emotional state;
numerous studies support the theory that the more easily and accurately
people can estimate their heart rate, the more empathic they are. This is
based on a concept called sensory interoceptive ability. Interoception is
the sensing of internal physiologic signals, and it plays a role not only in
survival (it allows us to detect hunger, pain, and temperature) but in the
accessing of positive emotions, including love, affection, and empathy.

In one study, participants watched video clips of social interactions
designed to assess their ability to gauge the characters' emotional states.
They were asked a series of questions, including those that required read-

ing another person's emotion ("What is Sandra feeling?"); questions that did not require such a skill ("What is Michael thinking?"); and a control question ("What was the weather like on that evening?"). Researchers found that those subjects who had strong interoceptive ability, as measured by their ability to count their heartbeats without taking their pulse, were better at reading characters' emotions, suggesting that "an accurate perception of internal sensations helps mind reading in emotional situations." As one researcher described, "[I]f your colleague 'Michael' is aggressive towards 'Sandra' . . . your body processes this by increasing your heart rate, perhaps making you feel awkward and anxious, enabling you to understand that Sandra is embarrassed. If you do not feel your heart rate increase, it may reduce your ability to understand that situation and respond appropriately."

Some people naturally possess higher interoceptive ability; others have less. But you can cultivate the ability to estimate your own heart rate and be attuned to your own physiological signals. In the process, you also bolster your ability to empathize, perceive, and collaborate.

PEAK PERFORMANCE IRL

If interoceptive ability facilitates connection with others, could it help us connect with ourselves? Australian and UK researchers recruited 18 male high-frequency traders to find out. High-frequency trading involves the buying and selling of futures contracts, with traders holding their trading positions for a short period of time—from a few hours to a few minutes or even seconds. These London-based traders spent their days immersed in a continuous stream of risky decision making, typically with very little time to consider their choices.

Data on each trader's average daily profit and loss (P&L) over the previous year was collected, and they were asked about how many years of experience they had in the financial market. Their ability to correctly estimate their heart rate was measured.

Analysis showed that interoceptive ability predicted traders' P&L as well as the number of years they had survived as a trader. In other words, the more accurate a trader was at predicting his heart rate, the greater the profits and the longer his financial career lasted.

Much of this comes down to intuition, which people often describe as listening to "gut instinct." In the case of the London traders, the researchers explained "that subtle physiological changes in their bodies provide cues helping them rapidly select from a range of possible trades the one that just 'feels right.' . . . Our results suggest that signals from the body — the gut feelings of financial lore — contribute to success in the markets."

BREATHING EXERCISE #9: ESTIMATING YOUR HEART RATE

Now is a prime opportunity to begin training without a pacer. A goal of *Heart Breath Mind* is for you to develop the ability to feel when you are in resonance, as well as to know how to breathe at your resonance frequency without any device.

Here are the basic steps for estimating your heart rate, which can help build interoceptive ability. Once you're able to do this, you can attempt it with a partner, friend, or colleague. Use the homework tracking sheet on page 238 for this exercise.

Step 1: Sitting quietly, set a timer for 30 seconds and, breathing normally (not at resonance frequency), try to count the number of times your heart beats. Don't feel your pulse; try to dial into your heart and see if you can guess it. After the timer goes off, double the number and write it down; this is your estimated heart rate.

Step 2: Next, take your pulse by counting the number of beats in your neck or wrist for 30 seconds and doubling it. How close was your estimate to reality?

Step 3: Do jumping jacks or march in place for 30 seconds. The goal of this step is to increase your heart rate, so if those specific movements are difficult for you, do something physical that does elevate your heart rate.

Step 4: Sit down again and try to estimate your heart rate again, using only your 30-second timer and your interoceptive abilities. (Note: Your heart will be beating faster than it was before.) Double the number and write it down. Then take your pulse and compare the numbers.

Step 5: Commence with resonance breathing for 2 minutes. Now, try to estimate your heart rate once more. Can you guess it within 10 beats? Five beats?

Step 6: The more you practice this, the stronger your interoceptive abilities become. Try estimating your heart rate while standing in line at the store, while waiting on hold for an important phone call, or while sitting in traffic. The little challenges will help you improve, not to mention help time pass by more quickly.

BREATHING EXERCISE #10: ESTIMATING ANOTHER PERSON'S HEART RATE

Heart rate estimation is a powerful tool that can be used by couples to more fully tune in to each other's feelings. It works for all sorts of pairs of individuals (called *dyads* in clinical language): romantic partners, family members, team members at work, or sports teammates. It's not just random guessing; the heart produces a magnetic field strong enough to be detected from several feet away. EKGs work by measuring this electrical signaling, but as humans, we can pick up on this magnetic energy as well. You will both need to be familiar with resonance breathing and need to commit to breathing together twice a week for 20 minutes. Have your homework tracking sheet (on page 240) ready.

Step 1: Sit down side by side. Your first step is to try to estimate your partner's heart rate. It will likely be difficult at first, but just try to tune into your intuition. It may help to hold hands or have part of your bodies touching; physical touch helps to increase the synchronization of heart rates. Write down your estimate.

Step 2: Next, have your partner measure his or her heart rate. This can be done by simply measuring the pulse for 30 seconds and doubling that number. Alternatively, you can use a heart rate tracker with a finger sensor or chest strap to monitor your heart rate. How close was your estimate to reality?

Step 3: Ask your partner to leave the room and either (a) do jumping jacks or march in place for 10 seconds to increase heart rate or (b) perform deep breathing to slow the heart rate. Because your partner is in another room, you will not be able to see if they have chosen to accelerate or decelerate.

Step 4: Have your partner rejoin you. Try to estimate his or her heart rate again using only your 30-second timer and your interoceptive abilities.

Step 5: Ask your partner to commence with resonance breathing for 2 minutes. Now try to estimate his or her heart rate once more. Can you guess it within 10 beats? Five beats?

If You Have Equipment That Detects Resonance or Heart Rate:

- Can I predict when my breathing partner is in resonance or has decelerated his or her heart rate?
- Make this a contest between the two of you: Who is more sensitive to the other's physiology?
- See how closely you can predict the other person's actual heart rate in specific moments.

BREATHING EXERCISE #11: INTERPERSONAL SYNCHRONIZATION TRAINING

In this exercise, you and your partner will be alternating days of breathing at one another's resonance frequency. It does not matter if the two of you have the same or different resonance frequency. You will meet to practice this on 2 separate days. On the first of your 2 training days, you will both breathe at Person A's resonance frequency for 20 minutes. On the second training day, you will both breathe at Person B's resonance frequency for 20 minutes. (Use a breathing pacer for guidance and your homework tracking sheet on page 240 to record.) If either of you experiences any discomfort, practice breathing at your own rates side by side.

If you have a breathing app, breathe together following the breathing rate of one individual. If you have access to an app or device that provides continuous feedback, take turns with who is producing the heart rate (EKG) line and who is following it.

FINDING RESONANCE TOGETHER

George and Tom were vice presidents of a company. The nature of their roles meant that, at all times, they each needed to fully understand the other's vision for their organization so that they could ensure the team was functioning in the most effective, efficient manner possible. Their success demanded seamless communication between the two of them. They worked well together, but both thought there was an opportunity to elevate their professional rapport, and they came to me interested in increasing their interoceptive ability as a means of getting there.

They began by attempting to estimate each other's heart rates. Over the course of their first afternoon, it took George 8 tries to correctly estimate Tom's heart rate; Tom needed 2 tries to predict George's heart rate. From there, they began breathing together twice a week for 20 minutes at a time. On Tuesdays, George would follow Tom's heart rhythms, and on Fridays, Tom would follow George's. After about 4 weeks, they began reporting feelings of increased connectivity. George began to be able to estimate Tom's heart rate with increasing frequency and accuracy. By week 10, George told me, "Sometimes, it's almost like we can understand each other without talking." Training themselves to assess each other's physiological cues, they reported improved communication and enhanced confidence in their intuition and leadership.

What You'll Experience

Strengthening your interoceptive ability helps you cultivate your intuition in a way that has far-reaching effects on all types of relationships, from the boardroom to your family's living room. When you practice resonance breathing side by side with someone, you're exercising the pathway for greater social engagement. It brings you in tune with what that person is feeling and thinking. I've observed many couples and colleagues as they have developed heightened abilities to perceive and connect with each other after several weeks of joint breathing practice. The activation of resonance through breathing transports everyone involved into a more open and receptive and less defensive state for communication and collaboration. With sufficient practice, your heart rates can synchronize, leading to richer feelings of closeness and interconnectedness. You may also notice a reduction in the frequency or intensity of arguments. That's because now, when you find yourself in a stressful situation, you're better able to recognize your internal state and how it is contributing to your feelings and behaviors, which can in turn make you more aware of what to say and what not to say when communicating with your partner. Consider it a new take on couples' therapy.

Additional Strategies

When you're in the heat of an argument with someone you care for, cognitive techniques like counting to 10 usually don't help. Instead, try tapping into the power of your physiology to calm down, stop the ruminating thoughts, and reconnect in a meaningful way.

To Foster Stronger Romantic Connections . . .

Monitor Your Heart Rate

In the heart of downtown Seattle on the University of Washington campus sits a building nicknamed the Love Lab. Couples visit the Love Lab (official name: The Gottman Institute) to put their relationships under a microscope. Under the leadership of John Gottman, PhD, and his wife, Julie Schwartz Gottman, PhD, partners learn science-backed strategies for strengthening connections, communicating effectively, co-parenting successfully, building intimacy, and more.

Part of the protocol includes taking part in a "conflict discussion" while connected to various physiological monitoring equipment, not unlike what I have in my office, measuring heart rate and blood flow. They may even sit in chairs outfitted to measure anxious fidgeting, affectionately known as the "Jiggle-o-meter." Once all the sensors are attached, the couple is asked to identify and discuss an area of continuing disagreement in their relationship.

Thanks to the rich physiological data they've been able to collect from thousands of couples during more than three decades of research, the Gottmans have developed several books' worth of innovative conflict-management recommendations, all based on the precise ways our bodies and brains shape how we communicate with our romantic partners. These tips go beyond the traditional "Never go to bed angry" advice. One of my favorites is this: when your heart rate rises above 100 beats per minute, take a break for at least 20 minutes.

Bet you've never heard that one before. Here's why it works: arguing overarouses your nervous system, increasing heart rate, shunting blood flow to the extremities, and preparing you to fight or flee. And, as we know from the police study in week 8, brain functioning is compromised in very region-specific ways: the prefrontal cortex, home of information storage and memory retention, gets cheated out of the blood and oxygen it requires to function. But that same area of the brain is also responsible for critical relationship-sustaining behaviors, including the neural wiring that allows us to be supportive, empathetic, and capable of forming a unified front — all things you want to have in the middle of a dispute with a loved one.

When your heart rate reaches 100, the Gottmans discovered, blood flow to the cortex becomes compromised in a way that returns you to your primitive brain, leaving you in attack-and-defend mode. Continuing to argue while in this state of sympathetic dominance, they say, is not only futile — they compare it to trying to carry on a productive conversation while running at a fast pace — it floods the body with stress hormones in a way that leads to volatile communication, which in turn paves the way for dysfunctional emotional patterns, which can ultimately be predictive of relationship demise.

The sympathetic nervous system needs at least 20 minutes of calm to reverse the flood of stress hormones and return to baseline. Then you can try reconnecting with your partner from a place of love and understanding.

Ideally, you will spend those 20 or more minutes attempting to soothe yourself. Resonance breathing can help. Gottman also suggests imagining yourself in your favorite, most serene space, whether that's with your toes buried in the warm sand of a faraway beach, by a clear, babbling brook in a forest, or in the familiar surroundings of your childhood backyard.

Exercise

Another option, if you have the time and ability, is to exercise. The exercise needs to be vigorous; a stroll around the block won't be enough. Intense physical exercise helps your body complete the fight-or-flight response that you have become stuck within. Remember Peter Levine, the psychologist who witnessed that wild animals like deer are able to enter a state of sympathetic dominance and then quickly regain balance? He described the process, as seen from afar through binoculars, as a vibration, twitching, or light trembling that occurs in the deer as they realize no danger is present. It starts near the ears and neck and travels down the body, exiting through the hind legs. "These little tremblings of muscular tissue are the organism's way of regulating extremely different states of nervous system activation," he writes, and the process repeats itself hundreds of times a day.

If you've ever watched a nature documentary or visited a zoo, you've likely seen this process occur, not realizing that the animal's vibrations were evidence of it shifting rather seamlessly from a state of hypervigilance to one of calm alertness. The human equivalent is vigorous exercise. Afterward, emotional regulation should feel much easier.

Monitor Your Heart Rate

It's immensely helpful to evaluate your heart rate tracker when employing these conflict resolution strategies. If your heart rate hits 100 during a meeting, discussion, or conflict, or even if it increases 20 beats above your personal baseline rate, stop and take a time-out, allowing your body to return to its natural state. If you opt to exercise, aim to push your heart rate to higher than 100 beats per minute.

Shifting Your Partner into Parasympathetic Dominance

Dr. Porges, the psychophysiologist behind the polyvagal theory, has said that when we're in a relationship with another person, we have the responsibility "to keep our autonomic nervous system out of a state of defense." Only then, he maintains, can we provide our partners, friends, and family with the sense of safety they require and deserve — the sense of safety needed to remain in a healthy state of parasympathetic dominance.

According to his theory, the most primitive parts of our nervous system make the decision whether we mobilize to fight, flee, or freeze. The decision is made involuntarily, without us even realizing it, via a process called neuroception. Dr. Porges describes this way of evaluating risk and safety as "detection without awareness." When we interact with other people, we do this by evaluating their facial features, voice, and touch for warning signs or any sign of emotion. We can use these features, then, to promote and facilitate a sense of safety in those who are important to us, helping shift them into a parasympathetic dominance. There are a few ways you can do this.

Look into their eyes and show expression in your face. According to Dr. Porges, we feel safe when the person with whom we are interacting shows us signs of interest, listening, or understanding. This is conveyed mostly by the upper part of the face, including eye contact, which helps downregulate the nervous system. (Dr. Porges notes that dogs display a similar social engagement system: when two dogs greet each other, they engage in a little dance that may initially involve running after and around each other, followed by a quick face-to-face check-in to ensure that this is play and not fighting.)

Respect the power of your voice. Monotone, low-frequency sounds like thunder, a lion's roar, or a loud, rumbling truck, are interpreted as signs of danger, as are monotone, high-frequency sounds like a person screaming in pain or a newborn crying out. A soft, higher-pitched voice with variations in tone and pitch is almost universally soothing. Porges says it likely has to do with the innate safety we feel as an infant when we hear our mother's voice. The sing-song quality of what is known as "mother-ese" amplifies feelings of safety. To a frightened baby, the words themselves don't matter nearly as much as the comforting, fight-or-flight dampening intonation.

One fascinating aspect of this involves nerves that spread into both the upper facial muscles and the muscles of the middle ear. When the person speaking to us appears angry, negative, or emotionless, the muscle tone of their middle ears is impacted in a way that prevents them from effectively hearing our voice. That's why it so often seems, in the heat of a dispute, like the other person has "checked out" or isn't listening to you; they physically cannot hear you as well! Your raised voice essentially bounces off their eardrums. "It doesn't matter if you yell at them [or] talk louder, which is often the parent's or instructor's reaction when someone isn't processing," Porges explains. "It just makes things worse because the system is really a system that reacts to features of safety."

All of this is to say, endeavor to keep your voice soft and calm and speak slowly if you want to make someone feel at ease. Polyvagal theory describes the ideal voice as prosodic, which means it has variations in tone, such as those used to differentiate a statement from a question or to stress the importance of certain words.

Use the power of touch. Touch stimulates the parasympathetic nervous system in a deeply soothing way. That's one reason babies instinctively wrap their hand around your finger, why massage can feel so calming, and why holding hands makes us feel safe. (It also may explain the antianxiety effect of weighted blankets.) Moderate pressure is ideal. You want to hold your partner's hand in a way that feels reassuring (as opposed to a limp, lifeless handhold, which is less than reassuring). Hug her or him with intention, not just a pat on the back.

Send calming images. A BBC-funded study found that watching a nature documentary incited feelings of joy, awe, and contentedness and reduced feelings of anger and stress. Why? One interpretation looks at it from an evolutionary perspective: seeing beautiful images of nature reminds us of being in nature, which reminds us, evolutionarily speaking, of the opportunity to find food and shelter — two very comforting things. Try sending your loved one a photo you think he or she would relate to: a stunning waterfall, a green mountain landscape, the vast Sahara Desert, a cute sloth. (This helps explain why Alex, the phobic flier from week 5, sometimes scrolled through vacation photos on her phone in-flight; she and her family loved visiting destinations known for their outdoor activities.)

Use effective means of communication. Face-to-face conversation is ideal, but FaceTime, Zoom, or Skype can work if logistics prevent you from being physically together. Avoid phone, text, or e-mail to work through conflict.

OPTIMIZATION STRATEGY: SHIFTING CHILDREN INTO PARASYMPATHETIC DOMINANCE

If you're a parent or interact frequently with children, you can use your new parasympathetic enhancing skills to communicate more effectively with them. At some point, almost all parents find themselves raising their voice with their kids, whether it's out of frustration, irritation, or just plain exhaustion. The next time you find yourself raising your voice with a child, think about the strategies listed for making a partner feel safe, and try to put them into practice. Yelling doesn't work for several reasons, not the least of which is that a child being yelled at sees an adult's face that looks angry. The upper face especially tends to feature a furrowed brow and narrowed eyes. The child perceives danger, and it kicks the child's nervous system into overdrive. In response, his or her middle ear muscles react by tuning out your voice. A more effective, physiology-based approach would be to calmly physically connect with the child (touching their shoulder or arm, for example), making eye contact, and speaking in a softer, slower, and, if possible, prosodic voice. End with a loving hug to simulate the parasympathetic nervous system fibers of everyone involved.

SHIFTING OTHERS INTO PARASYMPATHETIC DOMINANCE IRL

Jill Blakeway is a doctor of acupuncture and Chinese medicine, a licensed and board-certified acupuncturist, a sought-after NYC-based energy healer, and the author of *Energy Medicine: The Science and Mystery of Healing*. We first met through a mutual client of ours, an actress I'll call Sadie. One day Sadie came in for HRV-BRB after just having had an acupuncture treatment, and I noticed that she went into resonance noticeably more easily than usual. Curious, I reached out to Jill, who agreed to meet me at my office for a little experiment. Jill explained that when she practices, she tends to enter a flow state, and it's not uncommon for her to feel her own positive energy transfer through to the needles as she inserts them. She offered to let me connect her to my biofeedback equipment. I asked her to imagine what it feels like for her to treat her patients. Within 15 seconds, she was in resonance . . . and she'd never practiced HRV-BFB before! It wasn't just that she was finding her resonance breathing frequency; her brain waves and heart waves were synching up with each other, almost effortlessly so.

My theory is that her high HRV, finely honed through decades of energy work, allowed her to put herself in resonance on demand. That perhaps allowed Jill to more seamlessly transfer her energy to her patients, which, in turn, may have helped them calm their nervous systems and strengthen their braking systems for a period of time following their visits with her.

HIGHLIGHT ON HEALTH:
SEXUAL HEALTH, PLEASURE, AND HRV

Here's some exciting news: research confirms that people with higher HRV have sex more frequently. Not only that — it's *better* sex. In a recent *Journal of Sexual Medicine* study, 25 women ages 20 to 44 with arousal issues were shown a 6-minute erotic film sequence, then asked to complete a 22-minute psychophysiological technique called autogenic training, which involves using verbal commands to relax and control your physiology. Autogenic training is also known to increase HRV. The researchers associated increases in resting HRV with increases in subjective sexual arousal. Other studies back this up, finding that women with low HRV may be more likely to experience problems with arousal compared with women having average or above-average HRV.

Similarly, among men, higher HRV has been linked with greater erectile tumescence (stronger erections). Other research has tied greater HRV to increased likelihood of achieving orgasm through penile-vaginal sex for both men and women.

Several possible reasons underlie the findings, including the fact that in some women, the sympathetic nervous system may be working more than it has to. This type of overactivation may dampen arousal. Parasympathetic dominance, though, allows an individual to feel relaxed and calm — ideal precursors to satisfying sex. New research also shows that practicing at-home HRV-BFB led to increases in HRV that were related to increases in perceived genital sensations in women with arousal problems.

More intriguing HRV sexual health facts:

- Sex stimulates the vagus nerve, turning on the parasympathetic nervous system and helping you relax and feel open to pleasure.

Among its innumerable other responsibilities, this nerve carries messages of sexual pleasure from the vagina and cervix to the brain. Because the vagus nerve bypasses the spinal cord, women with complete spinal injury are sometimes able to have orgasms even in the absence of other lower body functioning.

- The parasympathetic nervous system is associated with pro-erectile properties and the sympathetic nervous system with anti-erectile ones. This makes sense, considering that an erection isn't critical in times of danger. During REM sleep, the sympathetic nervous system goes into rest mode, allowing parasympathetic characteristics to dominate. That's why nocturnal erections happen mainly during REM sleep. Women experience similar cases of nocturnal arousal 4 or 5 times a night during REM, as demonstrated by labial, vaginal, and clitoral engorgement.
- One reason kissing feels so enjoyable is because it stimulates the parasympathetic nervous system.

WEEK 9 ACTION PLAN

1. Continue your twice-a-day, 20-minute breathing sessions. Use the last 5 minutes of each session to develop your interoceptive abilities.
2. If you're working alone, practice estimating your heart rate, then engage in a brief bout of physical exercise and reattempt to estimate your heart rate. (Use your homework tracking sheet on page 238.) Next, breathe at your resonance frequency for 2 minutes and reevaluate your heart rate. Does it seem slower? Throughout the day, can you estimate your heart rate during specific moments or events? (Use the Homework Tracking Sheet.)
3. If working with a partner, begin by attempting to estimate each other's heart rates. Then, one of you should leave the room and engage in their chosen activity to alter their heart

rate. Then they should return to their partner and ask him or her to estimate their heart rate. Can you estimate your partner's heart rate in real time, such as when he or she is waiting in line at the grocery store, recounting an emotional conversation, and so on? In addition, practice resonance breathing together, alternating who leads and who follows, twice this week for 20 minutes. (Use your homework tracking sheet on page 240.)

4. Practice the various physiology-based techniques for shifting your partner and/or children and other loved ones into parasympathetic dominance.

A PEEK AHEAD

Don't forget to measure and record your HRV next week, during week 10.

13

▼

Week 10:

Anchoring Yourself in Resonance

Have you ever noticed that you become extremely drained and sometimes even irritable around certain people and in particular environments? Of course you have. We use different names for situations like these — "negative," "energy draining" — but if you think about it, those are just ways of saying that these people and environments shift you out of resonance and into a state of dissonance. Likewise, there are other people, places, and things that shift you into resonance fairly easily or even amplify your existing state of resonance.

Different people are sensitive to different forms of sensory input. Some of us find certain types of noise stressful and distracting; others find that their physiology is greatly impacted by bright light or by the energy that emanates from those around them.

The question, then, is, how do you cultivate resonance when you are surrounded by negative energy (or environments that diminish your energy) or encounter resonance detractors such as lack of sleep, bad traffic, or feeling overstretched? In this chapter, I'll share with you a technique for amplifying your resonance in the presence of potential distractors. It's called the Bubble, and it will help you anchor yourself to a sense of internal safety and calm. You've spent the last 9 weeks learning how to cultivate your resonance. Now it's time to develop the skills you need to amplify it.

THE STRESS OF ABSORBING OTHER PEOPLE'S EMOTIONS

Complainers. Narcissists. Boundary-crossers. The emotionally exhausting. These sorts of unconstructive personalities are all around us, and they're not going anywhere anytime soon.

Spending time with people who make us feel sad, angry, abused, or disrespected can lead to a host of health concerns, from high blood pressure to chronic pain. One long-term study, published in the *Journal of the American Medical Association*, that followed nearly 10,000 men and women for about 12 years found that those who described their closest personal relationship as negative faced an increased risk of heart disease and heart attack compared with their counterparts whose close relationships were not rated negative. Why? One theory is that alterations in autonomic functions cause cumulative "wear and tear" on vital organs.

RESONANCE DETRACTORS IRL

You don't even need to be face-to-face with a negative person to feel his or her resonance-detracting effects. A study conducted by Facebook and Cornell University found evidence of "massive-scale emotional contagion" on social media, meaning you can "catch" a bad mood just by scrolling through someone's feed. In the experiment, researchers manipulated the News Feed content seen by 689,003 Facebook users, with the goal of seeing if they could impact users' own posting habits. (As with many social media channels, when you first join Facebook, you agree to a Data Use Policy, which grants consent for this sort of research.) They found that when positive content was limited on subjects' News Feeds, those subjects in turn posted fewer positive—and more negative—posts themselves. When negative posts were limited, the opposite effect was observed; users posted more positive posts themselves and fewer negative.

An important point about absorbing other people's emotions: the more stressed you feel, the more apt you are to soak up their negativity. Autonomic dysregulation, depression, and anxiety wear down your defenses, rendering you even more vulnerable to negative energy that is outside of you.

Two types of individuals are especially sensitive: empaths and highly sensitive people (HSPs). Empaths are so named for their heightened ability to empathize with others. They understand others' emotions and feel for others, whether they are experiencing joy or one of life's many trials and tribulations. Empaths sense the energies emanating from other people, absorb them, and actually feel them in their own body. An empath who sees a child celebrating her birthday, for instance, actually feels the little girl's joy. Similarly, if a person is being shamed or bullied, an empath will absorb that energy and experience a shared physiologic reaction, too.

This level of empathy is an asset. Empaths have an innate ability to connect with others and perceive their emotions without any words being exchanged. I often describe this population as feeling the world more deeply. But while empaths feel other people's joy, they also feel their pain. While it's beautiful to be able to connect so easily with others, it can be disruptive when their energies rub off on you and shift you out of resonance when you need to perform.

Highly sensitive people (HSPs) are just that—highly sensitive to their surroundings. They're tuned in to sound, light, and other sensory components. They don't absorb other peoples' energies as fully and deeply as empaths. However, they are still thrown off by criticisms, negativities, and unexpected sensory components that shift them out of resonance. All empaths are HSPs, but not all HSPs are empaths.

OTHER RESONANCE DETRACTORS

- Commuting and traffic
- Digital distractions: phones, e-mail, news alerts, social media
- The news itself, filled with scary headlines and stories of violence, inequality, political turmoil, and the like
- Lack of sleep
- Feeling overcommitted or like you don't have enough time
- Investments, career opportunities, or other things that don't work out as planned

INTRODUCING THE BUBBLE

Often, when people reach the last few weeks of my protocol, they crave additional ways to anchor their resonance when confronted with various external energies. They are beginning to understand the power of their new performance state, and it's important to them to learn how to sustain it.

For this purpose, I recommend a technique that was inspired by my conversations with social worker and therapist Rae Tattenbaum, which I refer to as the Bubble. It has helped many of my clients become more resilient in the face of potential triggers. It is a form of a visualization designed to help you amplify your internal state of flow and hold on to that state of resonance, no matter what is going on around you. It is especially important for HSPs, empaths, and anyone who feels a desire to expunge negative energy that they have absorbed from the world around them.

Remember: It's impossible to avoid all stressors or to eradicate every factor that dampens your resonance. But you can take away their power and anchor your physiology. My goal is to teach you not how to shut down or close yourself off but rather to create an imperceptible shield of self-care. To do this, you must learn how to temporarily close those pores, let go, and then re-open them with a clean slate. This is precisely what the Bubble teaches you to do.

BREATHING EXERCISE #12: THE BUBBLE

Here are the basic steps for surrounding yourself with the Bubble. Once you become comfortable with the technique, you can begin using it strategically when you find yourself in a situation imbued with negative energy.

Step 1: Close your eyes. Imagine a bubble starting at your right ankle, slowly moving up your right leg to the knee and hip, then the right side of your torso. This bubble is soft and reassuring. Its mission is to surround you to keep you safe. Imagine it extending from the right side of your waist to your right arm and shoulder . . . your right ear . . . now the crown of your head. The bubble is like the lightest blanket, gently covering the right side of your body. Now feel it gently extending over your head to your left ear . . . your left shoulder and arm . . . the left side of your torso. Envision it stretching down to your left knee and connecting all the way to your left foot. The bubble is now surrounding your entire body. You are safe and protected.

Step 2: Now, focus on your heart. With the bubble surrounding your body, I want you to focus on the feeling of safety and love in your heart as you inhale, and then exhale as normal. Please do this once more: focus on the feeling of safety and love in your heart as you inhale, then exhale as normal.

Step 3: Next, as you inhale, focus on anything negative in your body —tension, stress, frustration, anxiety. As you exhale, push that negativity out of your body to the very edges of your bubble, letting it float into the atmosphere. Then do this once more: as you inhale, focus on any negative sensations in your body, then push them out through the mouth, beyond your body, and into the atmosphere as you exhale.

Step 4: Finally, return to the feelings of safety and love in your heart. Take 2 more breaths—on the inhale, gently bring your focus to the center of your heart and connect to how safe you feel and how much love you have within you. Exhale negativity, pushing it to the edges of your bubble. Imagine it crossing through the bubble and floating away into the atmosphere.

With continued practice, you will be able to turn this new tool into a verb; plenty of my clients refer to it as "Bubbling," as in "I Bubbled on a packed subway yesterday" or "The other day I Bubbled while sitting in my pediatrician's waiting room. There were so many anxious parents with their sick kids, and you could feel the stress in the room."

Optimization Strategy: Using the Bubble in Different Situations

Plenty of scenarios warrant you evaluating your internal state and releasing negative tensions through your Bubble. Yes, it can provide significant resonance protection when a negative person is nearby, but there are many other practical applications.

- *You're in a confined space from which you can't move or retreat,* such as a crowded subway or overbooked airplane. The Bubble allows you to define a personal boundary or protective space within a space.
- *You're preparing for a performance event.* For example, you could use this before an important speech to help you let go of anything weighing you down, to amplify your resonance, and to approach the event with the confidence that nothing can penetrate your peak performance state.
- *You want to recover from a stressful event.* My clients have found this tool to be particularly helpful in letting go of an emotionally charged interaction or other stressful moment.
- *You want to prevent a physiological symptom of stress from occurring.* Remember Nancy, my client who experienced migraines for

her entire adult life? As she progressed through her 10-week protocol, the frequency and severity of her migraines reduced, but she
still experienced occasional auras, which are sensory disturbances
like flashing lights and blind spots that, for some people, signal
an oncoming migraine. Whenever Nancy noticed an aura developing, she would use the Bubble, creating a protective shield and
breathing away the migraine to prevent it from fully manifesting.

- *You want to let go of a negative internal state.* Maybe you're at
  a low in your day and just can't shake it. You might feel anxiety brewing inside your heart and body. Your body wants to let
  go, but there is too much uncertainty in your environment. You
  can use the Bubble to reset, teach the body to embrace a sense of
  safety, and release the unwanted negative state.

PROTECT YOUR HARD WORK

Aidan was a sought-after photographer who was beginning to acquire a
large following. Increasingly, he found himself hired to shoot global events.
His subjects tended to be demanding, often requesting multiple retakes and
asking to see the shots on his camera. Even after 6 months in this new world,
he was still finding himself rattled by this behavior.

When showing up at a function, Aidan needed to be able to perform
at his best and prove himself to whatever audience he faced. He used the
Bubble technique, therefore, to deflect external demands and criticism. As a
photographer, Aidan was a highly visual person, so picturing himself being
encased in a bubble to cultivate feelings of safety and let go of rising tensions came naturally to him. With regular practice, he was able to practice
his Bubble right before starting to shoot, considering it another piece of
equipment, just like his tripod and camera bag. According to Aidan, the Bubble helped to optimize his ability to stay in his flow and let go of the negative energy that had previously undermined his attention and performance.

What You'll Experience

You've created a portable, personalized safe haven with the ability to help protect you from external sources of stress. My clients tell me that this feeling translates powerfully into their daily lives. You may find that negative or critical people no longer have the same ability to impact your physiology. This is because by week 10, you've strengthened your vagal tone as well as increased activity in the frontal lobe to the point where you likely have a much better ability to inhibit anxious or unproductive thoughts. You may also feel more comfortable expressing your own emotions and ideas, irrespective of other peoples' actions.

IF YOU'RE SICK OF SOAKING UP OTHER PEOPLE'S STRESS . . .

Ainsley was an empath who lived in New York and couldn't help but absorb the negative energy of those around her. She rode the subway to work, and it seemed like every day a new heated conversation or vehement address of personal views presented itself just feet, or sometimes inches, from her. Whether it was someone listening to impossibly loud music with no regard for anyone else, a squabbling couple, or a person seeking to express his or her political views on the platform of the "R" train station, no book or podcast was gripping enough to distract her or prevent her from soaking in the unpleasantness.

We needed to find a way to reduce her sensory overload to help her protect her energy levels and resonance, which she required to function optimally at her office. Ainsley began practicing her Bubble the moment she swiped her transit card; as the subway turnstile rotated to let her through, she "armored up," as she called it, cultivating her Bubble to shield her in a protective embrace. Inevitably, she still wound up sitting next to loud, boisterous, or otherwise opinionated passengers, but instead of letting them derail her energy, she wore her Bubble like an oversized pair of noise-canceling headphones and was able to maintain her calm and focus for the day ahead.

OPTIMIZATION STRATEGY: AMPLIFYING YOUR RESONANCE VIA GRATITUDE PRACTICE

Just as you learned how to induce feelings of safety in your partner during week 9, you can — and must — create a sense of safety in your own body in order to enhance your resonance. Practicing gratitude stimulates neural pathways to the heart, which are known to elicit calming effects and even increase parasympathetic HRV response. By focusing on gratitude during the same week that you practice your Bubble, you can intensify your resonance-defending effects.

In one landmark study, participants were assigned to one of three groups. One group wrote down up to five things they were thankful for ("waking up this morning"; "the Rolling Stones"). The second wrote down what they considered hassles in their daily life ("parking trouble"; "messy kitchen"). The control group wrote down neutral events ("learned CPR"; "cleaned out my shoe closet"). Not only did subjects in the gratitude group report feeling more optimistic and better about their lives as a whole, they reported fewer physical complaints than the other two groups. That same study also found that people who practice gratitude are more likely to offer other people emotional support.

A relatively simple way to practice gratitude is to create a gratitude journal like that used by the first group in the study. Once a day, write down as many people and things as you can for which you feel thankful. For a fun twist on the gratitude journal, write and deliver a letter to somebody who has been especially kind to you but whom you have never properly thanked. One study found that this exercise was potent enough to produce feelings of increased happiness for up to 1 month.

ANY QUESTIONS?

"I'm trying to Bubble while someone with negative energy is talking to me. I want to seem respectful and not completely tune out, but how do I listen and hop in my Bubble at the same time?"

Their words are grating on your nerves. Maybe you feel your heart pounding in your chest as they rail on about their grievances. Your physiology is begging you to escape, to flee, or perhaps to fight back against their holding you hostage to their monologue of hostility, narcissism, or neediness. You feel trapped. And now your whole body is on edge—tightened shoulders, shallow breathing—as their negativity becomes internalized within you.

I often hear this from people who prioritize other people's needs over their own. They want to deflect the negative energy that's right in front of them, but they worry that if they were to try to Bubble, they'd have trouble focusing and might inadvertently out themselves as not listening.

The fact that you're even asking this question shows me that you are starting to consider resonance as an internal state that you not only want to cultivate but also maintain. You've dedicated the last few months to creating and nurturing your resonance, and nobody has the right to take that away from you. This is a brilliant opportunity to start reprioritizing your needs; starting today, *you* take precedence.

Your self-care priorities must shift. When you feel yourself slipping out of resonance, I'd like you to practice Bubbling exactly as someone is facing you and speaking at you. (Energy-draining people tend to speak *at* you, not *with* you.) Remember, they cannot see your Bubble. It's almost as if you're opening an umbrella and placing it in front of you as a shield without them realizing it. You can still hear what they're saying, but their words are no longer hitting you like pellets of bad energy.

Are you able to let go of what they think and prioritize yourself? Are you able to deflect their energy and create a neutral or positive cognitive space?

As we discussed in week 8, your brain may try to get in your way. It might tell you that you're being rude or insensitive.

You're not.

You're practicing self-care.

You're anchoring your resonance.

OPTIMIZATION STRATEGY: PROMOTING SAFETY BY MAINTAINING SCHEDULES FOR SLEEPING AND EATING

The human body craves stability. This innate preference can be seen in children, who thrive on the comfort and routine of a consistent bedtime schedule (bath, brush teeth, pajamas, book, sleep), all the way up to an elderly person who wants nothing more than to be able to age in place in his or her longtime home rather than move to a nursing facility. The constancy and predictability of routine send a message of safety to our brains and bodies.

One way to fortify this message is by setting regular times for eating and sleeping, especially during periods of increased stress. Both habits help convey a sense of internal safety, which your nervous system interprets as "I can relax because I know exactly when sleep and nourishment are coming. I am safe." It's fine if your schedule veers a bit on the weekends, but do try to stay on track during the week.

HIGHLIGHT ON HEALTH: PANIC ATTACKS

If you've ever experienced a panic attack, you know how frightening and all-consuming they can be. You feel as if you can't breathe; your heart pounds out of your chest; you may become sweaty and have trouble thinking clearly. The symptoms are so disturbing, first-time sufferers may fear they're having a heart attack or dying. Though panic attacks typically last just a few minutes, they can feel overwhelming and interminable, sometimes appearing seemingly out of nowhere, sometimes with no clear trigger.

While we don't know for certain why panic attacks happen, they likely result from a perfect storm of physiological, psychological, environmental, and genetic factors. These episodes happen when the body experiences a sudden surge of adrenaline, something that's only supposed to happen when we perceive a threat or danger.

Fortunately, panic attacks respond well to treatment. Some people take a quick-acting antianxiety medication as soon as they feel an attack coming on, but pharmaceuticals don't address the root cause or causes of the panic. Cognitive behavioral therapy can help tremendously in terms of stopping these attacks at their source. Mind-body techniques like belly breathing or mentally repeating reassuring statements such as "I am safe. This is going to pass" can help you ride out the attack. The use of the word *safe* is key here. It is almost always the case when a panic attack occurs that there is no imminent danger. Rather, it's the thought or perception of danger that triggered the attack; the threat is imagined, but the response is real.

I once worked with a litigator who had been offered a job at a competing firm. The offer came at the same time she and her husband were starting to discuss in earnest their plans for having children. They also happened to be renovating their home. Around this time, she began experiencing unexplained chest pains and heart palpitations that would come on suddenly and without notice. Her internist ruled out any cardiac or hormonal conditions; nothing in her blood panel explained these attacks. The woman's doctor referred her to me for stress management.

As we delved into her experiences, the litigator, a peak performer in many aspects of life, revealed that she felt unsafe, not in terms of worrying she was going to be the victim of a crime or that she might be seriously ill, but rather she felt a lack of security. After years of enjoying a satisfying career and stable marriage, she now felt a lack of predictability in three major pillars in her life: work, family, and home. Even though the changes were exciting, they left her feeling uprooted.

We created a list of behavioral interventions to help restore her sense of internal safety. These included a consistent weeknight bedtime of 10 p.m. and a regular schedule of meals and snacks. She committed to a nonnegotiable 8 hours of sleep each night and practiced resonance breathing twice a day for 20 minutes. She also Heart Shifted from feeling unsafe to feeling calm and confident, and did Power 10s throughout the day for safety. The goal was to establish a physiological sense of safety in her body. The behavioral inputs, particularly at established time intervals, aimed to provide a stabilizing sense of structure and predictability for her body. The goal was to systematize the most basic inputs that regulate her physiology (sleep and eating) to increase her body's perception of safety versus danger. Within 3 weeks, her chest pains and feelings of panic disappeared and never returned.

WEEK 10 ACTION PLAN

1. Continue your twice-a-day, 20-minute breathing sessions. Spend the last 5 minutes of your practice Bubbling in a quiet, safe space.
2. After a few days, practice Bubbling in everyday life when you find yourself near negative people or in other resonance-detracting environments.
3. Commit to anchoring your resonance by prioritizing self-care and systematizing your eating, sleeping, and breathing sessions during the week.
4. Remeasure your HRV using your equipment this week. (Refer to page 36 for a refresher. Mark your results on the homework tracking sheet on page 241.)

PART III

▼

BEYOND 10 WEEKS

14

▼

Maintaining and Fueling Your Resonance

If you're reading these words, you've made it through the 10-week program and deserve a heartfelt congratulations. You have put in the effort and time required and have progressed from optimizing your baseline stress response to developing tools to enhance your physiological response to the various stressors that inevitably confront us all. These tools will become your intrinsic coping mechanisms, and you're now primed to use them to reset your body over and over, sometimes multiple times throughout the day. This will allow you to perform at your peak at any time, in any place, no matter what is occurring around you. Most important, you are in control of how your heart reacts to the environment.

Now you may be wondering: What's next?

You've got an incredible new skill set, one that grants you much more power and control over your physiology. How do you preserve your newfound focus and organization? How do you keep fueling your resonance? How do you sustain your ability to feel and let go?

It's time to transition from intervention to maintenance and prevention. In this final section of the book, I will focus on advanced techniques for amplifying resonance and elevating your performance.

Here are a few common questions I hear from clients after their 10-week "graduation."

Can I keep training?

By all means, continue your daily resonance frequency breathing. You can repeat the 10-week protocol, or you can select the techniques that make your heart and mind come alive and practice them regularly.

How often do I need to do the breathing sessions if I want to maintain the cognitive benefits?

You need to adhere to the 20 minutes twice-a-day schedule for at least 5 days per week. Ninety percent of my peak performers continue at this level; they find that when they breathe for less, their cognitive benefits dissipate.

How many breathing sessions per week do I need to maintain my stress management abilities?

You can modify your routine so that you are breathing at your resonance frequency for 20 minutes, 3 days a week (just 1 breathing session per day on those 3 days). If you choose this option, however, you will only maintain your newfound ability to quickly let go; your cognitive benefits will dissipate with less than 20 minutes twice per day, at least 5 days per week of practice. That said, if you opt for this reduced protocol and feel as if your letting-go skills are diminishing, you'll need to add a session or two.

How can I help myself get into resonance even faster?

Try mixing things up a bit. Start your day with one 20-minute resonance breathing session, then spread out the second 20 minutes of breathing throughout your day. Maybe try several Power 10s, connecting to the feeling of the stressor on the inhale and releasing it on the exhale for 10 consecutive breaths. (By now you've likely progressed to Power 5s or

Power 3s.) Add in a heart boost or two, connecting to your heart imprint on the inhale and releasing the negative emotions on the exhale. Toggling between the two types of practice is analogous to a runner mixing up endurance and interval training; each approach strengthens your skills in different ways. The cumulative effect, though, is the ability to elicit resonance more easily.

Can I start meditating again?

Go for it. At the start of the book, I asked you to hold off on meditating for the next 10 weeks as you learned how to breathe at your resonance frequency. Doing both at the same time could have felt needlessly overwhelming. Now that you've found your resonance, you can reintegrate meditation into your life. If you're continuing to breathe for 20 minutes twice a day, you can practice meditation following each resonance breathing practice. If you're opting for less breathing, you could try substituting 1 breathing session with a meditation session. Maybe try breathing in the morning and meditating at night, or vice versa. You'll find that your improved HRV will help you reach that relaxed state of parasympathetic dominance faster than ever.

ADDITIONAL LAYERS TO BUILD YOUR PRACTICE

Immersive Music

In week 7, I mentioned that those who wished to add music to their breathing practice could do so. Now that the 10-week training has culminated, feel free to continue using music as a backdrop to your practice, or perhaps add it if you haven't already. Make it more immersive with surround sound or high-quality over-the-ear headphones.

Daily HRV Monitoring in the Morning

During the past 10 weeks, I asked you to measure your HRV during weeks 1, 4, 7, and 10 only, to help keep you tuned into your physiology and avoid possible tech-related distractions. Now that you have completed your 10 weeks, you can begin experimenting with daily HRV measurements if you so choose. You'll want to create a monitoring routine and adhere to it at approximately the same time each morning in order to ensure consistent, accurate measurements. Your HRV is highest first thing in the morning, and I suggest assessing it as soon as possible after waking up — before you check your phone, before you drink your coffee, before you answer any e-mails or read the news. No resonance breathing is necessary; measure your HRV as you breathe normally. If you keep a detailed journal of your mood, eating, sleep habits, and stress level along with your daily HRV numbers, you'll be able to detect patterns after about 4 weeks. Athletes may find this particularly appealing, as they can use the data to assess their recovery from training.

HRV Monitoring During Sleep

Several products are available to help you track your HRV as you sleep. Some of them, like the Sleeprate sleep monitoring app (sleeprate.com), the Oura Ring (ouraring.com), and the Whoop Strap (whoop.com) provide or are compatible with wearable technology to monitor your HRV. Along with HRV, you can gather a significant amount of other data to help you improve your sleep routine or reach any sleep goals you may have: hours slept, number of breaths per minute, snoring, room temperature, and more, depending on the product.

White Light

You may enjoy supplementing your breathing sessions with a lightbox. Lightboxes mimic sunlight without the UV rays and come in all shapes and sizes. They usually provide 10,000 lux, about 100 times brighter than typical indoor lighting (a sunny day can be 50,000 lux or more). Our bodies make vitamin D when sunshine hits our bare skin, but thanks to all the time we spend indoors these days, a significant portion of the public is vitamin D deficient. Low stores of vitamin D can correlate with cognitive impairment and other health problems. By sitting in front of a white light lamp as you breathe, you can swiftly and safely get your fill without really having to do anything extra. Bright light is also nicely stimulating for dark winter periods. I like the Verilux HappyLight brand, but many effective models exist.

Annual Blood Panel

Ask your health care practitioner to test your vitamin D and magnesium annually, along with your thyroid function and possibly your hormone levels. All have the potential to impact mood and anxiety. If your levels are suboptimal, consult with your health care provider for a treatment plan.

High-Intensity Interval Training (HIIT)

Cardiovascular fitness and HRV are strongly correlated; the fitter your heart, the higher your HRV. (Conversely, the fitter you are, the lower your resting heart rate.) HIIT training, characterized by quick, intense bursts of exercise followed by brief periods of recovery, may be even better at improving your body's response to stress. Specifically, it increases vagal tone.

Cold-Exposure Training

Exposure to cold temperatures can increase HRV. This may be due to an evolutionary mechanism called the diving reflex, which is essentially a pattern of physiological survival responses that kick in when a person dives into cold water. The body responds to this sudden underwater immersion by conserving oxygen (via decreased heart rate) and prioritizing blood flow to the heart and brain. Emerging research suggests that the diving reflex can be triggered by applying cold water to the forehead, cheeks, and nose, so try splashing your face with very cold water before practicing resonance breathing to get an HRV jump start.

HARNESSING THE POWER
OF GROUP RESONANCE

When I started working with a collegiate basketball team several years ago, their coach expressed to me her desire to help her players sharpen their focus and improve their ability to play at a higher level for a longer period. Due to time constraints, we decided that I would train the players in groups of 5 for 30 minutes per session. We began by having each team member take turns sitting with me in front of their respective group. As a group, we would practice resonance breathing, with the rest of the team members following the lead member's resonance frequency. After 5 minutes, we would rotate to the next person, and so on.

Seven weeks into our training, I noticed something very interesting: the HRVs of members within specific groups began synchronizing. Each group had 1 player with the highest HRV. After 7 weeks of breathing together, the HRVs of the other women in each group began increasing to match the level of that player.

Why did this happen? My theory is that when these teams breathed together, they began to generate the same heart and brain frequencies, which put them in a state of physiological alignment. I call this group resonance. When multiple members of a group breathe together at their resonance pace, their hearts emit strong magnetic fields that are subconsciously detected by one another. In one fascinating study, female acquaintances sat on a couch together and watched an emotional movie. No speaking or other forms of direct interaction were permitted. It was found that simply being in the presence of others during an emotional moment caused various positive autonomic responses, such as heart rate, to sync. This phenomenon has not been empirically studied but deserves further research and exploration.

But a synchronization in HRV wasn't the only change that occurred among the basketball players. Toward the end of the 10-week training, their coach came to me and asked, "What did you do? The groups that trained together have become extremely close and are working so well together — far better than before." Players that hadn't tended to socialize together off the court with those in their breathing groups began doing so.

Think back to week 9, when we discussed the importance of making others feel safe. Techniques like using a soft voice, eye contact, gentle but firm touch — these were all ways of instilling a sense of safety in our partners, a prerequisite for them to achieve autonomic balance. I would venture to say that resonance breathing practiced in a group setting can have a similar effect. By shaping one another's physiology, you're exercising a pathway for greater social engagement. This leads to feelings of emotional closeness and connection and brings a group psychologically closer. That, in turn, facilitates greater perceptivity and improves team members' ability to collaborate. It doesn't need to be a literal team, as it was in the case of the basketball players; it could be a team of colleagues or a family unit. For example, I have seen the same phenomenon occur in teams that work together in the business world. In the aforementioned movie study, researchers found that those subjects who exhibited higher autonomic synchronization with one another also reported more similar emotional responses to the movies shown.

Based on a research study, when the human resources team at Google conducted more than 200 interviews with employees, they found there were five key dynamics that helped predict a team's success . . . and psychological safety was at the top of the list. Described as a feeling of being able to take risks without fear of punishment or being made to feel insecure or embarrassed, employees on teams with higher psychological safety were "more likely to harness the power of diverse ideas from their teammates . . . bring in more revenue, and [be] rated as effective twice as often by executives," according to the findings.

Group resonance may be a form of somatic bonding, attained via breathing exercises in a group setting. When our hearts and brains oscillate at the same rhythms as others, we may develop a physiological alignment that transcends working in the cubicle next door to one another or even sharing the same living space. In my experience working with sports and business teams, the group training facilitates openness, empathic responding, and perceptivity.

A Few Ideas for Training

Group resonance may be elicited doing exactly what it sounds like you should do — practice breathing together with your group. But it can also be acquired when members of a group or team commit to breathing practice independently. With either method, you may be able to generate similar heart rhythms to one another, leading to the same 0.1 Hz frequency in your hearts and brains. When that happens, members of a group may start to feel more open to one another and receptive of each other's ideas. This same phenomenon was described in week 9, when we learned how resonance breathing side by side with someone exercises the pathway for enhanced social engagement.

To enact this psychobiological approach to high-performance teams, you can try:

- regular weekly group breathing sessions (to promote bonding, creativity, collaboration, and receptiveness).
- group breathing sessions before important meetings or conferences or before making key decisions together.
- exercising together. Cardiovascular exercise improves HRV. Exercising together may help group members obtain similar benefits. In the business world, holding meetings or brainstorming sessions while exercising is sometimes called sweatworking for its ability to help promote bonding and generate ideas.

Note: While the science behind this particular application of group resonance is still developing, I've observed its success among clients and stand behind its ability to synchronize and unite team members of all varieties.

ENHANCING THE MIND

We've learned how HRV-BFB has the power to open the heart and help you reach peak levels of performance. One mechanism responsible for these effects is HRV's strength in boosting blood flow to the brain. The Vaschillos have hypothesized that resonance breathing at a frequency of 0.1Hz — that is, breathing at a rate of about 6 breaths per minute — may trigger resonance not only in the cardiovascular system but in the brain as well. In new research presented at the International Brain Stimulation Conference, they and their coauthors discussed the results of their study of 15 college students who were asked to breathe at 0.1 Hz for 5 minutes while cardiac activity was monitored and blood oxygen levels were monitored in nine regions of the brain. They found that when subjects were in resonance, the resonance-induced oscillations seen in the heart were also observed in all nine brain regions. Their conclusion: Paced breathing at 0.1 Hz leads to large fluctuations in the diameter of blood vessels and, ultimately, improves the level of oxygenation of the brain, which aids cognitive and emotional control.

These findings are supported by Thayer's neurovisceral integration model, which suggests that vagal tone may represent the optimization of the neural circuitry that governs emotional–cognitive performance. According to Thayer, daily resonance breathing practice increases heart rate oscillations, which in turn stimulate oscillatory activity in regions of the brain associated with emotional regulation. HRV-BFB, then, has the potential to improve not just cognitive functioning but overall emotional health.

Possibilities for Future Applications

Armed with the knowledge that HRV and brain blood flow are inextricably linked, more researchers are investigating possible applications in the fields of brain injury. Take postconcussion syndrome (PCS), for example. The majority of athletes with sports-related concussions recover within 7 to 10 days; nonathletes, within the first 3 months. But up to 10 percent of sports-related concussion patients and 33 percent of non-sports-related concussive patients continue to PCS. PCS is characterized by a constellation of symptoms such as headache, irritability, dizziness, insomnia, lack of concentration, memory difficulty, and fatigue. At least 3 or more of these symptoms are necessary for a diagnosis of PCS.

Previously considered a brain-based condition, we now know that concussion impacts more than cognitive functioning; it affects other physiological systems, including the heart and autonomic nervous system. Concussed patients exhibit exaggerated sympathetic branch activity and increased heart rates compared with controls. Parasympathetic underactivation may also play a role, preventing the brain from returning to homeostasis. Further hindering recovery, patients are frequently advised to refrain from physical exertion until their symptoms have subsided, but lack of physical activity may predispose those same individuals to fatigue and depression, possibly delaying recovery indefinitely.

Recent studies have explored the use of HRV-BFB with PCS, with encouraging outcomes. In one case study, a 42-year-old competitive athlete was diagnosed with PCS following a concussion incurred during practice. After 10 weeks of HRV-BFB, she exhibited clinically significant improvements in headache severity, mood, and other postconcussion symptoms. Not surprisingly, her HRV and vagal tone increased as well.

Other research has found HRV-BFB to be helpful in treating emotional dysregulation in individuals with severe acquired brain injury.

Interestingly, significant overlap exists between symptoms of PCS and post-traumatic stress disorder (PTSD), a condition that can develop after experiencing a shocking, frightening, or otherwise traumatic event. As with PCS, not everyone who experiences a traumatic event goes on to develop PTSD. But in those who do, the effects can be debilitating: flashbacks; nightmares or insomnia; feeling tense, angry, or easily startled; avoiding specific places and people out of fear of being triggered. Another parallel shared by the two disorders is that both are characterized by sympathetic dominance. Hyperactivity of the autonomic sympathetic branch has even been called "a cardinal feature of patients with PTSD . . . as evidenced by elevations in heart rate, blood pressure, skin conductance, and other psychophysiological measures." Accordingly, the physiological release of trauma that occurs during HRV-BFB (weeks 3 or 4 of my program) may improve physiological functioning among PTSD patients.

Findings such as these are encouraging HRV experts to explore the potential of HRV-BFB as the next wave of brain stimulation—a new approach to strengthening the autonomic nervous system by inducing resonance in the brain as well as the body. If so, that means we not only can continue using it to treat hundreds of medical conditions marked by autonomic dysregulation, such as depression, insomnia, asthma, and more, but can offer it as a tool to individuals struggling with traumatic brain injury and related disorders.

THIS IS ONLY THE BEGINNING . . .

Stress may be an inevitable part of work and life, but the effects of stress are far from inevitable. For decades, the science of peak performance has focused on cognitive and neurochemical factors. But if we know that stress originates in and lives in our physiology, why try to treat it in the mind only? By merging proven psychological and physiological techniques to enhance your HRV, you have upgraded the way your body reflexively responds under pressure. You have learned specific heart protocols for anticipating stress, managing stress in the moment, and recovering quickly from stress, effectively closing the gap between practice and performance. When you can manage your stress anytime, anywhere, and under any condition, you bring out the best in yourself and those around you as you perform at your highest level of ability at work, in your relationships, and throughout your entire life.

Most people find that once they get a taste of the benefits of resonance, their 20-minute breathing sessions transform from a box on their to-do list to a valued, rewarding ritual of everyday life. My sincere hope is that this training evolves from serving as two breathing bookends at the start and end of each day into a new way of life. Optimal benefits manifest when you integrate your resonance breathing as a way of life to maximize successes and rebound from setbacks.

This training has been life-changing for thousands of clients as well as myself, its effects reverberating from the personal to the professional, whether it's an Olympic athlete or NBA player; CEOs and investment executives; authors, musicians, and performers; or anyone who has longed to tighten their emotional regulation and take charge of their stress response, instead of their stress response controlling them.

With a new and deep understanding of heart rate variability, you now possess a systematic, time-oriented, physiology-first approach for tapping into a performance-enhancing state. I am so excited for you to use this potent internal state of resonance to positively impact not only your personal life and career but also any relationship that demands — and deserves — collaboration, empathy, and teamwork.

You've done something incredible: you have optimized your nervous system response for peak performance. Maybe you're like Brent, who learned to nimbly pivot from stress to calm confidence between meetings at work. Maybe you learned how to close the gap between practice and performance, like Shelly the runner, who tamed her nerves enough to earn a spot on Team USA. Or perhaps you were able to enhance an existing relationship by bolstering a sense of interconnectedness, like George and Tom, or start a brand-new one, like Meg did after she exorcised her ghost. Armed with finely tuned reflexes and a richer understanding of your physiology, you are in control of stress and not the other way around. Life feels fuller and more enjoyable. This is what happens when you tap into the power of resonance and succeed in connecting your heart, breath, and mind.

YOUR WEEK-BY-WEEK SNAPSHOT

Week 1: Finding Your Resonance Frequency

The basics: Inhale for 4, exhale for 6.

Find your resonance frequency. Experiment with the following variations:

- 3.4 seconds to inhale, 5.2 seconds to exhale (7 breaths per minute)
- 3.7 seconds to inhale, 5.5 seconds to exhale (6.5 breaths per minute)
- 3.8 seconds to inhale, 5.8 seconds to exhale (6.2 breaths per minute)
- 4 seconds to inhale, 6 seconds to exhale (6 breaths per minute)
- 4.2 seconds to inhale, 6.2 seconds to exhale (5.7 breaths per minute)
- 4.4 seconds to inhale, 6.6 seconds to exhale (5.5 breaths per minute)
- 4.8 seconds to inhale, 7.2 seconds to exhale (5 breaths per minute)

Week 2: Using Your Breath to Increase Energy

Feel your belly expand on the inhale and deflate on the exhale. You can try this seated or lying down. Strive to make the exhale longer than the inhale, as if you are blowing on hot soup.

Week 3: Letting Go of Your Stress and Expanding Your Emotional Range

Feel the stressor on the inhale, and release the stressor during the exhale while breathing at your resonance frequency.

Week 4: Healing the Broken Parts

Connect to the physiological sensation that accompanies your ghost (past pain) on the inhale, and release it on the exhale.

Week 5: Preparing for Challenge

Heart Shifting:

- Three series of 5 breaths. For the first 5 breaths, on the inhale, connect to and experience your negative emotion — stress, anger, frustration, fear — as it feels in your heart, and release that emotion from your heart on the exhale. For the second set of 5 breaths, focus on the crisp, fresh air on the inhale and the feeling of letting go on the exhale. For the third set of 5 breaths, connect to your ideal performance state, such as calm and confident, on the inhale, and let go of any negative emotions on the exhale.

Heart Shifting ghosts:

- Three series of 5 breaths. For the first 5 breaths, focus on the theme that you'd like to release, such as the need for control or perfection, on the inhale, and release it through your mouth on the exhale. For the second set of 5 breaths, focus on the crisp, fresh air on the inhale and the feeling of letting go on the exhale. For the third set of 5 breaths, connect with your desired state on the inhale and on letting go of the ghost state on the exhale.

Week 6: Mastering the Emotional Pivot

Pivoting with your heart:

- Connect to a heart imprint on the inhale, and release any stress or negative emotions on the exhale.

Heart Pivoting throughout the day:

- Three times a day, take 10 strategic breaths, connecting to a positive emotion on the inhale and exhaling a negative emotion or state. Try toggling between imprints — you might experiment with a sense of gratitude in the morning, with courage or perseverance in the afternoon, and with a sense of calm in the evening.

Week 7: Cultivating Resonance Under Fire

Resonance Under Fire Training:

- Select a specific stressor. Choose your favorite resonance breathing tool to manage stress. As you imagine the emotional state of being exposed to your stressor, practice your breathing strategy for 2 minutes. Are you able to elicit resonance? After this, try repeating the practice in the presence of your stressor. How quickly can you achieve resonance while under stress?

Week 8: Imprinting the Physiology of Success

Heart Visualization:

- Identify a specific goal that you wish to achieve in the next month. Tune into your heart — what emotions will fill your heart after you have achieved your goal? Write down the three emotions you will experience following achievement of your desired goal. These are your imprints. After defining your three imprints, take some time to sit with each of them. Explore the energy of the emotion. Your goal is to let your heart come alive with the feelings you envision awaiting you in the future while breathing at your resonance frequency.

Week 9: Using Your Heart Rhythms to Strengthen Your Relationships

Practice estimating your heart rate: How close is your estimate to reality? Now, do jumping jacks or march in place for 30 seconds to increase your heart rate. Sit down and try to estimate your heart rate again, followed by taking your pulse and comparing the numbers. Finally, resume resonance breathing for 2 minutes, and try to estimate your heart rate once more. Can you guess it within 10 beats? Five beats?

If you're working with a partner, try to estimate each other's heart rate. Then practice resonance breathing together, alternating who leads and who follows, twice this week for 20 minutes.

Week 10: Anchoring Yourself in Resonance

Practice the Bubble. First, focus on the feeling of safety and love in your heart as you inhale, and then exhale as normal. As you inhale, focus on anything negative in your body — tension, stress, frustration, anxiety. As you exhale, push that negativity out of your body to the very edges of your Bubble, letting it float into the atmosphere. Repeat once more. Finally, return to the feelings of safety and love in your heart.

YOUR HRV AND
HOMEWORK TRACKING NOTES

Week 1: Finding Your Resonance Frequency

Breathing Exercise #2: Personalize your breathing rate

Spend 2 minutes breathing at each of the following rates. Which rate feels the most comfortable and least effortful? (Circle your answer.)

a. 3.4 seconds to inhale, 5.2 seconds to exhale (7 breaths per minute)
b. 3.7 seconds to inhale, 5.5 seconds to exhale (6.5 breaths per minute)
c. 3.8 seconds to inhale and 5.8 seconds to exhale (6.2 breaths per minute)
d. 4 seconds to inhale, 6 seconds to exhale (6 breaths per minute)
e. 4.2 seconds to inhale and 6.2 seconds to exhale (5.7 breaths per minute)
f. 4.4 seconds to inhale, 6.6 seconds to exhale (5.5 breaths per minute)
g. 4.8 seconds to inhale, 7.2 seconds to exhale (5 breaths per minute)

Reminder: If you don't notice a discernible difference between one rate and the next or find it too difficult to track your breath to a fraction of a second, revert to the standard rate — 4 seconds in, 6 seconds out.

My resonance frequency is: _____ .

If you are opting to utilize HRV instrumentation, use your HRV sensor and the app on your phone and breathe at each of the following rates for 2 minutes while tracking your heart rate. Which of the rates felt the least effortful and produced the greatest heart rate oscillations on your equipment? (Circle your answer.)

   a. 3.4 seconds to inhale, 5.2 seconds to exhale (7 breaths per minute)
   b. 3.7 seconds to inhale, 5.5 seconds to exhale (6.5 breaths per minute)
   c. 3.8 seconds to inhale and 5.8 seconds to exhale (6.2 breaths per minute)
   d. 4 seconds to inhale, 6 seconds to exhale (6 breaths per minute)
   e. 4.2 seconds to inhale and 6.2 seconds to exhale (5.7 breaths per minute)
   f. 4.4 seconds to inhale, 6.6 seconds to exhale (5.5 breaths per minute)
   g. 4.8 seconds to inhale, 7.2 seconds to exhale (5 breaths per minute)

My resonance frequency is: _____ .

According to my _____ device, my HRV is . . .

Day 1 HRV _____

Day 2 HRV _____

Day 3 HRV _____

Day 4 HRV _____

(Remember, these measurements don't have to take place on Days 1, 2, 3, and 4, per se. You just need to make sure you test on the same four days this first week as you will in the subsequent testing weeks, at the same time every day, preferably just after waking. Measure while seated, feet on the floor, back straight but relaxed.)

My mean HRV for week 1 is: _____ .

Setting goals

What do you hope to achieve by completing the Heart, Breath, Mind training? Take some time to write down your goals.

_____

_____

_____

On a scale of 1 (lowest) to 10 (highest), how would you rate your current level of achievement for each goal, prior to picking up this book?

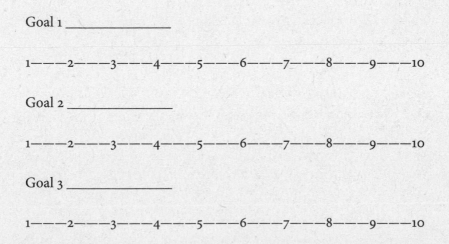

Goal 1 _____

1————2————3————4————5————6————7————8————9————10

Goal 2 _____

1————2————3————4————5————6————7————8————9————10

Goal 3 _____

1————2————3————4————5————6————7————8————9————10

Reflecting on those goals, what do you think might be getting in your way of achieving them?

Try filling in the blanks:

"I want to _____. But when I try, _____ happens."

or

"I wish I could _____, but _____ keeps getting in my way."

Week 2: Using Your Breath to Increase Energy

As you practice your belly breathing this week, do you notice any thoughts distracting you? If so, are you able to simply acknowledge them without engaging with them, and bring yourself back to the movement of your belly?

❑ Yes

❑ No

What are some steps you've been able to take this week to develop a healthy sleep routine?

Week 3: Letting Go of Your Stress and Expanding Your Emotional Range

Identifying your day-to-day stressors

Three reoccurring stressors in my life are:

1. _____

2. _____

3. _____

Please circle the stressor you would like to work on.

Mapping Out your Power 10s

What repeated stressors do you tend to experience in your morning or evening routine, or perhaps at work? Please list them below. These are the ideal times of day for you to plan to implement your Power 10s, in order to reduce your stress for the upcoming week.

1. _____

2. _____

3. _____

Heart Clearing

Use this space to journal about any Heart Clearing you may have experienced.

_____

_____

_____

Week 4: Healing the Broken Parts

Measure and record your HRV four times this week, on the same days as you chose during week 1 (ideally Monday, Wednesday, Friday, and Sunday.)

Measure at the same time every day, preferably just after waking. Measure while sitting upright in bed or in a chair with your back relaxed but straight.

According to my _____ device, my HRV is . . .

Day 1 HRV _____

Day 2 HRV _____

Day 3 HRV _____

Day 4 HRV _____

My mean HRV for week 4 is: _____.

Breathing Exercise #5: Letting go of deeply held triggers and beliefs

Step 1: In a few sentences, describe an experience from your past in which you felt a sense of disappointment, frustration, or anger that lasted for weeks, months, or more:

_____

_____

_____

Step 2: What sensations did you feel in your body during the experiences? For instance, did your heart rate increase, muscles tense, mind race, or body sweat?

_____

_____

_____

Step 3: *(Pacer needed, set to your resonance frequency.)* Practice connecting to the pain on your inhale and directing the stress outside of your body on the exhale.

Breathing Exercise #6: Catching and releasing your ghosts

Track your reactions to stress here for 3 days. Each night, write down as many moments as you can remember of feeling stress throughout the day.

◆ **Day 1**

_____

_____

_____

◆ **Day 2**

_____

_____

_____

◆ **Day 3**

_____

_____

_____

Rank the magnitude of each reaction on a scale of 1 (lowest) to 10 (highest). Go back and jot the number down next to each stressor.

After 3 days, review your data, circling anything you ranked as a 7 or higher — a ghost from your past may be lingering there.

For the rest of the week (the last 4 days), practice recognizing your ghosts as they occur and breathing through them. When you do, practice connecting to the ghost on the inhale, and releasing it on the exhale.

If you own a heart rate monitor such as a Fitbit, Apple Watch, or another heart rate tracker, try looking away from your device (to help mentally detach yourself) and take 5 breaths, feeling the stressor on the inhale and releasing it on the exhale. Now look at your heart rate monitor. Were you able practice decelerating your heart rate by 2 beats or more?

❑ Yes

❑ Not yet

Chasing ghosts with HRV technology

If using an HRV tracking device that provides real time feedback, how many beats are you able to decelerate the heart rate by on the exhale?

_____

Re-evaluating your goals

In Weeks 4, 7, and 10, you will be re-evaluating your goals.

On a scale of 1 (lowest) to 10 (highest), how would you rate your current level of achievement for each goal after completing the fourth week of training?

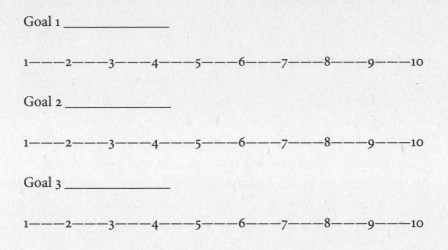

Goal 1 _____

1————2————3————4————5————6————7————8————9————10

Goal 2 _____

1————2————3————4————5————6————7————8————9————10

Goal 3 _____

1————2————3————4————5————6————7————8————9————10

Week 5: Preparing for Challenge

Breathing Exercise #7: Training your heart rhythms

Name a specific performance event or challenge that you have coming up:

_____

Step 1: Clear the heart
Take 5 breaths at your resonance frequency (using your pacer to match your inhale and exhale to your resonance frequency) to release negative emotions from your autonomic nervous system. On the inhale, connect to and experience your negative emotion — stress, anger, frustration, fear.

What does the emotion feel like in your heart? Crushing and heavy? Anxious and fearful? Lonely? Jot down your answer here:

_____

_____

On the exhale, focus on releasing that emotion *from your heart* by exhaling through your mouth and directing it out of your body.

Step 2: Clear the mind

For the second set of 5 breaths, focus on the crisp fresh air on the inhale and the feeling of letting go on the exhale.

Step 3: Shift the heart

Think about what you want to feel like during your performance or challenge and practice experiencing that heart state on the inhale. Do you want to feel excited? Perhaps calm and composed? What physiological state will be most conducive to your peak performance? Jot down your answer here:

_____

Now, during your third set of 5 breaths, connect to your ideal performance state on the inhale and let go of any negative emotions on the exhale. In the absence of any negative emotions, you can also focus on the feeling of letting go on the exhale.

◆ **Dominant resonance symptom**

Your dominant resonance symptom is the feeling or sensation that stands out when you are in resonance.

What is your dominant resonance symptom? _____

Week 6: Mastering the Emotional Pivot

Heart Pivoting

Step 1: Physiological recall

Name three times in your life in which you felt love, gratitude, awe, or a similarly pleasurable physiological sensation in your heart. Write down those memories, or heart imprints, here:

Heart imprint #1 _____

Heart imprint #2 _____

Heart imprint #3 _____

Step 2: Increasing accessibility
Choose one heart imprint to focus on (circle it above.) Begin your resonance breathing, connecting to your chosen imprint on the inhale and releasing stress on the exhale.

Step 3: Bridging the gap
This week, try activating the heart imprint in neutral situations like while riding the train, standing in line for groceries, or waiting on hold on the phone. Are you able to boost your mood by focusing on your heart imprint on the inhale and letting go of stress on the exhale in approximately 10 breaths?

❏ Yes

❏ Not yet

Step 4: Pivoting with the heart
Once you're able to shift from a neutral mood to a positive one, you can try Heart Pivoting from a negative internal state to positive one. As stress occurs, try to connect to your heart imprint on the inhale, and let go of the negative emotion you're experiencing (or a state that isn't helping you to achieve your desired performance) on the exhale. Try to stay nonjudgmental as you do so.

Are you able to boost your mood by focusing on your heart imprint on the inhale and letting go of stress on the exhale in approximately 10 breaths?

❏ Yes

❏ Not yet

Week 7: Cultivating Resonance Under Fire

Measure and record your HRV 4 times this week, on the same days as you chose during weeks 1 and 4. Measure at the same time every day, preferably just after waking. Measure while sitting upright in bed or in a chair with your back relaxed but straight.

According to my _____ device, my HRV is . . .

Day 1 HRV _____

Day 2 HRV _____

Day 3 HRV _____

Day 4 HRV _____

My mean HRV for week 7 is: _____ .

Making stress your friend

Step 1: Create a list of stressors:

Stressor #1 _____

Stressor #2 _____

Stressor #3 _____

Stressor #4 _____

Stressor #5 _____

Choose one stressor to focus on (circle it above.)

Step 2: Choose your most empowering breathing tool for managing stress. Options include (circle your favorite):

- Quieting the mind by focusing on the inhale and exhale (or, alternatively, counting the seconds of your inhale and exhale). (Weeks 1 and 2)
- Breathing away your stress by feeling the stressor on the inhale and letting it go on the exhale. (Week 3)
- Connect to the physiological sensation that accompanies your ghost (past pain) on the inhale and release it on the exhale. (Week 4)
- Preparing for stress in advance by practicing the Heart Shift, which involves 15 consecutive breaths to communicate to your heart how you want to respond in the moment. (Week 5)
- Improving your HRV by pairing positive emotions on the inhale with exhaling negative emotions away. (Week 6)

Step 3: Rank your current level of stress on a scale of 1 to 10, with 1 being the lowest and 10 the highest.

1————2————3————4————5————6————7————8————9————10

Imaginal exposure

Spend 2 minutes imagining or discussing the emotional impact of your chosen stressor.

Next, practice your preferred breathing method for 3 minutes. Check in with yourself. Are you in resonance?

❏ Yes

❏ Not yet

Rate your current stress level on a scale of 1 to 10, with 1 being the lowest and 10 the highest.

1———2———3———4———5———6———7———8———9———10

Were you able to reduce your stress response by at least 2 integers within 10 breaths?

❑ Yes

❑ Not yet

In vivo exposure

View, listen, or otherwise expose yourself to your chosen stressor for 2 minutes. As you continue to be exposed to the stressor, practice your preferred form of breathing. Check in with yourself. Are you in resonance?

❑ Yes

❑ Not yet

Rate your current stress level. Were you able to reduce your stress level?

❑ Yes

❑ Not yet

Re-evaluating your goals

On a scale of 1 (lowest) to 10 (highest), how would you rate your current level of achievement for each goal after completing the seventh week of training?

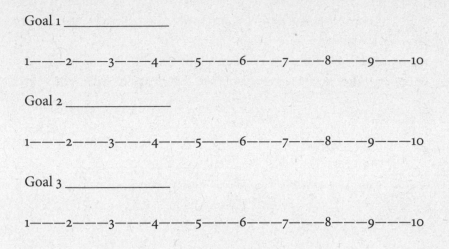

Goal 1 _____

1———2———3———4———5———6———7———8———9———10

Goal 2 _____

1———2———3———4———5———6———7———8———9———10

Goal 3 _____

1———2———3———4———5———6———7———8———9———10

Week 8: Imprinting the Physiology of Success

Breathing Exercise #8: Imprinting the physiology of success

Step 1: Name a specific goal that you wish to achieve in the next month.

_____

_____

_____

Step 2: Next, try to switch off your outcome-focused brain and tune into your heart. Dive deep. What emotions will flood your heart after you have achieved your goal? What do you feel? Write down the three emotions you will experience following the achievement of your desired goal. These are your imprints.

_____

_____

_____

Step 3: Take some time to sit with each of these imprints. One at a time, allow each emotion to just sit there in your heart like an actual person pulling up a chair to the dinner table. Explore the energy of the emotion and get to know it. Note how it feels to sit next to this emotion and just be with it.

Imprint #1 _____

Imprint #2 _____

Imprint #3 _____

Create a resonance playlist

Songs that make me feel alive and in resonance include:

_____

_____

_____

Week 9: Using your Heart Rhythms to Strengthen Your Relationships

Breathing Exercise #9: Estimating your heart rate

Step 1: Sitting quietly, set a timer for 30 seconds and, breathing normally (not at resonance frequency), try to count the number of times your heart beats. Don't feel your pulse; try to dial into your heart and see if you can guess it. After the timer goes off, double the number and write it down; this is your estimated heart rate.

My estimated heart rate is _____ beats per minute.

Step 2: Take your pulse by counting the number of beats in your neck or wrist for 30 seconds and doubling it. How close was your estimate to reality?

My actual heart rate is _____ beats per minute.

Step 3: For 30 seconds, do jumping jacks, march in place, or some other physical activity that elevates your heart rate.

Step 4: Sit down again and try to estimate your heart rate again, using only your 30-second timer and your interoceptive abilities. Double the number and write it down.

My estimated heart rate is _____ beats per minute.

Then take your pulse and compare the numbers.

My actual heart rate is _____ beats per minute.

Step 5: Initiate resonance breathing for 2 minutes. Now, try to estimate your heart rate once more.

My estimated heart rate is _____ beats per minute.

Then take your pulse and compare the numbers.

My actual heart rate is _____ beats per minute.

Can you guess it within 10 beats? Five beats?

I came within _____ beats per minute.

Step 6: Practice estimating your heart rate while standing in line at the store, while waiting on hold for an important phone call, or in traffic.

Breathing Exercise #10: Estimating another person's heart rate

Step 1: Sit down side by side with your partner. Try to estimate your partner's heart rate. It may help to hold hands or have part of your bodies touching; physical touch helps to increase the synchronization of heart rates. Write down your estimate.

I estimate that my partner's heart rate is _____ beats per minute.

Step 2: Have your partner measure his or her heart rate.

My partner's actual heart rate is _____ beats per minute.

How close were you to accurately predicting your partner's heart rate?

I came within _____ beats per minute.

Step 3: Ask your partner to leave the room and either a) do jumping jacks or march in place for 10 seconds to increase heart rate or b) perform deep breathing to slow heart rate. Because your partner is in another room, you will not be able to see if they have chosen to accelerate or decelerate.

Step 4: Have your partner rejoin you. Try to estimate his or her heart rate again, using only your 30-second timer and your interoceptive abilities.

I estimate that my partner's heart rate is _____ beats per minute.

Step 5: Ask your partner to commence with resonance breathing for 2 minutes. Now, try to estimate his or her heart rate once more.

I estimate that my partner's heart rate is _____ beats per minute.

Have your partner measure his or her heart rate.

My partner's actual heart rate is _____ beats per minute.

Were you able to you guess it within 10 beats? Five beats?

I came within _____ beats per minute.

Week 10: Anchoring Yourself in Resonance

Measure and record your HRV four times this week, on the same days as you chose during weeks 1, 4, and 7. Measure at the same time every day, preferably just after waking. Measure sitting upright in bed or in a chair with your back relaxed but straight.

According to my _____ device, my HRV is . . .

Day 1 HRV _____

Day 2 HRV _____

Day 3 HRV _____

Day 4 HRV _____

My mean HRV for week 10 is: _____ .

Resonance detractors

My resonance detractors are:

_____

_____

_____

Re-evaluating your goals

On a scale of 1 (lowest) to 10 (highest), how would you rate your current level of achievement for each goal after completing the tenth week of training?

Goal 1 _____

1————2————3————4————5————6————7————8————9————10

Goal 2 _____

1————2————3————4————5————6————7————8————9————10

Goal 3 _____

1————2————3————4————5————6————7————8————9————10

ACKNOWLEDGMENTS

My clients have taught me the multiple applications and benefits of resonance. I'm deeply appreciative to them for trusting me with their health and performance and also for teaching me about the vast applications of this process for health, performance, and physical optimization.

This book came to fruition through the support and insights of many. First and foremost, I'd like to thank my agent, Laura Nolan; my editor, Deb Brody; and the talented team at Houghton Mifflin Harcourt. I am grateful for your support, insights, and guidance throughout the development process. To Leslie Goldman, my writing partner, I have been inspired by your hard work, dedication, and enthusiasm every step of this journey. Thank you for being my teammate and a warrior of the heart and mind. My deepest appreciation to Dr. Jill Blakeway, a gifted healer and the founder of the Yinova Clinic, for helping me fulfill my dreams of sharing resonance with the world.

I am grateful to my biofeedback mentors and colleagues who have graciously extended their time, clinical acumen, biofeedback expertise, and friendship with me. To Drs. Paul Lehrer, Evgeny Vaschillo, and Bronya Vaschillo, I am profoundly appreciative for having had the opportunity to be trained by you. Your inspiration and support changed the course of my career and life and served as the foundation for my love for resonant frequency biofeedback. To Dr. Sue Wilson, thank you for your humor, your phenomenal insight and expertise, and most of all your infinite support. You are part of my biofeedback family. To Dr. Donald Moss, thank you for helping me to develop my voice as an author in the field of biofeedback and encouraging me to write. To Drs. Rob Pandina and Marsha Bates, thank you for giving me the opportunity to pursue my research and application of biofeedback with athletes.

Similar to raising a child, I believe that the love for a craft is reared and cultivated by a community. In this sense, I have grown professionally through the inspiration of two specific biofeedback communities, the Biofeedback Foundation of Europe and the Association for the Advancement of Applied Physiology and Biofeedback. Drs. Erik Peper and Monika Fuhs, thank you for sharing your time and passion for biofeedback with me and for promoting the education of biofeedback around the world. To my colleagues at Thought Technology LTD, thank you for your support of my work and continual creative collaborations. Thank you to Larry Klein for your infinite passion for biofeedback and friendship, as well as to Hal Myers and Carole Klein for your guidance and enthusiasm for my work over the years. I feel deeply honored to work with gifted researchers and clinicians, many of whom I consider teammates and friends at the Association for Applied Psychophysiology and Biofeedback: Michelle Cunningham, Dr. Ethan Benore, Dr. Inna Khazan, Dr. Fred Schaffer, Dr. Patrick Steffen, Dr. Mari Swingle, Dr. Angelika Sadar, Dr. Brad Lichenstein, Dr. Dennis Romig, Christina Brown-Bochicchio, and Andrew VanWasshnova. To my colleagues in the biofeedback community—Dr. Tim Herzog, Dr. Ben Strack, Dr. Michael Linden, Dr. Steve Baskin, Dr. Lindsay Shaw, Dr. Shilagh Mirgrain, Dr. Richard Harvey, and Dr. Bob Whitehouse — thank you for collaboration, friendship, and enthusiasm for biofeedback. I am grateful to a community of additional colleagues in New York, including Adam Robinson, Andrew Zimmermann, Dr. Dennis Goodman, Dr. Larry Thomas, Joenine Roberts, Wendy Cassidy, and Dr. Sherry Wulkan for their creative contributions and insights to my work. Thank you to Josh Waitzkin for your energy and inspirations throughout the years.

In addition, I feel deep gratitude for the team members and colleagues at my practice in Manhattan. Thank you to Andrew Sether and Andrea Rydel for your support and practice of biofeedback over the years. Diana Bednarek, my executive assistant, I am grateful for your invaluable feedback on this book and for keeping me focused on a day-to-day basis.

Most important, thank you to my husband, Keith, for your love and support. This book wouldn't have been possible without you.

NOTES

PREFACE

PAGE

3 *Most people are under:* Fred Shaffer, Rollin McCraty, and Christopher L. Zerr, "A Healthy Heart Is Not a Metronome: An Integrative Review of The Heart's Anatomy and Heart Rate Variability," *Frontiers in Psychology* 5 (2014): 1040, doi: 10.3389/fpsyg.2014.01040.

5 *This is the branch:* Leah M. Lagos, "A Manual for Implementing Heart Rate Variability Biofeedback with Collegiate Athletes" (PhD diss., Rutgers, The State University of New Jersey, 2009), https://rucore.libraries.rutgers.edu/rutgers-lib/28473/PDF/1/play/.

In 2018, the most: Cosette Jarrett, conversation with the author, April 17, 2019.

The American Institute: The American Institute of Stress, "Stress Research," https://www.stress.org/stress-research.

7 *In doing so, the Vaschillos:* Paul M. Lehrer, Evgeny Vaschillo, and Bronya Vaschillo, "Resonance Frequency Biofeedback Training to Increase Cardiac Variability: Rationale and Manual for Training," *Applied Psychophysiology and Biofeedback* 25, no. 3 (2000): 177–91, doi: 10.1023/A:1009554825745.

1. THE IMPORTANCE OF TRAINING YOUR HEART

14 *a body in rest-and-digest mode:* Rollin McCraty, "Heart-Brain Neurodynamics: The Making of Emotion," *The Neuropsychotherapist* 6 (2003): 68–89, doi: 10.12744/tnpt(6)068-089.

19 *communication between the brain:* HeartMath Institute, "Heart-Brain Communication," https://www.heartmath.org/research/science-of-the-heart/heart-brain-communication.

   Vagus is: Rice University, "Vagus Nerve," https://www.caam.rice.edu/~cox/wrap/vagusnerve.pdf.

   The vagus nerve: Sigrid Breit et al., "Vagus Nerve as Modulator of the Brain–Gut Axis in Psychiatric and Inflammatory Disorders," *Frontiers in Psychiatry* 9, no. 44 (2018), doi: 10.3389/fpsyt.2018.00044.

2. BUILDING A LIFE OF RESONANCE

24 *6 breaths per minute:* Leah Lagos et al., "Heart Rate Variability Biofeedback as a Strategy for Dealing with Competitive Anxiety: A Case Study," *Biofeedback* 36, no. 3 (2008); 109–15, https://www.drleahlagos.com/docs/biof_heart_rate-1-Dr.%20Lagos.pdf.

   subjects were divided: Patrick R. Steffen et al., "The Impact of Resonance Frequency Breathing on Measures of Heart Rate Variability, Blood Pressure, and Mood," *Frontiers in Public Health* 5 (2017): 222, doi: 10.3389/fpubh.2017.00222.

25 *successfully been used:* Richard Gevirtz, "The Promise of Heart Rate Variability Biofeedback: Evidence-Based Applications," *Biofeedback* 41, no. 3 (2013): 110–20, doi: 10.5298/1081-5937-41.3.01.

   In an Italian study: Luciano Bernardi et al., "Effect of Rosary Prayer and Yoga Mantras on Autonomic Cardiovascular Rhythms: Comparative Study," *British Medical Journal* 323, no. 7327 (2001): 1446–49, doi: 10.1136/bmj.323.7327.1446.

26 *Stamina increases:* Lagos et al., "Heart Rate Variability Biofeedback as a Strategy for Dealing with Competitive Anxiety."

   The depth and rate: M. Mather and J. Thayer, "How Heart Rate Variability Affects Emotion Regulation Brain Networks," *Current Opinion in Behavioral Sciences* 19 (2018): 98–104, doi: 10.1016/j.cobeha.2017.12.017.

3. HOW TO USE THIS BOOK

34 *low HRV in general:* Lagos et al., "Heart Rate Variability Biofeedback as a Strategy for Dealing with Competitive Anxiety."

39 *Rick Harvey, PhD:* Rick Harvey, conversation with the author, August 17, 2019.

41 *with regular practice:* Jim Lagopoulos et al., "Increased Theta and Alpha EEG Activity During Nondirective Meditation," *Journal of Alternative and Complementary Medicine* 15, no. 11 (2009): 1187–92, doi: 10.1089/acm.2009.0113.

4. WEEK 1: FINDING YOUR RESONANCE FREQUENCY

53 *the most accurate reflection:* Elite HRV, "What Are HRV Score, RMSSD, ln(RMSSD), SDNN, NN50, and PNN50?" https://elitehrv.com/hbm-about-hrv-scores.

55 *when college-age:* Erik Peper et al., "How Posture Affects Memory Recall and Mood," *Biofeedback* 45, no. 2 (2017): 36–41, doi: 10.5298/1081-5937-45.2.01.

62 *strong predictor of health:* Donald Moss and Fredric Shaffer, "The Application of Heart Rate Variability Biofeedback to Medical and Mental Health Disorders," *Biofeedback* 45, no. 1 (2017): 2–8, doi: 10.5298/1081-5937-45.1.03.

HRV was deemed a better predictor: Hisako Tsuji et al., "Impact of Reduced Heart Rate Variability on Risk for Cardiac Events: The Framingham Heart Study," *Circulation* 94 (1996): 2850–55, doi: 10.1161/01.cir.94.11.2850.

High blood pressure (also called hypertension): American Heart Association, "How to Help Prevent Heart Disease at Any Age," last modified April 1, 2015, https://www.heart.org/en/healthy-living/healthy-lifestyle/how-to-help-prevent-heart-disease-at-any-age.

Up to 30 percent: Stanley S. Franklin et al., "White-Coat Hypertension: New Insights from Recent Studies," *Hypertension* 62 (2013): 982–87, doi: 10.1161/HYPERTENSIONAHA.113.01275.

A study in the aptly named: Marion Tomičić et al., "Deep Breathing: A Simple Test for White Coat Effect Detection in Primary Care," *Blood Pressure* 24, no. 3 (2015): 158–63, doi: 10.3109/08037051.2014.997102.

5. WEEK 2: USING YOUR BREATH TO INCREASE ENERGY

65 *The average person takes:* Ann Brown, "How Many Breaths Do You Take Each Day?," The EPA Blog, posted April 28, 2014, https://blog.epa.gov/2014/04/28/how-many-breaths-do-you-take-each-day/.

Relentless stress: Mather and Thayer, "How Heart Rate Variability Affects Emotion Regulation Brain Networks."

66 *No baby around:* Erik Peper, "Breathing Reduces Acid Reflux and Dysmenorrhea Discomfort," The Peper Perspective, posted October 4, 2018, https://peperperspective.com/2018/10/04/breathing-reduces-acid-reflux-and-dysmenorrhea-discomfort/.

68 *Exhaling too quickly:* Inna Khazan and Fred Shaffer, "Practical Strategies for Teaching Your Clients to Breathe," lecture, 2018, slide 7, https://www.aapb.org/files/public/2018/AnnMtg/Handouts/BOS29_Khazan_Shaffer.pdf.

This is called overbreathing: Ibid.

71 *It was written:* Herbert Benson with Miriam Z. Klipper, *The Relaxation Response,* updated and expanded ed. (New York: HarperCollins, 2001): xii.

Dr. Benson's book: Ibid., xxii.

76 *Dr. Peper and another:* Erik Peper and Merrie MacHose, "Symptom Prescription:

Inducing Anxiety by 70% Exhalation," *Biofeedback and Self-Regulation* 18, no. 3 (1993): 133–39, doi: 10.1007/bf00999790.

Researchers at the University of Salzburg: Gabriela G. Werner et al., "High Cardiac Vagal Control Is Related to Better Subjective and Objective Sleep Quality," *Biological Psychology* 106 (2015): 79–85, doi: 10.1016/j.biopsycho.2015.02.004.

77 *Compared with people:* Jiawei Yin et al., "Relationship of Sleep Duration with All-Cause Mortality and Cardiovascular Events: A Systematic Review and Dose-Response Meta-Analysis of Prospective Cohort Studies," *Journal of the American Heart Association* 6, no. 9 (2017), doi: 10.1161/JAHA.117.005947.

Just one night: Caroline Doyle et al., "Associations Between Objective Sleep and Ambulatory Blood Pressure in a Community Sample," *Psychosomatic Medicine* 81, no. 6 (2019): 545–56, doi: 10.1097/psy.0000000000000711.

hospitals reported: Amneet Sandhu, Milan Seth, and Hitinder S. Gurm, "Daylight Savings Time and Myocardial Infarction," *Open Heart* 1, no. 1 (2014), doi: 10.1136/openhrt-2013-000019.

such as C-reactive protein: Michael A. Grandner et al., "Extreme Sleep Durations and Increased C-Reactive Protein: Effects of Sex and Ethnoracial Group," *Sleep* 36, no. 5 (2013): 769–79, doi: 10.5665/sleep.2646.

and testosterone: Rachel Leproult and Eve Van Cauter, "Effect of 1 Week of Sleep Restriction on Testosterone Levels in Young Healthy Men," *JAMA* 305, no. 21 (2011): 2173–74, doi: 10.1001/jama.2011.710.

78 *Keep your thermostat:* The National Sleep Foundation, "The Ideal Temperature for Sleep," https://sleep.org/articles/temperature-for-sleep/.

79 *That's because caffeine:* The National Sleep Foundation, "How Caffeine Works," https://www.sleep.org/articles/what-does-caffeine-do-2/.

Large amounts of caffeine: Rackel Aguiar Mendes de Oliveira et al., "Coffee Consumption and Heart Rate Variability: The Brazilian Longitudinal Study of Adult Health (ELSA-Brasil) Cohort Study," *Nutrients* 9, no. 7 (2017): 741, doi: 10.3390/nu9070741.

Magnesium is a mineral: Wilhelm Jahnen-Dechent and Markus Ketteler, "Magnesium Basics," *Clinical Kidney Journal* 5, Suppl. 1 (2012): i3–i14, doi: 10.1093/ndtplus/sfr163.

Melatonin is a hormone: The National Sleep Foundation, "What Is Melatonin?," https://www.sleep.org/articles/melatonin/.

81 *Research out of the Medical University:* Waleed O. Twal, Amy E. Wahlquist, and Sundaravadivel Balasubramanian, "Yogic Breathing When Compared to Attention Control Reduces the Levels of Pro-inflammatory Biomarkers in Saliva: A Pilot Randomized Controlled Trial," *BMC Complementary and Alternative Medicine* 16 (2016): 294, doi: 10.1186/s12906-016-1286-7; Sundaravadivel Balasubramanian, Jacobo E. Mintzer, and Amy E. Wahlquist, "Induction of Salivary Nerve Growth Factor by Yogic Breathing: A Randomized Controlled Trial," *International Psychogeriatrics* 27, no. 1 (2015): 168–70, doi: 10.1017/S1041610214001616.

Salivary NGF has potent: Karl Schenck et al., "The Role of Nerve Growth Factor (NGF) and Its Precursor Forms in Oral Wound Healing," *International Journal of Molecular Sciences* 18, no. 2 (2017): 386, doi: 10.3390/ijms18020386.

It also gets shuttled: Alessandra Berry, Erika Bindocci, and Enrico Alleva, "NGF, Brain and Behavioral Plasticity," *Neural Plasticity* 2012, doi: 10.1155/2012/784040.

Researchers at the Trinity College: Michael Christopher Melnychuk et al., "Coupling of Respiration and Attention via the Locus Coeruleus: Effects of Meditation and Pranayama," *Psychophysiology* 55, no. 9 (2018), doi: 10.1111/psyp.13091.

82 *This discovery is:* Sara Lazar, conversation with the author, July 29, 2019.

The most common GI disorder: Maria Henström et al., "Functional Variants in the Sucrase–Isomaltase Gene Associate with Increased Risk of Irritable Bowel Syndrome," *Gut* 67, no. 2 (2018): 263–70, doi: 10.1136/gutjnl-2016-312456.

Nearly all people: Erik Peper, Lauren Mason, and Cindy Huey, "Healing Irritable Bowel Syndrome with Diaphragmatic Breathing," The Peper Perspective, posted June 23, 2017, https://peperperspective.com/2017/06/23/healing-irritable-bowel-syndrome-with-diaphragmatic-breathing/.

Chest breathing is: Michigan Medicine, "Diaphragmatic Breathing for GI Patients," https://www.uofmhealth.org/conditions-treatments/diaphragmatic-breathing-gi-patients.

A case report: Erik Peper, Lauren Mason, and Cindy Huey, "Healing Irritable Bowel Syndrome with Diaphragmatic Breathing," *Biofeedback* 45, no. 4 (2017): 83–87, doi: 10.5298/1081-5937-45.4.04.

6. WEEK 3: LETTING GO OF YOUR STRESS AND EXPANDING YOUR EMOTIONAL RANGE

100 *healthy, young, active women:* Nina S. Stachenfeld et al., "Water Intake Reverses Dehydration Associated Impaired Executive Function in Healthy Young Women," *Physiology & Behavior* 185, no. 1 (2018): 103–11, doi: 10.1016/j.physbeh.2017.12.028.

7. WEEK 4: HEALING THE BROKEN PARTS

103 *"the deer are alert":* Peter A. Levine, *Waking the Tiger: Healing Trauma* (Berkeley, CA: North Atlantic Books, 1997), 97.

104 *In the 1990s, psychophysiologist:* Home of Dr. Stephen Porges, "Innovation Timeline," https://www.stephenporges.com/timeline.

105 *Levine explains:* Levine, *Waking the Tiger,* 100.

116 *mindful breathing technique called urge surfing:* Sarah Bowen and Alan Marlatt, "Surfing the Urge: Brief Mindfulness-Based Intervention for College Student Smokers," *Psychology of Addictive Behaviors* 23, no. 4 (2009): 666–71, doi: 10.1037/a0017127.

9. WEEK 6: MASTERING THE EMOTIONAL PIVOT

132 *Ultramarathoner Courtney Dauwalter:* Courtney Dauwalter, conversation with the author, August 13, 2019.

133 *Such a skill set:* Jaclyn M. Stoffel and Jeff Cain, "Review of Grit and Resilience Literature within Health Professions Education," *American Journal of Pharmaceutical Education* 82, no. 2 (2018): 6150, doi: 10.5688/ajpe6150/.
This capacity to: Ibid.
Psychological resilience: HeartMath Institute, "Resilience, Stress and Emotions," https://www.heartmath.org/research/science-of-the-heart/resilience-stress-and-emotions/.
It sounds implausible: Sarah D. Pressman, Matthew W. Gallagher, and Shane J. Lopez, "Is the Emotion-Health Connection a 'First-World Problem'?," *Psychological Science* 24, no. 4 (2013): 544–49, doi: 10.1177/0956797612457382.
Research tells us: Michele M. Tugade and Barbara L. Fredrickson, "Resilient Individuals Use Positive Emotions to Bounce Back from Negative Emotional Experiences," *Journal of Personality Social Psychology* 86 (2004): 320–33, doi: 10.1037/0022-3514.86.2.320.

138 *demonstrated this beautifully:* Bethany E. Kok and Barbara L. Fredrickson, "Upward Spirals of the Heart: Autonomic Flexibility, as Indexed by Vagal Tone, Reciprocally and Prospectively Predicts Positive Emotions and Social Connectedness," *Biological Psychology* 85, no. 3 (2010): 432–36, doi: 10.1016/j.biopsycho.2010.09.005.

142 *HRV plays a role:* Christopher P. Fagundes et al., "Spousal Bereavement Is Associated with More Pronounced Ex Vivo Cytokine Production and Lower Heart Rate Variability: Mechanisms Underlying Cardiovascular Risk?," *Psychoneuroendocrinology* 93 (July 2018): 65–71, doi: 10.1016/j.psyneuen.2018.04.010.

143 *A dysregulated autonomic:* Minxuan Huang et al., "Association of Depressive Symptoms and Heart Rate Variability in Vietnam War–Era Twins: A Longitudinal Twin Difference Study," *JAMA Psychiatry* 75, no. 7 (2018): 705–12, doi: 10.1001/jamapsychiatry.2018.0747.
New research published: Ibid.
Additionally, recent neurocardiology: HeartMath Institute, "Heart-Brain Communication."
at least one episode: National Institute of Mental Health, "Major Depression," https://www.nimh.nih.gov/health/statistics/major-depression.shtml.
millions more live: Harvard Health Publishing, "Six Common Depression Types," https://www.health.harvard.edu/mind-and-mood/six-common-depression-types

10. WEEK 7: CULTIVATING RESONANCE UNDER FIRE

145 *As blood is shunted:* Judith P. Andersen and Harri Gustafsberg, "A Training

Method to Improve Police Use of Force Decision Making: A Randomized Controlled Trial," *SAGE Open* 6, no. 2 (2016): 1–13, doi: 10.1177/2158244016638708.
This does not bode well: Ibid.
nor does it facilitate: Brian R. Johnson, *Crucial Elements of Police Firearm Training* (Flushing, NY: Looseleaf Law Publications, Inc., 2008).
With so much blood: Andersen and Gustafsberg, "A Training Method to Improve Police Use of Force Decision Making."

146   *Compounding matters:* Ibid.
the SET included: Ibid.

147   *officers appearing capable:* Ibid. Also confirmed in conversation with Judith Andersen, on April 22, 2018.

149   *Stanford psychologist:* Kelly McGonigal, "How to Make Stress Your Friend," TEDGlobal video, June 2013, https://www.ted.com/talks/kelly_mcgonigal_how_to_make_stress_your_friend?language=en.
Stress, McGonigal says: Clifton B. Parker, "Embracing Stress Is More Important than Reducing Stress, Stanford Psychologist Says," *Stanford News,* May 7, 2015, https://news.stanford.edu/2015/05/07/stress-embrace-mcgonigal-050715/.
This sort of mentality: Ibid.
But when people find: Ibid.
Put another way: Ibid.

156   *Make sure to give yourself:* National Sleep Foundation, "Does Your Body Temperature Change While You Sleep?" https://www.sleep.org/articles/does-your-body-temperature-change-while-you-sleep/.

159   *middle-of-the-night awakenings:* M. Moline et al., "Impact of Middle-of-the-Night Awakenings on Health Status, Activity Impairment, and Costs," *Nature and Science of Sleep* 6 (2014): 101–11, doi: 10.2147/NSS.S66696.

160   *Between 7 and 9 percent:* Amit Shah and Viola Vaccarino, "Heart Rate Variability in the Prediction of Risk for Posttraumatic Stress Disorder," *JAMA Psychiatry* 72, no. 10 (2015): 964–65, doi:10.1001/jamapsychiatry.2015.1394.
The numbers are even higher: Ibid.
What renders those: National Alliance on Mental Illness, "Posttraumatic Stress Disorder," last reviewed December 2017, https://www.nami.org/learn-more/mental-health-conditions/posttraumatic-stress-disorder.

161   *Science's ability to predict:* Shah and Vaccarino, "Heart Rate Variability in the Prediction of Risk for Posttraumatic Stress Disorder."
US government is actively: Paul Dennis, Lana Watkins, Patrick Calhoun, et al, "Posttraumatic Stress, Heart Rate Variability, and the Mediating Role of Behavioral Health Risks," *Psychosomatic Medicine* 76, no. 8 (2014):629–37. doi: 10.1097/PSY.0000000000000110; U.S. Department of Veterans Affairs, "What the Heart Can Tell Us About the Mind: Heart Rate Variability and PTSD," *VA Research Currents,* August 26, 2014, https://www.research.va.gov/currents/summer2014/summer2014-25.cfm.

system dysregulation is considered: Shah and Vaccarino, "Heart Rate Variability in the Prediction of Risk for Posttraumatic Stress Disorder."

As the official: Military Health System, "People with PTSD May Have Overactive 'Fight or Flight' Response."

Newer research suggests: Amit J. Shah et al., "Posttraumatic Stress Disorder and Impaired Autonomic Modulation in Male Twins," *Biological Psychiatry* 73, no. 11 (2013): 1103–10, doi: 10.1016/j.biopsych.2013.01.019; Arpi Minassian et al., "Association of Predeployment Heart Rate Variability with Risk of Postdeployment Posttraumatic Stress Disorder in Active-Duty Marines," *JAMA Psychiatry* 72, no. 10 (2015): 979–86, doi: 10.1001/jamapsychiatry.2015 .0922.

11. WEEK 8: IMPRINTING THE PHYSIOLOGY OF SUCCESS

162 *When the casts:* Brian Clark, conversation with the author, April 24, 2019.

163 *After the 1984 Olympics:* Thomas Newmark, "Cases in Visualization for Improved Athletic Performance," *Psychiatric Annals* 42, no. 10 (2012): 385–87, doi: 10.3928/00485713-20121003-07.

improved speed: Marc S. J. Boschker, Frank C. Bakker, and B. Rietberg, "Retroactive Interference Effects of Mentally Imagined Movement Speed," *Journal of Sports Sciences* 18, no. 8 (2000): 593–603, doi: 10.1080/02640410050082305.

greater pass accuracy: M. Afrouzeh et al., "Effectiveness of PETTLEP Imager on Performance of Passing Skill in Volleyball," *Journal of Sports Medicine and Physical Fitness* 55, nos. 1-2 (2015): 30–36, https://www.minervamedica.it/en/jour nals/sports-med-physical-fitness/article.php?cod=R40Y2015N01A0030#.

clear the bar: C. J. Olsson, B. Jonsson, and L. Nyberg, "Internal Imagery Training in Active High Jumpers," *Scandinavian Journal of Psychology* 49, no. 2 (2008): 133–40, doi: 10.1111/j.1467-9450.2008.00625.x.

A prevailing theory: Tracy C. Ekeocha, "The Effects of Visualization & Guided Imagery in Sports Performance," master's thesis, Texas State University (2015), https://digital.library.txstate.edu/bitstream/handle/10877/5548/EKEOCHA-THESIS-2015.pdf?sequence=1.

athletes with visual impairments: Kate A. T. Eddy and Stephen D Mellalieu, "Mental Imagery in Athletes with Visual Impairments," *Human Kinetics Journal* 20, no. 4 (2003), doi: 10.1123/apaq.20.4.347.

169 *Dr. Paul Lehrer studied:* Paul Lehrer, Yuki Sasaki, and Yoshihiro Saito, "Zazen and Cardiac Variability," *Psychosomatic Medicine* 61, no. 6 (1999): 812–21, doi: 10.1097/00006842-199911000-00014.

170 *Enjoyable music:* Hayley Jarvis, "Brainwaves Show How Exercising to Music Bends Your Mind," Brunel University London, February 19, 2018, http://www.bru nel.ac.uk/news-and-events/news/articles/Brainwaves-show-how-exercising-to-music-bends-your-mind.

171 *Researchers have postulated:* Noboru Kobayashi, "The Soothing Effect of the

Mother's Heart–Part 2," Child Research Net (2003), https://www.childresearch. net/aboutCS/mediscience/24.html.

In fact, we know: Ibid.

172   *The phenomenon of:* Rongjun Yu, "Choking Under Pressure: The Neuropsychological Mechanisms of Incentive-Induced Performance Decrements," *Frontiers in Behavioral Neuroscience* 9, no. 19 (2015), doi: 10.3389/ fnbeh.2015.00019.

One widely held: Sylvain Laborde, Philip Furley, and Caroline Schempp, "The Relationship Between Working Memory, Reinvestment, and Heart Rate Variability," *Physiology & Behavior* 139 (2015): 430–36, doi: 10.1016/j.phys-beh.2014.11.036.

Working memory plays: Child Mind Institute, "What Is Working Memory?," https://childmind.org/article/what-is-working-memory/.

Neurovisceral theory suggests: Sylvain Laborde, Philip Furley, and Caroline Schempp, "The Relationship Between Working Memory, Reinvestment, and Heart Rate Variability"; Ryan J. Giuliano, "Parasympathetic and Sympathetic Activity Are Associated with Individual Differences in Neural Indices of Selective Attention in Adults," *Psychophysiology* 55, no. 8 (2018), doi.org/10.1101/173377.

173   *An entrepreneur about to:* Rongjun Yu, "Choking Under Pressure."

baseline HRV level predicted: Ibid.

12. WEEK 9: USING YOUR HEART RHYTHMS TO STRENGTHEN YOUR RELATIONSHIPS

175   *Friends and strangers:* Ari Z. Zivotofsky and Jeffrey M. Hausdorff, "The Sensory Feedback Mechanisms Enabling Couples to Walk Synchronously: An Initial Investigation," *Journal of NeuroEngineering and Rehabilitation* 4, no. 28 (2007), doi: 10.1186/1743-0003-4-28.

We often yawn: Beverley J. Brown et al., "A Neural Basis for Contagious Yawning," *Current Biology* 27, no. 17 (2017), doi: 10.1016/j.cub.2017.07.062.

When two people in love: Karen Nikos-Rose, "Lovers' Hearts Beat in Sync, UC Davis Study Says," US Davis, February 8, 2013, https://www.ucdavis.edu/news/lov ers-hearts-beat-sync-uc-davis-study-says/.

Being touched by: Pavel Goldstein, Irit Weissman-Fogel, and Simone G. Shamay-Tsoory, "The Role of Touch in Regulating Inter-Partner Physiological Coupling During Empathy for Pain," *Scientific Reports* 7, no. 1 (2017): 3252, doi: 10.1038/ s41598-017-03627-7.

176   *As two people sleep:* Heenam Yoon et al., "Human Heart Rhythms Synchronize While Co-Sleeping," *Frontiers in Physiology* 10 (March 11, 2019), doi: 10.3389/ fphys.2019.00190.

When a mother gazes: Ruth Feldman et al., "Mother and Infant Coordinate Heart Rhythms Through Episodes of Interaction Synchrony," *Infant Behavior and Development* 34, no. 4 (2011): 569–77, doi: 10.1016/j.infbeh.2011.06.008.

177 *subjects who had strong:* "Listening to Your Heart May Help You Read Minds," Anglia Ruskin University, May 2, 2017, https://www.anglia.ac.uk/news/listening-to-your-heart-may-help-you-read-minds.

178 *interoceptive ability predicted:* Narayanan Kandasamy et al., "Interoceptive Ability Predicts Survival on a London Trading Floor," *Scientific Reports* 6, 32986 (2016), doi: 10.1038/srep32986.
   "that subtle physiological changes": Ibid.

179 *It's not just random:* Rollin McCraty et al., "The Coherent Heart: Heart–Brain Interactions, Psychophysiological Coherence, and the Emergence of System-Wide Order," *Integral Review* 5, no. 2 (2009), https://integral-review.org/issues/vol_5_no_2_mccraty_et_al_the_coherent_heart.pdf.
   EKGs work by: Alan Watkins, *Coherence: The Secret Science of Brilliant Leadership* (London: Kogan Page, 2014), 42.

182 *In the heart of downtown:* The Gottman Institute, "Inside the Family Research Lab, a.k.a. 'The Love Lab,'" video, 4:46, https://www.gottman.com/love-lab/.

183 *They may even sit:* Ibid.
   Thanks to the rich: Zach Brittle, "Manage Conflict—Part 4," The Gottman Institute, June 4, 2015, https://www.gottman.com/blog/manage-conflict-part-4/.
   heart rate rises above 100: Ibid.
   that same area of the brain: John Grey, "How to Repair the Little Things So They Don't Become Big Things," The Gottman Institute, August 30, 2017, https://www.gottman.com/blog/repair-little-things-dont-become-big-things/.
   When your heart rate reaches 100: Ibid.
   Continuing to argue: Ellie Lisitsa, "The Four Horsemen: Criticism, Contempt, Defensiveness, and Stonewalling," The Gottman Institute, April 3, 2013, https://www.gottman.com/blog/the-four-horsemen-recognizing-criticism-contempt-defensiveness-and-stonewalling/.

184 *The sympathetic nervous system needs:* Ellie Lisitsa, "Weekend Homework Assignment: Physiological Self-Soothing," The Gottman Institute, March 1, 2013, https://www.gottman.com/blog/weekend-homework-assignment-physiological-self-soothing/.
   Gottman also suggests: Ibid.
   The exercise needs: Erik Peper, "Are You Out of Control and Reacting in Anger? The Role of Food and Exercise," The Peper Perspective, October 6, 2017, https://peperperspective.com/2017/10/06/are-you-out-of-control-and-reacting-in-anger-the-role-of-food-and-exercise/.
   "These little tremblings": Levine, *Waking the Tiger,* 97–98.
   Afterward, emotional regulation: Erik Peper, "Are You Out of Control and Reacting in Anger?"

185 *Dr. Porges, the psychophysiologist:* "The Neuroscience & Power of Safe Relationships—Stephen W. Porges—The Smart Couple Podcast 116," The

Relationship School, April 19, 2017, https://relationship school.com/podcast/the-neuroscience-power-of-safe-relationships-stephen-w-porges-sc-116/.

Dr. Porges describes: "The Polyvagal Theory for Treating Trauma: A Teleseminar Session with Stephen W. Porges, PhD, and Ruth Buczynski, PhD," National Institute for the Clinical Application of Behavioral Medicine (transcribed): 11, https://drrebeccajorgensen.com/wp-content/uploads/2014/02/stephen_porges_interview_nicabm.pdf.

we feel safe when: Shari M. Geller and Stephen W. Porges, "Therapeutic Presence: Neurophysiological Mechanisms Mediating Feeling Safe in Therapeutic Relationships," *Journal of Psychotherapy Integration* 24, no. 3 (2014): 178–92. doi: 10.1037/a0037511.

This is conveyed: "Dr. Stephen Porges on Face to Face Social Engagement," PsychAlive video, April 23, 2018, https://youtu.be/lxS3bv32-UY.

dogs display a similar: Ibid.

186   *Monotone, low-frequency:* International Misophonia Research Network, "Stephen Porges (Polyvagal Perspective and Sound Sensitivity Research)," https://misophonia-research.com/stephen-porges/.

The sing-song quality: Margot Slade, "Stephen W. Porges, PhD: Q&A About Freezing, Fainting, and the 'Safe' Sounds of Music Therapy," Everyday Health, October 16, 2018, https://www.everydayhealth.com/wellness/united-states-of-stress/advisory-board/stephen-w-porges-phd-q-a/.

To a frightened baby: Ibid.

That's why it: Integrated Listening Systems, Randall Redfield and Karen Onderko interview with Stephen Porges, podcast, February 17, 2016, https://integratedlistening.com/blog/2016/02/17/stream-the-dr-porges-podcast/.

Polyvagal theory describes: Integrated Listening Systems, "A Therapeutic Model Based on Physiological State," https://integratedlistening.com/ssp-safe-sound-protocol-clinical-resources/.

importance of certain words: Anne-Marie R. DePape et al., "Use of Prosody and Information Structure in High Functioning Adults with Autism in Relation to Language Ability," *Frontiers in Psychology* 3 (2012): 72, doi: 10.3389/fpsyg.2012.00072.

Touch stimulates: M. A. Diego and T. Field, "Moderate Pressure Massage Elicits a Parasympathetic Nervous System Response," *International Journal of Neuroscience* 119, no. 5 (2009): 630–38, doi: 10.1080/00207450802329605.

187   *effect of weighted blankets:* Hsin-Yung Chen et al., "Physiological Effects of Deep Touch Pressure on Anxiety Alleviation: The Weighted Blanket Approach," *Journal of Medical and Biological Engineering* 33, no. 5 (2013): 463–70, http://www.jmbe.org.tw/files/1961/public/1961-5094-1-PB.pdf.

Hug her or him: Jonathan Jones, "Why Physical Touch Matters for Your Well-Being," *Greater Good Magazine,* November 16, 2018, https://greatergood.berkeley.edu/article/item/why_physical_touch_matters_for_your_well_being.

A BBC-funded: Dacher Keltner, Richard Bowman, and Harriet Richards, "Exploring the Emotional State of 'Real Happiness.' A Study into the Effects of Watching Natural History Television Content," University of Berkeley, California; BBC Worldwide Global Insight Team, https://asset-manager.bbcchannels.com/workspace/uploads/bbcw-real-happiness-white-paper-final-v2-58ac1df7.pdf.
Face-to-face conversation: "Dr. Stephen Porges on Face to Face Social Engagement," PsychAlive video.

188 *That perhaps allowed:* Jill Blakeway, *Energy Medicine: The Science and Mystery of Healing* (New York: Harper Wave, 2019): 44–45.

189 *Here's some exciting news:* Stuart Brody and Ragnar Preut, "Vaginal Intercourse Frequency and Heart Rate Variability," *Journal of Sex & Marital Therapy* 29, no. 5 (2003): 371–80, doi: 10.1080/00926230390224747; S. Brody, R. Veit, and H. Rau, "A Preliminary Report Relating Frequency of Vaginal Intercourse to Heart Rate Variability, Valsalva Ratio, Blood Pressure, and Cohabitation Status," *Biological Psychology* 52, no. 3 (2000): 251–57, doi: 10.1016/s0301-0511(99)00048-4.
25 women ages 20: Amelia M. Stanton et al., "One Session of Autogenic Training Increases Acute Subjective Sexual Arousal in Premenopausal Women Reporting Sexual Arousal Problems," *Journal of Sexual Medicine* 15 (2018): 64–76, doi: 10.1016/j.jsxm.2017.11.012.
Autogenic training is: Amelia M. Stanton et al., "Heart Rate Variability Biofeedback Increases Sexual Arousal Among Women with Female Sexual Arousal Disorder: Results from a Randomized-Controlled Trial," *Behaviour Research and Therapy* 115 (2019): 90–102, doi: 10.1016/j.brat.2018.10.016.
Other studies back this up: Amelia M. Stanton et al., "Heart Rate Variability: A Risk Factor for Female Sexual Dysfunction," *Applied Psychophysiology and Biofeedback* 40, no. 3 (2015): 229–37, doi: 10.1007/s10484-015-9286-9.
Similarly, among men: Christopher B. Harte, "The Relationship Between Resting Heart Rate Variability and Erectile Tumescence Among Men with Normal Erectile Function," *Journal of Sexual Medicine* 10, no. 8 (2013): 1961–68, doi: 10.1111/jsm.12197.
Other research has tied: Rui M. Costa and Stuart Brody, "Greater Resting Heart Rate Variability Is Associated with Orgasms Through Penile-Vaginal Intercourse, But Not with Orgasms from Other Sources," *Journal of Sexual Medicine* 9, no. 1 (2012): 188–97, doi: 10.1111/j.1743-6109.2011.02541.x.
This type of overactivation: Amelia Stanton, conversation with the author, May 6, 2019.
New research: Amelia M. Stanton et al., "Heart Rate Variability Biofeedback Increases Sexual Arousal Among Women with Female Sexual Arousal Disorder."

190 *Among its innumerable:* Barry R. Komisaruk et al., "Women's Clitoris, Vagina and Cervix Mapped on the Sensory Cortex: fMRI Evidence," *Journal of Sexual Medicine* 8, no. 10 (2011): 2822–30, doi: 10.1111/j.1743-6109.2011.02388.x.

Because the vagus: Barry R. Komisaruk and Beverly Whipple, "Functional MRI of the Brain During Orgasm in Women," *Annual Review of Sex Research* 16, no. 1 (2005): 62–86, https://www.tandfonline.com/doi/abs/10.1080/10532528.2005.10559 829.

Women experience similar: Irwin Goldstein, "The Central Mechanisms of Sexual Function," Boston University School of Medicine, https://www.bumc.bu.edu/sex ualmedicine/publications/the-central-mechanisms-of-sexual-function/.

One reason kissing: Kory Floyd et al., "Kissing in Marital and Cohabiting Relationships: Effects on Blood Lipids, Stress, and Relationship Satisfaction," *Western Journal of Communication* 73, no. 2 (2009): 113–33, doi: 10.1080/10570310902856071.

13. WEEK 10: ANCHORING YOURSELF IN RESONANCE

193 *high blood pressure:* Rodlescia S. Sneed and Sheldon Cohen, "Negative Social Interactions and Incident Hypertension Among Older Adults," *Health Psychology* 33, no. 6 (2014): 554–65, doi: 10.1037/hea0000057.

chronic pain: Laurie Dempsey Wolf and Mary C. Davis, "Loneliness, Daily Pain, and Perceptions of Interpersonal Events in Adults with Fibromyalgia," *Health Psychology* 33, no. 9 (2014): 929–37, doi: 10.1037/hea0000059.

One long-term study: Roberto De Vogli, Tarani Chandola, and Michael Gideon Marmot, "Negative Aspects of Close Relationships and Heart Disease," *Archives of Internal Medicine* 167, no. 18 (2007): 1951–57, doi: 10.1001/archinte.167.18.1951.

A study conducted by Facebook: Adam D. I. Kramer, Jamie E. Guillory, and Jeffrey T. Hancock, "Experimental Evidence of Massive-Scale Emotional Contagion Through Social Networks," *PNAS* 111, no. 24 (2014): 8788–90, doi: 10.1073/pnas.1320040111.

194 *Two types of individuals:* Judith Orloff, "The Differences Between Highly Sensitive People and Empaths," *Psychology Today,* June 3, 2017, https://www.psychologyto day.com/us/blog/the-empaths-survival-guide/201706/the-differences-between-highly-sensitive-people-and-empaths.

198 *flashing lights and blind spots:* American Migraine Foundation, "Understanding Migraine with Aura," July 6, 2017, https://americanmigrainefoundation.org/re source-library/understanding-migraine-aura/.

200 *Practicing gratitude stimulates:* Laura Redwine et al., "Pilot Randomized Study of a Gratitude Journaling Intervention on Heart Rate Variability and Inflammatory Biomarkers in Patients with Stage B Heart Failure," *Psychosomatic Medicine* 78, no. 6 (2016): 667–76, doi: 10.1097/PSY.0000000000000316.

participants were assigned: Robert A. Emmons and Michael E. McCullough, "Counting Blessings Versus Burdens: An Experimental Investigation of Gratitude and Subjective Well-Being in Daily Life," *Journal of Personality and Social Psychology* 84, no. 2 (2003): 377–89, doi: 10.1037/0022-3514.84.2.377.

this exercise was potent: Martin E. P. Seligman et al., "Positive Psychology Progress: Empirical Validation of Interventions," *American Psychologist* 60, no. 5 (2005): 410–21 doi: 10.1037/0003-066X.60.5.410.

202 *Though panic attacks:* National Institute of Mental Health, "Panic Disorder: When Fear Overwhelms," last modified 2016, https://www.nimh.nih.gov/health/publica tions/panic-disorder-when-fear-overwhelms/index.shtml.

203 *a perfect storm:* Mayo Clinic, "Panic Attacks and Panic Disorder," last modi- fied May 4, 2018, https://www.mayoclinic.org/diseases-conditions/panic-attacks/ symptoms-causes/syc-20376021.

14. MAINTAINING AND FUELING YOUR RESONANCE

210 *They usually provide:* Michael C. Miller, "Seasonal Affective Disorder: Bring on the Light," Harvard Health Publishing, last modified October 29, 2015, https:// www.health.harvard.edu/blog/seasonal-affective-disorder-bring-on-the- light-201212215663.
Low stores of vitamin D: Andjelka Pavlovic et al., "The Association Between Serum Vitamin D Level and Cognitive Function in Older Adults: Cooper Center Longitudinal Study," *Preventive Medicine* 113 (2018): 57–61, doi: 10.1016/j. ypmed.2018.05.010.

211 *Specifically, it increases:* Pooja Bhati and Jamal Ali Moiz, "High-Intensity Interval Training and Cardiac Autonomic Modulation," *Saudi Journal of Sports Medicine* 17, no. 3 (2017): 129–34, doi: 10.4103/sjsm.sjsm_2_17.
Exposure to cold: Manuela Jungmann et al., "Effects of Cold Stimulation on Cardiac-Vagal Activation in Healthy Participants: Randomized Controlled Trial," *JMIR Formative Research* 2, no. 2 (2018), doi: 10.2196/10257.
This may be due: Ibid.
The body responds: Julia K. Choate, "Using Stimulation of the Diving Reflex in Humans to Teach Integrative Physiology," *Advances in Physiology Education* 38, no. 4 (2014): 355–65, doi: 10.1152/advan.00125.2013.
Emerging research: Jungmann et al., "Effects of Cold Stimulation on Cardiac-Vagal Activation in Healthy Participants."

212 *When multiple members:* Rollin McCraty, "New Frontiers in Heart Rate Variability and Social Coherence Research: Techniques, Technologies, and Implications for Improving Group Dynamics and Outcomes," *Frontiers in Public Health* 5 (2017): 267, doi: 10.3389/fpubh.2017.00267.
It was found: Yulia Golland, Yossi Arzouan, and Nava Levit-Binnun, "The Mere Co-Presence: Synchronization of Autonomic Signals and Emotional Responses Across Co-Present Individuals Not Engaged in Direct Interaction," *PLoS One* 10, no. 5 (2015), doi: 10.1371/journal.pone.0125804.

213 *In the aforementioned movie:* Ibid.
"more likely to harness the power": Julia Rozovsky, "The Five Keys to a Successful

Google Team," re:Work, November 17, 2015, https://rework.withgoogle.com/blog/five-keys-to-a-successful-google-team/.

215   *The Vaschillos have hypothesized:* Evgeny Vaschillo et al., "New Approach for Brain Stimulation," *Brain Stimulation* 12, no. 2 (2019): 393, doi: 10.1016/j.brs.2018.12.263.

In new research: Evgeny and Bronya Vaschillo, conversation with the author, October 16, 2019.

They found that: Ibid.

Their conclusion: Ibid.

These findings are supported: Gewnhi Park and Julian F. Thayer, "From the Heart to the Mind: Cardiac Vagal Tone Modulates Top-Down and Bottom-Up Visual Perception and Attention to Emotional Stimuli," *Frontiers in Psychology* 5, no. 278 (May 1, 2014), doi: 10.3389/fpsyg.2014.00278.

HRV-BFB, then, has the: Mather and Thayer, "How Heart Rate Variability Affects Emotion Regulation Brain Networks."

PCS is characterized by a constellation of symptoms: Harvey S. Levin et al., "Neurobehavioral Outcome Following Minor Head Injury: A Three-Center Study," *Journal of Neurosurgery* 66 (1987): 234–43, doi: 10.3171/jns.1987.66.2.0234.

216   *compared with controls:* B. Gall, W. S. Parkhouse, and D. Goodman, "Exercise Following a Sport Induced Concussion," *British Journal of Sports Medicine* 38, no. 6 (2004), 773–77, doi: 10.1136/bjsm.2003.009530; Brent Gall, Wade Parkhouse, and David Goodman, "Heart Rate Variability of Recently Concussed Athletes at Rest and Exercise," *Medicine and Science in Sports and Exercise* 36, no. 8 (2004), 1269–74, doi: 10.1249/01.MSS.0000135787.73757.4D.

possibly delaying recovery indefinitely: Leah Lagos et al., "Heart Rate Variability Biofeedback for Postconcussion Syndrome: Implications for Treatment," *Biofeedback* 40, no. 4 (2012): 150–53, doi: 10.5298/1081-5937-40.4.05.

Not surprisingly, her HRV: Ibid.

Other research has found HRV-BFB: Sonya Kim et al., "Emotion Regulation After Acquired Brain Injury: A Study of Heart Rate Variability, Attentional Control, and Psychophysiology," *Brain Injury* 33, no. 8 (2019): 1012–20, doi: 10.1080/02699052.2019.1593506.

Interestingly, significant overlap: Leah Lagos, "Distinguishing Mild Traumatic Brain Injury and Stress Responses: Implications for Heart Rate Variability Biofeedback Training," *Biofeedback* 43, no. 1 (2015): 4–5, doi: 10.5298/1081-5937-43.1.04.

or otherwise traumatic: National Institute of Mental Health, "Post-Traumatic Stress Disorder," https://www.nimh.nih.gov/health/topics/post-traumatic-stress-disorder-ptsd/index.shtml.

But in those who do: Ibid.

Hyperactivity of the: Jonathan E. Sherin and Charles B. Nemeroff, "Post-Traumatic

Stress Disorder: The Neurobiological Impact of Psychological Trauma," *Dialogues in Clinical Neuroscience* 13, no. 3 (2011): 263–78, https://www.dialogues-cns.org/contents-13-3/dialoguesclinneurosci-13-263/.

Findings such as these: Evgeny and Bronya Vaschillo, conversation with the author, May 3, 2019.

INDEX

Accessibility, of heart imprint, 136

Achievable goals, 59

Action plans, 40

    Anchoring Yourself in Resonance, 204

    Cultivating Resonance Under Fire, 161

    Finding Your Resonance Frequency,
      63–64

    Healing the Broken Parts, 118–19

    Imprinting the Physiology of Success, 174

    Letting Go of Your Stress and Expanding
      Your Emotional Range, 102

    Mastering the Emotional Pivot, 144

    Preparing for Challenge, 131

    technology use, 39–40

    Using Your Breath to Increase Energy, 83

    Using Your Heart Rhythms to Strengthen
      Your Relationships, 190–91

Acupuncture, 188–89

Acute stress, 148

Adenosine, 100

Adrenaline, 148, 154–55, 203

Aging, effects of, 81

American Heart Association, 62

American Institute of Stress, 5

Amplitude, of heart rate oscillations, 4

Anchoring Yourself in Resonance (week 10),
    192–204

    action plan, 204

    activity snapshot, 222

    breathing exercise, 196–98

    Bubble technique, 195–98

    experience of, 199

    HRV and homework tracking notes,
      241–42

    optimization strategies, 197–98,
      200–202

    physical health effects, 202–4

    resonance detractors, 195

stress with absorbing others' emotions, 193–95

Andersen, Judith, 146–47

Anger. *See also* Negative emotions
breathing to suppress, 73
and communicating with children, 187–88
with Heart Clearing experience, 96
images that reduce, 187
letting go of, 85, 109
overbreathing and experience of, 68
pivoting away from, 134

Angst, 87

Animals
freezing as stress response for, 104
recovery from stress by, 103–4, 184

ANS. *See* Autonomic nervous system

Antianxiety medication, 203

Anxiety. *See also* Negative emotions
chest breathing and, 66–67
competitive/preperformance, 172–74
connecting to, 87
Healing the Broken Parts and, 114
Heart Shifting to reduce, 123–24
hormone levels and, 211
HRV-BFB training to reduce, 16, 20, 30
HRV tracking as cause of, 38–39
and Imprinting the Physiology of Success exercise, 167
and Inhale for 4, Exhale for 6 exercise, 51
letting go of, 85, 88, 91, 109, 198
Mini Heart Pivots to reduce, 142
overbreathing and experience of, 68
pivoting away from, 134
resonance breathing and, 7, 25, 26
with sympathetic dominance, 66–67
and vulnerability to negative energy, 194

Apple Watch, 112

Asthma, 25, 62, 217

Athletes
HRV-BFB training for, 6–7
HRV monitoring for, 210
postconcussion syndrome in, 215–16

Attack-and-defend mode, 183

Auditory processing, 118, 186

Auras, migraine, 198

Autogenic training, 189

Autonomic nervous system (ANS). *See also* Parasympathetic nervous system; Sympathetic nervous system
baroreflex and functioning of, 17–18
in Cultivating Resonance Under Fire Training, 154
dysregulation/dysfunction in, 95, 114, 143, 194, 216–17
heart in, 4–6
heart rate variability and, 4, 15, 34
in HRV-BFB training, 8, 216–17
incomplete fight-or-flight response in, 105
negative emotions and, 89
in physiological stress response, 2
and resonance breathing, 26

Ave Maria prayer, reciting, 25

Awareness
and neuroception, 185
somatic, 2, 34

Awe
Heart Pivoting with, 135–36
heart rate variability and experience of, 138–39
images eliciting, 187

Awesome Breathing app, 36

Baroreceptors, 16, 19

Baroreflex
described, 16
flow and, 115
heart rate variability and sensitivity of, 61
HRV-BFB training and, 24, 43, 45
resonance breathing and, 26, 50, 89
strengthening of, 16–19, 95, 114

Bath, in bedtime routine, 156

Bedtime routines, 156, 202

Befriending stress, 150–51, 157–58, 234–35

Behavioral approaches, 2

Behaviors, aligning motivations and, 28–29

Beliefs, deeply held, letting go of, 109–10, 228–29

Belly breathing. *See* Diaphragmatic breathing
Belly Breathing exercise, 69–70
Belly Breathing in Bed technique, 79–80
Benson, Herbert, 14, 71
Big's Backyard Ultra, 132
Biofeedback
    defined, 7
    video-enhanced, 158–59
Biofeedback (journal), 82–83
Biohacking, 27–28
Blakeway, Jill, 188
Blood panel, 211
Blood pressure, 115
    baroreflex and, 61–62
    high, 25, 26, 62, 156, 193
Blood Pressure (journal), 62
Blood vessels, constriction of, 1
Blood volume, resonance frequency and, 55
Blue light, 78
Body sensations
    with chest breathing, 75–76
    stressor-associated, 109–10
Brain. *See also* Prefrontal cortex
    bond between heart and, 14–15
    HRV and blood flow to, 215
    meditation and cortical thickness in, 81–82
    resonance breathing and frontal lobe of, 26
Breathe2Relax app, 36
Breathe app, 36
Breath holding, 67, 74, 88–89
Breathing. *See also* Using Your Breath to Increase Energy (week 2)
    basic tips, 54
    chest, 23, 65–67, 73–76, 82
    diaphragmatic (*See* Diaphragmatic breathing)
    and heart rate, 3, 16, 49
    and heart rate variability, 15, 17f
    in HRV-BFB training, 8
    incorrect, 65
    in physiological stress response, 1, 2
    to release ghosts, 111–12
    resonance (*See* Resonance breathing)
Breathing exercises
    Belly Breathing, 69–70
    Bubble, 196–98
    Catching and Releasing Your Ghosts, 110–13
    for Cultivating Resonance Under Fire Training, 151
    Estimating Another Person's Heart Rate, 179–80, 240–41
    Estimating Your Heart Rate, 178–79, 238–39
    in HRT-BFB training, 23, 32
    Imprinting the Physiology of Success, 164–65, 237–38
    Inhale for 4, Exhale for 6 exercise, 51
    Interpersonal Synchronization Training, 180–81
    Letting Go of Deeply Held Triggers and Beliefs, 109–10, 228–29
    Personalize Your Breathing Rate, 52–53
    Release Emotion through Resonance Frequency Breathing, 88–92, 99–101
    Training Your Heart Rhythms, 122–23, 231–32
Breathing practice, post-training, 209–11
Breathing rate, 3, 82
Breathing sessions. *See also* Daily breathing sessions
    group, 214
    for HRV-BFB training, 40–43
    in maintenance and prevention phase, 208, 217
Breath Pacer app, 36
Breath pacing (breathing pacer) apps
    finding resonance frequency with, 50
    selecting, 34–36
    with sound, 117–18
Broken heart syndrome, 142
Bubble technique, 193, 195–98, 222
    appropriate situations for, 197–98
    experience of using, 199
    healing painful experiences with, 21

and listening to others, 201–2
purpose of, 195–96
Buddha breathing. *See* Diaphragmatic
    breathing
Buddhism, 134, 169

Caffeine, 79, 100
Calm, sense of
    belly breathing and, 67
    in Bubble technique, 193
    Heart Pivoting toward, 142
    with letting go of emotions, 91
    with parasympathetic dominance, 189
    and recovery from stress, 104, 184
    with resonance, 28, 50, 125
Cancer, 67
Carbon dioxide, exhaling, 68
Cardiac health, heart rate variability and,
    61–62
Cardiac resilience, 4
Cardiovascular disease, 77
Cardiovascular reactivity, 146–48, 150, 154,
    173
Cardiovascular recovery, 133, 138, 173–74
Catching and Releasing Your Ghosts exer-
    cise, 110–15
    experience of, 113–15
    with HRV technology, 112, 230
    recording, 229–30
Challenges. *See* Preparing for Challenge
    (week 5)
Chest breathing, 23, 65–67
    by individuals with IBS, 82
    with negative/stressful thoughts, 74
    sensations related to, 75–76
    technology and, 66–67, 73
Chest strap HRV sensors, 36, 37
Childre, Doc, 14
Children
    schedules for, 202
    shifting, into parasympathetic dominance,
        187–89
    synchronization between mothers and,
        176

"Choking under pressure," 172–74
Chronic pain, 193
Chronic stress, 148, 161
"Clocks" (song), 170–71
Cognitive approaches
    to healing painful experiences, 20, 21
    to stress management, 2, 85
Cognitive behavioral therapy, 203
Cognitive functioning, 154, 208
Cognitive reframing, 85
Cognitive resistance, 165–67
Cold-exposure training, 211
Coldplay, 170–71
Commitment, to HRV-BFB training,
    41–43
Communication, 187
Competition, Heart Visualization for, 168–69
Competitive anxiety, 172–74
Composure
    with flow, 115
    heart imprints related to, 136
    stress and, 72–73
Concussion, 215–16
Confidence
    during adversity, 133
    after Heart Clearing, 97
    Bubble technique to improve, 197
    with flow, 115
    heart imprints related to, 136
    with resonance, 50
Confined spaces, Bubble technique in, 197
Conflict resolution, 182–87
Contentedness, images eliciting, 187
Control, need for, 106
Coping skills, 149
Cornell University, 193
CorSense HRV Sensor, 37
Cortical thickness, meditation and,
    81–82
Cortisol, 148, 154–55
Counting, worrying and, 51
Courage, Heart Pivoting with, 142
Cravings, food, 116–17, 156
C-reactive protein, 77

Csikszentmihalyi, Mihaly, 115
Cultivating Resonance Under Fire (week 7),
    145–61
  action plan, 161
  activity snapshot, 221
  befriending your stress, 150–51
  Cultivating Resonance Under Fire Train-
    ing, 147–48, 152–53
  experience of, 154–55
  exposure practices, 152–53
  HRV and homework tracking notes,
    234–37
  optimization strategies, 155–60
  physical health effects, 160–61
  and physiology of stress, 148–50
  for police officers, 145–47
Cultivating Resonance Under Fire Training,
    147–48, 221
  experience of, 154
  exposure practices in, 152–53
  and physiology of stress, 149
  transferring, to other stressors,
    158

Daily breathing sessions
  extending length of, 101
  flow during, 115–16
  for HRV-BFB training, 40–43
  sleepiness after, 80
  timing of, 72
Dauwalter, Courtney, 132–33
Daylight Saving Time, 77
Day-to-day stressors
  identifying, 86–87, 226–27
  letting go of, 110–11
Decision making, 14, 15, 154
Deer, recovery from stress by, 103–4, 184
Dehydration, 100
Depression
  baroreflex and, 18
  chest breathing and, 67
  heart rate variability and, 4, 142–43
  HRV-BFB training and, 217
  and postconcussion syndrome, 216

resonance breathing and, 25, 26
  and vulnerability to negative energy, 194
DHEA, 149
Diabetes, 4, 62, 156
Diaphragm, 65–66
Diaphragmatic breathing (belly breathing),
    8, 40
  in bed, 79–80
  breaking up negative thoughts with,
    74–75
  chest breathing vs., 65–67
  experience of, 73–74
  heart rate variability and, 26
  importance of, 67–69
  and physical endurance, 69
  physical health effects of, 81–83
  relaxation response with, 71
  slimming garments and, 71
Diet, heart rate variability and, 100–101
Disappointment, 24, 106, 109
Disordered eating, 116–17
Diving reflex, 211
Dogs, social engagement system for, 185–86
Dominant resonance symptom, 125–26,
    232
Dopamine, 143
Doubt, 87, 165, 167, 168
Driving, breathing sessions while, 72
Dyads, 179

Eating schedule, 202
EGCG (epigallocatechin-3-gallate), 101
Elite HRV app, 37, 38
Emotion(s). *See also specific types*
  in Imprinting the Physiology of Success
    exercise, 164–65
  in incomplete fight-or-flight response
    theory, 105
  releasing, through resonance breathing,
    88–90, 99–101
  stifling, 73
  stress with absorbing others', 193–95, 199
Emotional contagion, 193–94
Emotional flexibility, 114

Emotionally charged situations, activating
heart imprint in, 137
Emotional Pivoting. *See also* Heart Pivoting
technique
during breathing session, 40
heart rate variability and, 133
power of, 139–40
practicing, 137
stages of, 133–37
Emotional range, expanding, 86. *See also*
Letting Go of Your Stress and Expanding Your Emotional Range (week 3)
Emotional regulation, 8, 138, 215
Emotional well-being, 26, 214–17
Empaths, 194, 199
Empathy
after Heart Clearing experience, 97–98
for empaths, 194
heart rate estimation and, 176–78
releasing ghosts and, 114–15
resonance breathing and, 26–27
Emwave device, 38
Endurance, physical, 69
Energy. *See also* Using Your Breath to In-
crease Energy (week 2)
deep breathing and, 69
negative, 192, 194, 196, 201–2
Energy Medicine (Blakeway), 188
Engagement. *See* Social engagement
Epigallocatechin-3-gallate (EGCG),
101
Equipment, for HRV-BFB training, 35–40,
50–51
Erection tumescence, 189, 190
Estimating Another Person's Heart Rate ex-
ercise, 179–80, 240–41
Estimating Your Heart Rate exercise, 178–79,
238–39
Eustress, 154–55
EvuTPS app, 38
Executive functioning
Cultivating Resonance Under Fire Train-
ing and, 154
dehydration and, 100

with Heart Pivoting, 139
heart rate variability and, 14–15
Exercise
and conflict resolution, 184
group, 214
sleep and timing of, 79
Exhale
in belly breathing, 68
incomplete, 89
Inhale for 4, Exhale for 6 breathing exercise, 51
inhale to exhale ratio, 23
letting go on, 88, 99
Exposure
cold-exposure training, 211
imaginal, 146, 152–53, 235–36
stress exposure training, 146–47
in vivo, 152, 153, 236
Eye contact, 185–86

Facebook, 193–94
FaceTime, 187
Facial expressions, 185–88
Fear. *See also* Negative emotions
of disappointing others, 106
and Imprinting the Physiology of Success, 167
letting go of, 91, 113
pivoting away from, 134
and psychological safety, 213
as sensation associated with pain, 23
of showing emotion, 86
of underperforming, 172
Fight-or-flight response, 2
anxiety and, 39
being stuck in, 6, 8, 19, 87, 89, 184
brain during, 14
chest breathing as activator of, 67
during conflict discussions, 183
embracing your stress and, 87
incomplete exhale and, 89
incomplete fight-or-flight theory, 96,
103–5
letting go of stress and, 8

Fight-or-flight response (*cont.*)
  sensory distortions during, 145–46
  sympathetic nervous system and, 5, 6
  vagal tone and, 19
Finding Your Resonance Frequency (week
    1), 49–63
  action plan, 63–64
  activity snapshot, 219
  beginning, 50–51
  breathing exercises, 51–55
  experience of, 61
  goal setting, 57–61
  HRV and homework tracking notes,
    223–26
  physical health effects of, 61–62
  and posture, 55–57
Fine motor skills, during fight-or-flight re-
    sponse, 146
Fingertip-scanning HRV apps, 36–38
Fitbit, 112
Flow, 3, 4, 115–16. *See also* Resonance
Focus
  belly breathing and, 81–82
  HRV-BFB training to improve, 30
Food cravings, 116–17, 156
Framingham Heart Study, 62
Frederickson, Barbara, 138–39
Freezing, as stress response, 104
Frequency
  musical, 169
  resonance (*See* Resonance frequency)
Frontal lobe, 26
Frustration. *See also* Negative emotions
  and Bubble technique, 196
  and embracing your stress, 87
  psychological resilience and, 133
  releasing, 88, 109
Full oxygen exchange, 67
Future events, visualization of,
    166–67

Game Day Moments technique, 155
Ghost imprints, 96
  catching and releasing, 106, 110–13

effect of, on relationships, 112–13
  Heart Shifting with, 127–31, 220–21
  identifying, 108, 109, 112
Global Brain Health Institute, 81
Goals
  for Imprinting the Physiology of Success
    exercise, 164–65
  re-evaluating, 230–31, 236–37, 242
  setting, 57–61, 225–26
Google, 213
GoPro Hero5 camera, 37
Gottman, John, 183, 184
Gottman, Julie Schwartz, 183
Gottman Institute, 182–83
Gratitude
  amplifying resonance with, 200
  for Heart Clearing experience, 98
  Heart Pivoting with, 135–36, 142
  heart rate variability and experience of,
    133, 138–39
Green tea, 100–101
Group resonance, 212–14
Guilt, 2. *See also* Negative emotions
Gustafsberg, Harri, 146–47
Gut instinct, 178

Hand holding, 186, 187
"Happy" (song), 169
Harvard Medical School, 14, 71
Harvard University, 6, 81–82
Harvey, Rick, 39
Headaches
  baroreflex and, 18
  HRV-BFB training to prevent, 94–95
  releasing ghosts and, 114
  resonance breathing and, 26, 42
Healing the Broken Parts (week 4), 103–19
  action plan, 118–19
  activity snapshot, 220
  after end of romantic relationship, 107–8
  breathing exercises, 109–13
  experience of, 113–16
  HRV and homework tracking notes,
    227–31

identifying traumatic experiences, 105–6
incomplete fight-or-flight theory,
    103–5
physical health effects, 116–18
Heart
    in autonomic nervous system, 4–6
    bond between brain and, 14–15
    clearing of, 121–23, 128
    feeling memories in, 130–31, 135–36
    high HRV and health of, 4
    in HRV-BFB training, 8
    muscle memory of, 13–14, 74, 121–22
    neurochemicals secreted by, 143
    resonance of mind and, 28–31
    visualization with, 163–64
Heart attack
    in broken heart syndrome, 142
    HRV and outcome after, 62
    negative close relationships and risk of,
        193
    sleep quality and, 77
Heartbeat, maternal, 171
Heart boost technique, 209
Heart Clearing experience
    empathy and relationship quality after,
        97–98
    healing painful experiences with, 21,
        95–97
    journaling about, 227
    prevalence of, 98
    support after, 115
Heart disease
    chest breathing and risk of, 67
    heart rate variability and, 4, 62
    negative close relationships and risk of,
        193
Heart imprint
    activating, 136–37
    defined, 136
    for Imprinting the Physiology of Success
        exercise, 165, 167
    increasing accessibility of, 136
    refreshing, 143–44
HeartMath Institute, 14

Heart Pivoting technique, 134–41, 221, 232–33
    bridging gap in, 136–37
    in Cultivating Resonance Under Fire
        Training, 152, 153, 157
    defined, 134
    experience of, 138
    to get unstuck, 140–41
    increasing accessibility to heart imprints,
        136
    Mini Heart Pivots, 142
    nonjudgment during, 135
    physiological recall in, 135–36
    power of, 139–40
    Power Pivots, 156
    in real time, 137
    reasoning behind, 138–39
Heart rate, 33. *See also* Synchronization
    (heart rate)
    breathing and, 3, 16, 49
    estimating another person's, 179–80,
        240–41
    estimating your, 178–79, 238–39
    monitoring, during conflict, 182–85
    in physiological stress response, 1, 2
Heart rate estimation
    for another person, 179–80, 240–41
    and empathy, 176–78
    for yourself, 178–79, 238–39
Heart rate monitors, 112, 180, 185
Heart rate oscillations
    emotional well-being and, 26
    resonance frequency and, 16, 24, 25, 34, 49
    stress and, 3–4
Heart rate variability (HRV)
    and autonomic nervous system, 5
    baseline, recording of, 37
    breathing and, 15, 17f
    cardiac health and, 61–62
    daytime, and sleep quality, 76–77
    defined, 3, 33
    and depression, 142, 143
    diet and, 100–101
    high vs. low, 3–4
    measuring, 39, 40

Heart rate variability (*cont.*)
monitoring, in maintenance and prevention phase, 209–10
and post-traumatic stress disorder, 160–61
and psychological resilience, 133
and sexual health, 189–90
and stress, 15
understanding, 33–34
weekly mean, 34, 35, 39, 40, 227–28, 234
Heart rate variability biofeedback training (HRV-BFB training). *See also specific topics and techniques*
after 10-week "graduation," 208–9
for athletes, 6–7
benefits of, 8–9
daily breathing sessions, 40–42
effects of, 217–18
equipment for, 35–40
for group resonance, 214
healing painful experiences with, 20–22
and heart–brain bond, 14–15
at home, 34–35
improving emotional health with, 214–17
in-office sessions, 15–19, 34
making commitment to, 41–43
objectives of, 8
tips for, 43–45
and vagus nerve, 19
Heart rhythms
strengthening relationships with (*See* Using Your Heart Rhythms to Strengthen Your Relationships [week 9])
training your, 120, 122–23, 231–32
Heart Shifting technique, 120–22, 204, 220
for anxiety reduction, 123–24
breathing exercise for, 122–23
experience of, 124–26
with ghost imprints, 127–31, 220–21
and muscle memory of heart, 13–14, 121–22
opportunities for using, 121
Heart Visualization, 164–65, 222
cognitive resistance to, 165
for competitive moments, 168–69

experience of, 167–68
focusing on future events in, 166–67
music with, 170–71
Hertz (unit), 25
High blood pressure (hypertension)
absorbing other people's emotions and risk of, 193
heart rate variability as predictor of, 62
resonance breathing and, 25, 26
sleep deprivation and, 156
High-frequency trading, 177–78
High heart rate variability, 3–4
autonomic nervous system and, 34
heart and breathing rate oscillations with, 17f
prefrontal cortex activity with, 14–15
resilience and, 133
sexual arousal and, 189
High-intensity interval training (HIIT), 211
Highly sensitive people (HSPs), 194–95
Homework Tracking Notes, 45, 223–42
Hormones, 77, 211. *See also* Stress hormones
"How to Make Stress Your Friend" (TED Talk), 149
HRV. *See* Heart rate variability
HRV4Training app, 37, 38
HRV apps, 37–40
HRV-BFB training. *See* Heart rate variability biofeedback training
HRV sensors, 36–37, 53–54
HRV technology
action plan for using, 39–40
chasing ghosts with, 112, 230
Estimating Another Person's Heart Rate exercise with, 180
finding resonance frequency with, 53–54
HSPs (highly sensitive people), 194–95
Hugging, 187, 188
Hyperventilation, 54
Hypervigilance
in incomplete fight-or-flight response theory, 103, 105

with sympathetic dominance, 66–67
and vagal tone, 19

IBS. *See* Irritable bowel syndrome
Ideal breathing rate, 3
Imagery training, 162–63
Imaginal exposure, 146, 152–53, 235–36
Immune system, belly breathing and, 81
Imprinting the Physiology of Success (week 8), 162–74
    action plan, 174
    activity snapshot, 222
    breathing exercise, 164–65, 237–38
    cognitive resistance, 165–67
    experience of, 167–68
    HRV and homework tracking notes, 237–38
    music to amplify physiological experience, 169–72
    optimization strategy, 168–69
    physical health effects, 172–74
    and visualization with heart, 163–64
Incomplete exhale, 89
Incomplete fight-or-flight theory, 96, 103–5
Inhale
    in belly breathing, 68
    connecting to stressor on, 88, 99
    inhale to exhale ratio, 23
Inhale for 4, Exhale for 6 breathing exercise, 51
Inhibitory control, heart rate variability and, 15
Inner critic, quieting, 90, 135, 140–41
In-office HRV-BFB training sessions, 15–19, 34
Insomnia
    baroreflex and, 18
    and Healing the Broken Parts, 114
    HRV-BFB training to treat, 217
    middle-of-the-night awakenings, 159–60
    resonance breathing to treat, 25, 27–28
Interbeat interval, 33
International Brain Stimulation Conference, 215

Interoception, 176
Interoceptive ability
    building, 178–79
    and empathy, 176–77
    experience of strengthening, 182
    and peak performance, 177–78
Interpersonal Synchronization Training, 180–81
Intuition, 178, 179
In vivo exposure, 152, 153, 236
Irritability, 192, 215
Irritable bowel syndrome (IBS)
    belly breathing and, 82–83
    letting go of ghosts and symptoms of, 114
    resonance breathing and, 25
ithlete HRV app, 38

JAMA Psychiatry, 143
Journaling, 115, 200
Journal of the American Medical Association, 193
Joy, 137–39, 187

Kissing, 190
Kok, Bethany, 138–39

Lacey, Beatrice, 14
Lacey, John, 14
Laughter, 160
Learning
    after resonance breathing, 41
    and heart rate variability, 14, 15
    rehearsal and rate of, 167
Lehrer, Paul, 6–7, 14, 15, 169
Letters of gratitude, 200
Letting go
    Bubble technique for, 197
    difficulty with, 85–86
    of ghost imprints, 106
    to heal painful experiences, 20–22
    maintaining ability to let go, 208
    of negative emotions/internal state, 137, 138, 198

Letting go (*cont.*)
  paradox of, 38–39
  for peak performance, 17
Letting Go of Deeply Held Triggers and Be-
    liefs exercise, 109–10, 228–29
Letting Go of Your Stress and Expanding
    Your Emotional Range (week 3), 84–102
  action plan, 102
  activity snapshot, 220
  breathing exercise, 88–90
  difficulty with letting go, 85–86
  embracing stress, 87–88
  experience of, 90–92
  Heart Clearing experience, 95–98
  HRV and homework tracking notes,
    226–27
  identifying day-to-day stressors, 86–87
  optimization strategy, 92–94
  physical health effects, 94–95
  practical strategies, 99–101
Levine, Peter, 103, 105, 184
Light
  blue, 78
  sleep quality and, 77–78
  white, 210–11
Lightbox, 210–11
Listening, Bubble technique and, 201–2
Love
  Heart Pivoting with, 135–36
  physiological synchronization with loved
    ones, 175
Love Lab (Gottman Institute), 182–83
Low heart rate variability, 4, 15
  cardiac health and, 62
  as PTSD risk factor, 161
  and risk of depression, 143
  as sign of stress, 33–34
L-theanine 100–101
Lungs, 65, 67

Magnesium, sleep quality and, 79
Magnetic field, heart's, 179, 212
Mantras, reciting
  baroreflex strengthening with, 25

and experience of stress, 85
to shift physiology, 126–27
Mapping Out Your Power 10s exercise, 94,
    227
Marlatt, G. Alan, 116
Massachusetts Institute of Technology, 81–82
Massage, 186
Mastering the Emotional Pivot (week 6),
    132–44
  action plan, 144
  activity snapshot, 221
  Heart Pivoting technique, 134–41
  HRV and homework tracking notes,
    232–33
  optimization strategy, 142
  physical health effects, 142–44
  and physiology of resilience, 132–34
Maternal heartbeat, 171
Mattress topper, cooling, 78
McCraty, Rollin, 14
McGonigal, Kelly, 149
Measurable goals, 59
Meditation
  cortical thickening with, 81–82
  and HRV-BFB training, 43
  in maintenance and prevention phase, 209
  nonjudgment in, 134–35
  resonance state during, 24
Melancholy, 96, 107
Melatonin, 78, 79
Memory(-ies)
  feeling vs. thinking about, 130–31
  and heart rate variability, 14, 15
  HRV-BFB training to improve, 30
  of painful experiences, 20–21
  physiological recall of, 135–36, 143–44
  poor, 156
  storing of, fight-or-flight response and,
    146
  working, 15, 101, 172, 173
Mental health, heart and, 142
Mental health professionals, support from,
    115, 150
Mice, freezing stress response for, 104

Middle ear, 186, 188
Middle-of-the-night awakenings, 159–60
Migraine headaches, 94–95
Military Health System, 161
Mind
   clearing, in Heart Shifting, 121, 123, 128
   resonance of heart and, 28–31
   wandering, 56–57, 101
Mind–body connection, 8, 71, 203
Mind-set, 2, 55–56
Mini Heart Pivots, 142
Moab 240 ultramarathon, 132
Mobilization strategies, 104
Mood
   after letting go, 90–91
   emotional contagion over social media,
      193
   Heart Pivoting and, 136–37
   hormone levels and, 211
   HRV-BFB training to improve, 30
   as indicator of resonance state, 57
   parasympathetic nervous system and, 60
   resonance breathing and, 24
Morning, HRV monitoring in, 209–10
Mother, synchronization between child and,
   176
"mother-ese," 186
Motivations, aligning behaviors and, 28–29
Movement, shifting physiology with, 126–27
Multitasking, 43
Music
   amplifying physiological experience with,
      169–72
   brain stimulation when processing, 118
   in breathing practice, 101, 209
   making a resonance playlist, 170, 238
   maternal heartbeat and, 171
   shifting physiology with, 126

NBA (National Basketball Association), 69
Negative emotions
   connecting to and releasing, 126–27
   and embracing stress, 87
   and HRV-BFB training, 2
   letting go of, 85–86, 89, 137, 138
   pivoting from, 134–35
Negative energy, 192, 194, 196, 201–2
Negative internal state, letting go of, 198
Negative relationships, physical health and,
   193
Negative self-talk, 106, 135
Negative thoughts, belly breathing to break
   up, 74–75
Nerve growth factor (NGF), 81
Nervous system
   muscle strength and, 162–63
   stress and, 92–93
Neuroception, 185
Neuroplasticity, 149
Neurovisceral integration model, 172–73, 215
Neutral situations, activating heart imprint
   in, 136–37
New Year's resolutions, 59
NGF (nerve growth factor), 81
Nocturnal arousal, 190
Nonjudgment, 134–35, 137
Noradrenaline, 81
Norepinephrine, 143

Ohio University, 162
Olympic Games, 163, 173
On-boarding, for HRV-BFB training, 43
Optimization strategies
   Anchoring Yourself in Resonance, 197–98,
      200–202
   Cultivating Resonance Under Fire, 155–60
   Imprinting the Physiology of Success,
      168–69
   for improving sleep, 79–80
   Letting Go of Your Stress and Expanding
      Your Emotional Range, 92–94
   Mastering the Emotional Pivot, 142
   Preparing for Challenge, 127–31
   Using Your Heart Rhythms to Strengthen
      Your Relationships, 187–89
Orgasm, 189
Oscillations, heart rate. *See* Heart rate oscil-
   lations

Oura Ring, 210
Out of breath, feeling, 54
Overbreathing, 68
Overeating, 116–18
Oxygen, inhaling, 67, 68
Oxytocin, 143

Paced Breathing app, 36
Pain, 23, 68, 193
Painful experiences. *See also* Traumatic
    experiences
  connecting to, 110
  evaluation of, 111
  healing, with HRV-BFB training, 20–22
  releasing, 109–10
Pajamas, sweat-wicking, 78
Panic, 20
Panic attacks, 114, 202–4
Paralysis by overanalysis, 14
Parasympathetic dominance, 2
  in meditation, 209
  and sexual pleasure, 189–90
  shifting children into, 187–89
  shifting partner into, 185–87
Parasympathetic nervous system, 5
  after concussion, 216
  Heart Clearing and, 96, 97
  in HRV-BFB training, 15, 32, 60
  and incomplete fight-or-flight response
    theory, 104
  and inhale to exhale ratio, 23
  laughter and, 160
  preperformance anxiety and, 173
  resonance frequency and, 49
  touch to stimulate, 186–87
PCS (postconcussion syndrome), 215–16
Peak performance
  flow and, 115–16
  heart rate variability and, 3–4
  HRV-BFB training to achieve, 30
  interoceptive ability and, 177–78
  letting go for, 17
  physiological stress response and, 2
Peper, Erik, 75–76

Perfectionism, 56, 106
Performance. *See also* Peak performance
  Bubble technique to prepare for, 197,
    198
  Heart Shifting before, 120–22
  impaired, stress and, 92–93
  posture and, 55–56
  stress at home and, 29–30
Performance goals, 42
Performance training, 1, 6, 7
Peripheral vision, fight-or-flight response
    and, 145
Perseverance, 142
Personalize Your Breathing Rate exercise,
    52–53, 223–25
PGA Tour, 69
Phobias, 128–30
Photographs, 126, 187
Physical endurance, 69
Physical exercise
  and conflict resolution, 184
  group, 214
  sleep and timing of, 79
Physical health
  Anchoring Yourself in Resonance and,
    202–4
  Cultivating Resonance Under Fire and,
    160–61
  Finding Your Resonance Frequency and,
    61–62
  Healing the Broken Parts and, 116–18
  Imprinting the Physiology of Success and,
    172–74
  Letting Go of Your Stress and Expanding
    Your Emotional Range and, 94–95
  Mastering the Emotional Pivot and,
    142–44
  negative relationships and, 193
  positive emotions and, 133–34
  Preparing for Challenge and, 128–31
  Using Your Breath to Increase Energy and,
    81–83
  Using Your Heart Rhythms to Strengthen
    Your Relationships and, 189–90

Physical resilience, 133
Physiological flexibility, 4
Physiological recall, 135–36, 143–44
Physiological stress response, 1–2
  Bubble technique for preventing, 197–98
  controlling, 30–31, 49–50
  and high-intensity interval training, 211
Pitch, vocal, 186
Polar H7 Bluetooth Heart Rate Sensor for
    the Chest, 37
Polar H10 Bluetooth Heart Rate Sensor for
    the Chest, 37
Police officers, 145–47
Polyvagal theory, 104, 185–86
Porges, Stephen, 104, 165–66, 185–86
Positive emotions
  moving to, 134–35
  music to elicit, 169–70
  physical health and, 133–34
  resonance breathing and connection to, 26
  sensing of, 138–39
Possibility, sense of, 136
Postconcussion syndrome (PCS), 215–16
Post-training breathing practice, 209–11
Post-traumatic stress disorder (PTSD)
  heart rate variability and, 160–61
  postconcussion syndrome and, 216
  resonance breathing and, 25
Posture, 55–57, 66
Power 3 strategy, 208
Power 5 strategy, 208
Power 10 strategy, 204
  implementing, 92–94
  in maintenance and prevention phase,
    208–9
  Mapping Out Your Power 10s exercise, 94,
    227
Power Pivots technique, 156
Pranayama, 71
Prefrontal cortex
  and Cultivating Resonance Under Fire
    Training, 154
  effect of resonance on, 26
  in fight-or-flight response, 146, 183

HRV and activity of, 14–15
  visual processing in, 117–18
Preparing for Challenge (week 5), 120–31
  action plan, 131
  activity snapshot, 220–21
  breathing exercise, 122–24
  experience of, 124–26
  Heart Shifting technique, 120–22
  HRV and homework tracking notes,
    231–32
  optimization strategy, 127–31
  with photos, music, mantras, or move-
    ment, 126–27
  physical health effects, 128–31
Preperformance anxiety, 172–74
Prosodic voice, 186
Psychobiological approach to team perfor-
    mance, 214
Psychological resilience, 133–34
Psychological safety, 213
Psychological well-being, 6
Psychology, in performance training, 6, 7
PTSD. *See* Post-traumatic stress disorder

Rebound headaches, 95
Reflection, to identify ghost imprints, 111
Rehearsal, 167–68
Relationships. *See also* Using Your Heart
    Rhythms to Strengthen Your Relation-
    ships
  building empathy to enhance, 97–98
  effect of ghost imprints on, 112–13
  HRV-BFB training to improve, 29, 32
  resonance breathing to improve, 42
  romantic, healing after end of, 107–8
Relaxation response, 71
Relaxation Response, The (Benson), 71
Release Emotion through Resonance Fre-
    quency Breathing exercise
  experience of, 90–92
  implementing, 89–90
  practical strategies for, 99–101
Relevant goals, 59
Reminders, HRV-BFB training, 44

REM sleep, 190
Repetition, 167–68
Resilience, 86, 89
  cardiac, 4
  defined, 133
  HRV-BFB training and, 18
  with Imprinting the Physiology of Success
    exercise, 167
  and incomplete fight-or-flight response
    theory, 104–5
  physiology of, 132–34
  psychological, 133–34
Resistance, cognitive, 165–67
Resonance. *See also* Anchoring Yourself in
    Resonance; Cultivating Resonance Un-
    der Fire (week 7)
  during daily breathing sessions, 115–16
  described, 49
  dominant symptom of, 125–26, 232
  entering, 16, 208–9
  extending time spent in, 138
  finding, with another person, 181
  group, 212–14
  and HRV-BFB training, 3
  identifying your state of, 124–26
  music as trigger for, 169
  practicing gratitude to amplify, 200
  words that elicit, 60–61
Resonance breathing, 23–31
  during conflicts, 184
  effects of, 26–28
  experience of, 28
  with Heart Pivoting, 138
  and heart rate oscillations, 25, 34
  learning after, 41
  learning techniques for, 23–25
  prayer/mantra recitation and, 25
  releasing emotion through, 88–92, 99–101
  and resonance of heart and mind, 28–31
  in urge surfing, 117
Resonance detractors, 192–95, 241–42
Resonance frequency
  blood volume and, 55
  defined, 15, 16, 49

finding, 24 (*See also* Finding Your Reso-
    nance Frequency [week 1])
Resonance playlist, 238
Resonant goals, 60
Rest-and-digest system, 14–15. *See also* Para-
    sympathetic nervous system
RMSSD (root mean square of successive dif-
    ferences), 53
Romantic relationships
  effect of ghost imprints on, 112–13
  healing after end of, 107–8
  shifting partner into parasympathetic
    dominance, 185–87
  strengthening, 182–87
Root mean square of successive differences
    (RMSSD), 53
R-R interval (RRI), 33
Rumination, 6, 172
Rutgers University, 7, 14

Safety, sense of
  in Bubble technique, 193, 196–98
  gratitude practice to enhance, 200
  and panic attacks, 203–4
  performance optimization with,
    165–66
  and shifting others into parasympathetic
    dominance, 185, 186
  sleeping and eating schedules to promote,
    100, 202
  and team success, 213
Saliva production, 81
San Francisco State University, 39, 75
Scarcity, traumatic experiences related to,
    106
Scents, amplifying physiological imprints
    with, 171–72
SDNN (standard deviation of time between
    heartbeats), 53
Seattle University of Washington,
    182–83
Second-wind effect, 69
Self-care, 196, 201–2
Self-doubt, 87

Self-talk
negative, 106, 135
and resilience, 133
Sensors, HRV, 36–37, 53–54
Sensory input, sensitivity to, 192
Sensory interoceptive ability, 176
SET (stress exposure training), 146–47
Sexual arousal, 189, 190
Sexual health, 189–90
Sheets, sweat-wicking, 78
Silence, for HRV-BFB training, 45
Sitting, posture during, 55–56, 66
Sitting still, difficulty with, 63
Skipped sessions, in HRV-BFB training, 44–45
Skype, 187
Sleep
and ability to manage stress, 156–57
HRV monitoring during, 210
improving quality of, 76–80
resonance breathing and, 27–28
synchronization with partner during, 176
Sleep agreement, 156–57
Sleep deprivation, 156–57
Sleepiness, after breathing sessions, 80
Sleeping schedules, 202
Sleeprate app, 210
Slimming garments, 71
S.M.A.R.T. goals, 59–60
S.M.A.R.T.R. goals, 60
Snakes, freezing stress response for, 104
Social engagement
for dogs, 185–86
and group resonance, 213, 214
and interoceptive ability, 182
and letting go, 86
Social media, emotional contagion on, 193–94
Somatic awareness, 2, 34
Somatic bonding, 213
Somatic experiencing, 135
Sound, during HRV-BFB training, 45, 117–18
Specific goals, 59

Stamina
belly breathing and, 69
HRV-BFB training and, 18
resonance breathing and, 26
Standard deviation of time between heartbeats (SDNN), 53
Stress
from absorbing others' emotions, 193–95, 199
acute vs. chronic, 148
befriending, 150–51, 157–58, 234–35
chronic, 148, 161
and composure, 72–73
dysregulation due to, 84–85
embracing, 87–88
and heart rate variability, 4, 15
high, shifting physiology during, 126–27
impaired performance due to, 92–93
letting go of, 86
low heart rate variability as sign of, 33–34
and performance at work, 29–30
physiology of, 148–50
pivoting to positive internal state under, 133
and sympathetic nervous system, 5–6
training heart to react to, 121
Stress exposure training (SET), 146–47
Stress hormones. *See also specific hormones*
cascade of, 148, 149
in conflict discussions, 184
with eustress, 154–55
and physiologic stress response, 1, 2, 148
Stress management, 8, 15–16, 32, 217. *See also* Letting Go of Your Stress and Expanding Your Emotional Range (week 3)
Stressors
day-to-day, 86–87, 226–27
ghost imprints and, 109–10
managing response to, 149
selecting, to befriend, 150–51
task-specific, 158
transferring Cultivating Resonance Under Fire Training to other, 158
in United States, 5

Stress triggers. *See also* Ghost imprints
  letting go of, 109–10, 228–29
  and Mapping Out Your Power 10s, 94
  recognizing, 87–88
Stroke, sleep quality and, 77
Sweatworking, 214
SweetBeat HRV app, 37
Sweetwater HRV app, 38
Sympathetic dominance
  chest breathing and, 66–67
  during conflict discussions, 183–84
  heart and, 5–6
  with PTSD, 216
  shifting from, 104
  sleep quality and, 77
  in stress response, 148
Sympathetic nervous system, 5
  after concussion, 216
  dampening, with HRV-BFB training, 15
  dysregulation due to, 85
  and preperformance anxiety, 173
  and sleepiness, 80
Synchronization (heart rate)
  with group resonance, 212–13
  Interpersonal Synchronization Training,
    180–81
  with loved ones, 175, 176
  touch and, 175, 179

Task-specific stressors, 158
Tattenbaum, Rae, 195
Teams, group resonance for, 212–14
Team USA Track & Field, 124
Technology
  chest breathing and use of, 66
  for measuring heart rate variability (*See*
    HRV technology)
  sleep quality and, 78, 156
Temperature, sleep quality and, 78, 156
Testosterone, 77
Thayer, Julian, 14, 172–73, 215
Timely goals, 59
Timing, of breathing sessions, 72
Tired, HRV-BFB training when, 43

Touch
  heartbeat synchronization and, 175, 179
  stimulating parasympathetic nervous sys-
    tem with, 186–87
Training space, HRV-BFB, 44
Training Your Heart Rhythms exercise,
  122–23, 231–32
Trauma, defined, 105
Traumatic experiences
  Heart Clearing and, 95–97
  identifying, 105–6
  letting go of negative emotions after,
    85–86
Trinity College Institute of Neuroscience,
  81
Turtles, freezing stress response for, 104

Uncertainty, 165–66
United States, stressors in, 5
University of California, 76
University of Salzburg, Austria, 76
University of South Carolina, 81
Upside of Stress, The (McGonigal), 149
Urge surfing, 116–17
Using Your Breath to Increase Energy (week
  2)
  action plan, 83
  activity snapshot, 220
  breathing exercise, 69–73
  and diaphragmatic vs. chest breathing,
    65–67
  experience of, 73–76
  HRV and homework tracking notes, 226
  importance of belly breathing, 67–69
  and improving sleep, 76–80
  optimization strategies, 79–80
  physical health effects, 81–83
Using Your Heart Rhythms to Strengthen
  Your Relationships (week 9), 175–91
  action plan, 190–91
  activity snapshot, 222
  breathing exercises, 178–81
  empathy and heart rate estimation,
    176–78

experience of, 182
and foster stronger romantic connections, 182–87
HRV and homework tracking notes, 238–41
optimization strategy, 187–89
physical health effects, 189–90
US Open, 147

Vagal tone
after HRV-BFB training, 24, 216
heart rate variability and, 19
high-intensity interval training and, 211
inhibition of unproductive thoughts and, 199
in neurovisceral integration model, 215
Vagus nerve
effect of resonance on, 26
function of, 19
HRV training and, 20
and sexual pleasure, 189–90
Vaschillo, Bronya, 7, 14, 15, 25, 215
Vaschillo, Evgeny, 7, 14, 15, 25, 69, 215
Verilux HappyLight, 211
Veterans, PTSD for, 160–61
Vibration twitching, 184
Video-enhanced biofeedback, 158–59
Visual amplifiers, 172
Visualization. *See also* Heart Visualization
in Bubble technique, 195–97
of future events, 166–67
with heart, 163–64
and heart rate variability, 15

physical effects of, 162–63
for self-soothing during conflicts, 184
in stress exposure training, 146
and uncertainty, 165–66
Visual processing, 118, 145
Vitamin D, 211
Vocal pitch, 186

Waking the Tiger (Levine), 103
Weekly mean heart rate variability, 34, 35, 39, 40, 227–28, 234
Weighted blankets, 187
Weight management, 116–17, 156
Well-being
emotional, 26, 214–17
psychological, 6
White-coat hypertension, 62
White light, 210–11
Whoop Strap, 210
Williams, Pharrell, 169
Withdrawal headaches, 95
Word choice, for goal setting, 60–61
Working memory
EGCG and, 101
and heart rate variability, 15
and preperformance anxiety, 172, 173
Worrying, 51, 74
Wristbands, with HRV sensors, 36–37

Yale University, 81–82
Yoga, 24

Zoom, 187